P9-CSA-773

Miller Center Series
on the American Presidency

The Trusteeship Presidency

CHARLES O. JONES

☆THE☆ TRUSTEESHIP PRESIDENCY

Jimmy Carter and the United States Congress

Louisiana State University Press
Baton Rouge and London

Manufactured in the United States of America

Designer: Laura Roubique Gleason
Typeface: Times Roman
Typesetter: Focus Graphics
Printer: Thomson-Shore, Inc.
Binder: John H. Dekker & Sons, Inc.

10 9 8 7 6 5 4 3 2 1

Library of Congress Cataloging-in-Publication Data

Jones, Charles O.
The trusteeship presidency: Jimmy Carter and the United States Congress/Charles O. Jones.
p. cm.—(Miller Center series on the American presidency)
Includes index.
ISBN 0-8071-1426-X
1. Carter, Jimmy, 1924–. 2. United States—Politics and government—1977–. 3. United States. Congress—History—20th century. I. Title. II. Series.
E873.2.J66 1988
973.926—dc19 87-24379
CIP

Figure 4 was originally published in "Carter and Congress: From the Outside In," *British Journal of Political Science*, XV (July, 1985), 269–98. Tables 8 and 10 were originally published in *The United States Congress: People, Place, and Policy* (Homewood, Ill., 1982), 58, 429.

To my mother and
the memory of my father

Contents

Illustrations

FIGURES

TABLES

On the Series

From its creation the Miller Center has devoted a major portion of its efforts to the American presidency and especially the nature of the presidency, particular presidencies, and urgent problems that confront the institutional presidency. In pursuit of such a threefold inquiry, scholars at the Center are engaged in both theoretical and empirical intellectual endeavors. Theoretical inquiry calls for philosophical and intellectual powers of the first order. Empirical research requires a body of facts and information that for any given administration is often obscured for decades from public understanding.

To supply the resource material for understanding the presidency, the Center has turned to oral histories, most notably an extensive history of the Carter White House. However, the Center's commitment to a new kind of oral history begins but does not end with that project. Preceding that effort was an impressive study of the Ford administration in which nine members of the "inner family" came to Charlottesville for two days of debriefing. The group included such leaders as Richard Cheney, Donald Rumsfeld, and James Lynn.

Looking to the future, the Center is committed to continuing attention to presidential studies through oral histories of American presidencies since the Carter administration. The goal is to use whenever possible the same approach to the Reagan and subsequent administrations. However, use of the oral history techniques at the Center is not restricted to studies of the White Houses of certain postwar presidents. Thanks to the example of the Carter Project, oral history is part and parcel of the overall Miller Center approach. Shorter and more concentrated studies are being conducted of each postwar presidency drawing on the participation of some twenty intimates of each president. The full texts of such debriefings are held at the Center, but edited versions are published in single-volume histories. It is fair to say, therefore, that a distinguishing characteristic of the Miller Center is an oral history emphasis responding in part to Elliot Richardson's injunction: "Those of us who have had long tenure in government actually know more than we know we know not only from the standpoint of institutional memory but with respect to principles of governance. However, someone must help us give birth to such insights." The Miller Center has viewed its oral history enterprise as among its foremost responsibilities.

When James Sterling Young joined the staff of the Miller Center in 1978, he was determined to institute what he defined as a new kind of oral history. He had observed some of the efforts in the major oral history projects at Columbia University, where he was a vice-president and professor of government. In the last days of the Carter presidency, Professor Young began extending invitations to members of the Carter White House to visit the Miller Center.

At first, the Carter people were uncertain about devoting the necessary two or three days (including travel time) to the project. A few key people such as Jody Powell made the effort and thereafter engaged in "word-of-mouth advertising." What seemed to attract them was the serious way in which Professor Young organized the agenda, structuring it within a common format for each participant. Young was systematic about preparatory conversations—repeated telephone calls and private meetings with the subjects and dinner and breakfast meetings before the first day of formal discussion.

Another attraction was the quality of the questioners who included not only University of Virginia political scientists but outside scholars of international repute such as Professor Richard Neustadt of Harvard, Professor Richard Fenno of the University of Rochester, former Mount Holyoke president David Truman, and Professor William Leuchtenburg of the University of North Carolina. Some thirty scholars joined in the Carter history:

Henry J. Abraham, University of Virginia
James W. Ceaser, University of Virginia
Inis L. Claude, Jr., University of Virginia
Elmer E. Cornwell, Brown University
Richard F. Fenno, Jr., University of Rochester
Michael B. Grossman, Towson State University

Donald H. Haider, Jr., Northwestern University
Erwin C. Hargrove, Vanderbilt University
Charles O. Jones, University of Virginia
Donald F. Kettl, University of Virginia
Martha J. Kumar, Towson State University
William E. Leuchtenburg, University of North Carolina
Paul C. Light, University of Virginia
David B. Magleby, Brigham Young University
Thomas E. Mann, American Political Science Association
H. Clifton McCleskey, University of Virginia
Richard A. Melanson, Kenyon College
Frederick C. Mosher, University of Virginia
Richard E. Neustadt, Harvard University
David M. O'Brien, University of Virginia
Peter A. Petkas, Miller Center
Don K. Price, Harvard University
Robert J. Pranger, American Enterprise Institute
Steven E. Rhoads, University of Virginia
Emmette S. Redford, University of Texas
Bert A. Rockman, University of Pittsburgh
Francis E. Rourke, Johns Hopkins University
Larry J. Sabato, University of Virginia
David A. Shannon, University of Virginia
Robert A. Strong, Miller Center and Tulane University
David B. Truman, Mount Holyoke (ret.)
Jeffrey Tulis, Princeton University
Stephen J. Wayne, George Washington University

Miller Center Staff

James S. Young, Chair
Kenneth W. Thompson
W. David Clinton III
Joseph F. Devaney
Lowell S. Gustafson
Daniel C. Lang

Thus, the quality of participants recruited by Professor Young matched the systematic organization of the project.

Full credit for the Carter Oral History Project belongs to James Sterling Young. He conceived of the study, designed and organized it, recruited the participants, and kept major objectives consistently before us all. At each stage, he was ably assisted especially by Professor Robert A. Strong of Tulane University, now associate professor of political science at Tulane, and by Joseph F. Devaney.

It goes without saying that the monographs on the Carter presidency that follow are the result of the Young approach to oral history. The data on which they rest and the insights on the Carter presidency hark back to a concept that Professor Young conceived and formulated before any of the interviews or writings in the project were conducted. Without the intellectual resources and research materials made available through the oral history, none of the projected books in the Carter series could have been written.

Kenneth W. Thompson

Foreword

Each presidency nowadays gets studied in two rounds. First, during incumbency, it gets closely studied by Washington observers, especially by journalists whose job it is to keep watch on the White House and keep the world informed of what they learn. Many years after incumbency—usually after the principals have died and their confidential papers have been released—it gets reexamined in the light of history, mainly by scholars who comb through the documents the president and his people have left behind. During the long lull between these two rounds of study it may be reviewed, defended, or attacked in memoirs, biographies, and other writings. But not much new is learned about it—or in much depth—until the presidential library has been opened and restrictions on the important papers have been lifted.

In the typical pattern an outgoing presidency loses the attention of journalists and is all but ignored by scholars. It vanishes from the news as the incoming presidency claims press attention and, while scholars wait for access to the documents, disappears into history. The way it looked when last seen, through the eyes of Washington observers, tends to become the accepted portrait. Then, as its documents come to light, things will be discovered that were missed, misconstrued, or not considered newsworthy when it was in office; and sometimes, as in the case of the Eisenhower presidency, the portrait that emerges from the second round differs greatly from the one that emerged from the first.

But what might be learned from the people whose presidency it was, by interviewing them when they leave office? Exit interviews have been done as a matter of policy by government archivists but not by scholars who study the presidency. Oral history interviews have been conducted for presidential libraries and private collections, but only rarely by scholars who study the presidency. Interviews with White House staff members have long been recognized as an important part of presidential scholarship. But interview studies of an outgoing presidency have fallen outside the normal pattern.

The Trusteeship Presidency and the companion volumes to follow in this series on the Carter presidency are a departure from the pattern. Here a presidency is studied after Washington observers have finished examining it but before the time has come for reexamining it in the light of history and before research on the presidential papers has begun. These studies are based mainly on interviews with the people whose presidency it was, conducted shortly after they left office.

These interviews were undertaken as a new kind of oral history effort by the White Burkett Miller Center of Public Affairs at the University of Virginia. Former president Carter and his principal White House aides were asked to spend a day or two each in private but recorded discussion with a panel of scholars for the purpose of reviewing, reflecting on, and responding to queries about their presidency. With the generous cooperation of Mr. Carter and his staff, twenty-one such sessions were held, most of them in 1981 and 1982. Each session was organized around a single individual or staff group in the Carter White House and consisted of at least five hours of recorded discussion time with a panel of three or more scholars. At least one session was held with each of the principal persons and staff groups. In addition to the former president, the senior-level staff members, most of their deputies, and a number of staff assistants below the deputy level were interviewed. Charles O. Jones participated in most of the sessions, including two with the members of the congressional liaison staff, as a member of the panel. I directed the project and chaired the sessions.

The Carter Presidency Project was not undertaken with the object of writing books about the thirty-ninth presidency, much less books of revisionist import. Indeed, most of the scholars who participated in the project probably began with the assumption that the essential picture of the Carter White House that had come through to us in news and commentary during incumbency was correct and would be confirmed in the interviews. But as the interviews proceeded significant disparities emerged. Facets of this presidency came to light under questioning by scholars that had not figured in news and commentary. Contemporary Washingtonian assumptions about power in this White House did not always prove out. Seen from the middle distance of history, in the whole of its four-year term the Carter presidency did not seem quite the same presidency it seemed to observers on the scene, day to day during incumbency. New ways of understanding this presidency became possible and new interpretations of its performance in office suggested themselves.

So the idea jelled, roughly at midcourse in the project, of commissioning a series of monographs in which a few of the participating scholars would report the insights they had gained from the oral history interviews. The respondents gave permission, in most cases on a background basis only, for the transcripts to be used as source material for this purpose. Upon completion of the monograph series, copies of the Miller Center's twenty-one bound volumes of interview transcripts will be furnished to the presidential library in Atlanta, where, as part of the nation's oral history archives, they will be made available to all for reading and research under such terms as the respondents may wish to stipulate. Until that time, in order to assure the anonymity of those respondents who requested it, the interview material is cited in this book by the volume number of the transcript rather than by the name of the respondent.

The main data base for the monographs was created by the cooperative effort of some thirty-three scholars and of former president Carter and some fifty persons who were associated with him in a staff capacity. Space does not permit acknowledgment of the particular contribution made by each of these individuals. I single out five without whose cooperation and active support the monograph series inaugurated by Professor Jones's *The Trusteeship Presidency* could not have come to pass. Jimmy Carter's personal cooperation and support for the idea of the project were essential to its successful completion. He is the first former president to have subjected himself and his staff to the kind of scrutiny and questioning we gave them. He did this generously and conscientiously and asked no favor in return. Jody Powell responded to a number of my requests for specific help, and his counsel and assistance were vital in keeping the interview process going. Kenneth W. Thompson, in addition to contributing as a participant in virtually all the interview sessions, secured the financial and institutional commitments to a project about whose outcome many had reason to be skeptical. His support through thick and thin, even when we sometimes differed about how to proceed, was key to both the inception and the completion of the project. Robert A. Strong and Joseph F. Devaney made indispensable contributions as chief research assistants on the project.

The subject of study here is a presidency outside the familiar mold.

Carter was the first president to be elected from the Deep South since before the Civil War, the first to be elected under the new presidential selection system of the 1970s, and the first true outsider—having no previous experience in Washington—to be elected since Woodrow Wilson. If the ways of Washington were new to Jimmy Carter and most of his Georgia lieutenants when they came to the White House, the ways of their presidency were new to Washingtonians, too. Very little about the thirty-ninth presidency resembled any other one in the memory of Washington observers. And there is little evidence to suggest that Carter and his people meant to cultivate any such resemblance.

There were the Republican presidencies of the recent past. There was the "hidden-hand" presidency of Eisenhower, a former general and diplomat, who brought to the White House his considerable experience in leading politicians while seeming not to. Carter's was no such presidency, and did not mean to be. There was the "imperial" presidency of Nixon, bent upon taking over the government but losing control instead. Carter was at great pains not to resemble that presidency. There was the vetoing presidency of Gerald Ford, confronted with an "imperial" Democratic Congress in the wake of Vietnam and Watergate. Carter's was no such presidency, and did not mean to be.

Neither did the Carter presidency follow in the expected pattern of the Democratic presidencies. After Roosevelt's New Deal, Truman's Fair Deal, Kennedy's New Frontier, and Johnson's Great Society, here was a Democratic president who not only spurned labels but presented a large legislative agenda with a distinctly conservative cast. Carter moved to retrench and reform—not to extend—the welfare state that other Democrats had built; to curb and roll back the regulatory state that other Democrats had built; to reduce intervention in the private sector as a way of solving public problems in the long run; to deregulate and start returning to reliance on market forces in order to achieve desired economic ends. To some, this looked like more than minor deviancy from Democratic doctrine. It looked like an attack on interest-group liberalism itself, and many in the liberal wing of the Democratic party responded accordingly.

Not only programmatically but politically also the Carter presidency fell outside the familiar Democratic mold. While asking a great deal of the government, especially of Congress, in the way of new policy, the administration seemed in the eyes of many Washington observers to be short on political skills and strategies to achieve its policy objectives. The Carter White House seemed not to go by the Roosevelt-Truman-Kennedy-Johnson book on the politics of persuasion. It scored low on the standard Washington political aptitude and achievement tests. If the thirty-ninth presidency was not a hidden-hand, or an imperial, or a veto presidency, neither was it a "political presidency"—to use Barbara Kellerman's term—of Democratic vintage. And in all probability Carter did not mean to have a presidency of that kind, either.

The kind of presidency Carter's wasn't became a major theme in news and commentary from Washington beginning with his inaugural walk from the Capitol to the White House and continuing throughout his term in office. In the first round of study, during incumbency, much was learned from Washington observers about the way the thirty-ninth presidency did *not* go about getting things done, what it did *not* do to push its policies through, what it did *not* do to project its power. Far less was learned about the kind of presidency it was, the way it did go about getting things done, what it did do to push its policies through, the way in which it did use a president's power to persuade—and why so. These aspects are the focus of this series of retrospectives on the Carter presidency.

Each president has his own way of approaching the opportunities and problems of office, and each has his own way of pursuing his purposes. His way is bound to capitalize on what he is good at, to minimize what he is not good at, and to reflect what he has learned from experience about what works and what does not work. What was Carter's way? Each presidency has a *modus operandi* of its own, a methodology of governance. What were those of the thirty-ninth? Many Washington observers and presidential scholars have strong ideas about the right way and the wrong way to organize and conduct a presidency. But presidents and the people who work with them in the White House have their ideas too—and theirs get implemented. How was the Carter presidency organized and conducted, and why so? And, once these questions are answered, what does the election and defeat of this kind of presidency have to teach about the nature and problems of governance in the American Republic in our time?

These questions will not be answered for many years yet, not until scholars have probed the presidential papers. But the interviews with the people who constituted and conducted the thirty-ninth presidency brought the answers much nearer than they were when the first round of study of this administration came to an end in January, 1981.

When Carter came to Washington with comfortable Democratic majorities in Congress, it was predicted, by Washington observers who should have known better, that harmony between the Capitol and the White House would replace the adversarialism of the Nixon-Ford era. Carter was not long in office when it became apparent that more than ordinary effort would have to be made in order to obtain affirmative congressional responses to his large legislative agenda, which included such politically difficult items as the Panama Canal treaties (opposed by a majority of the people) and a comprehensive energy policy (opposed by hordes of lobbyists). Having such an agenda and confronting a resurgent Congress that was organized and minded to assert independence from the executive, Carter would clearly have to campaign hard for passage of his policies, inside Washington and outside. How Carter and his people responded to this necessity, why they responded as they did, and the consequences of their response are the subjects of Charles O. Jones's *The Trusteeship Presidency*.

In this pathfinding study, Jones illuminates facets of the Carter presidency that have heretofore escaped notice and that challenge some of the conventional interpretations of presidential-congressional relations in the Carter years. He delineates a presidency that put high priority on pushing for passage of its policies, was highly attentive to the need for building coalitions for this purpose, and was methodical not haphazard in its approach. He shows a president who was no legislative politician but who was by no means lacking in a methodology for pursuing his purposes in Congress. This methodology—mostly missed by president-watchers in Washington—was, Jones shows, rooted in Carter's political ideas and experience, it capitalized on what he was good at and minimized what he wasn't good at, and was fairly consistently pursued throughout his term in office.

The Trusteeship Presidency is the study of a president who wanted to—indeed had to—motivate Congress to act against the grain of its politics. Increasingly, in my view, this is what presidential leadership will entail. Seen in this light, the trusteeship presidency of Jimmy Carter, so well illumined in this book, deserves study by more people than scholars.

James Sterling Young

Preface and Acknowledgments

Presidents differ as people, and the conditions under which they enter the White House vary dramatically. Jimmy Carter was who he was and he came to Washington under special circumstances—the first elected president following Watergate. This book offers an interpretation of the Carter presidency that is attentive to the political and policy context of its existence. It seeks to explain more than criticize, to understand more than judge.

The study itself grows out of a series of oral history interviews with the senior White House staff, most of which were held at the White Burkett Miller Center of Public Affairs, University of Virginia. The president was also interviewed in Plains, Georgia. I participated in most of these sessions and had transcripts available for them all. I have used unattributed quotations from the transcripts, but the influence of these sessions extends beyond the actual words used by the participants. An interpretation of Carter's relations with Congress evolved as I listened and then reflected on how and why the staff organized and worked as they did. The interpretation is mine, not theirs; but it is the result of a reconstruction of what they had to say.

I confess to all the standard preconceptions about Jimmy Carter's political naïveté. Being a student of Capitol Hill politics, I was impatient with his lack of appreciation for the workings of Congress. I came to realize, however, that it was important for me as a scholar to comprehend Carter's perspective on politics. That could be done only if I were to see Washington through the president's eyes. I began by identifying the president as basically antipolitical. Eventually I understood that he had a politics that differed from what I had come to accept as standard for a president working with Congress. The task then was to identify Jimmy Carter's politics. Once I allowed myself that shift in focus—from what he was against to what he favored—things began to fall into place. I found the time-honored concept of the *trustee* to be serviceable. Indeed, the very notion of trusteeship politics suited the post-Watergate era.

What follows is a study of Jimmy Carter's relations with Congress from 1977 to 1980; it is partial for several reasons. First, it relies primarily on the unique sessions with Carter aides and the president. The perspective offered here grows out of the discussions with those centrally involved in managing the Carter White House. Second, it follows that I have not sought to analyze Carter's congressional approach from the perspective of Capitol Hill or of the departments and agencies. That would be a useful exercise, to be sure, but it is not attempted here. Third, I have not tried to provide a "nuts and bolts" description of congressional contact and lobbying by the Carter White House. I do offer a few cases to illustrate Carter's choice of issues and the problems encountered—typically I selected those matters that were discussed most frequently in the oral history sessions. But this book is neither a "how to do it" nor a "how not to do it" manual. The focus throughout is on the special political conditions associated with the Carter presidency and the trusteeship interpretation of his role that influenced the president's relations with Congress.

I incurred many debts in completing this book. James Sterling Young directed the Carter Presidency Project at the Miller Center. He deserves the credit he will receive for conceiving this unique contribution to future scholarship on the presidency. He read this manuscript twice and provided the kind of critique that was essential for me to develop the interpretation set forth herein.

I received financial and administrative aid from several sources. The Miller Center provided summer salary for this and other projects related to my study of the presidency. I was also provided office space and superb secretarial assistance. Deans Merrill Peterson and Hugh Kelly of the Faculty of Arts and Sciences at the University of Virginia arranged for supplemental grants, for which I am grateful.

I wrote the final draft during a sabbatical leave in 1984–1985, supported by the University of Virginia and a fellowship from the John Simon Guggenheim Memorial Foundation. Other support along the way came from a visiting scholarship at the American Enterprise Institute

(Spring, 1983) and the research funds and leave arrangements of the Robert Kent Gooch Chair in Government and Foreign Affairs, University of Virginia. I can only hope that the product merits the confidence demonstrated by these awards.

I also want to thank Richard F. Fenno, Jr., Bert A. Rockman, and David B. Truman, who read the manuscript and provided excellent suggestions. Few authors have been better served. Several of the suggestions for reorganizing material were particularly helpful to me.

There would have been nothing for anyone to read without the services of Nancy Lawson and Anne Hobbs. I am very grateful for their talents in producing readable text from my cut-and-paste creations. Other Miller Center staff—Clyde Lutz, Shirley Kohut, and Reed Davis—provided the kind of assistance a scholar needs but often does not get. Vera Jones and others among my colleagues at Virginia and elsewhere sustained me in seeing this project through to publication. Given the circumstances, I could not have done without their support.

I also wish to acknowledge the professional and meticulous editing of my manuscript by Barbara O'Neil Phillips of the Louisiana State University Press. The index was prepared by Linda Webster.

My intention was to produce a realistic analysis of the purpose, structure, and methods of Carter's relations with Congress. My hope is that this account will contribute to a balanced judgment about the Carter years.

The Trusteeship Presidency

☆1☆

The Carter Model: Trusteeship Politics in the White House

"Reporters covering his trips around the country during his first year or so said he was almost incapable of saying nice things about members of Congress even as he traveled among their constituents. One United States senator's office had arranged for Carter to say a few words of endorsement for the senator when Carter was in the senator's home state. Expensive television and video machinery had been rented and set up to capture Carter's few words of praise, hoping that they might be usable in the 1978 election race. But Carter came and talked and went but never uttered the expected words of praise. Washington was full of such anecdotes." In recounting this incident, presidential scholar Thomas E. Cronin observes: "It was as if he didn't like politics, and yearned to be above both politics and politicians." This very view was expressed even more forcefully by one of the president's aides from Georgia: "He doesn't like politicians. He really just doesn't like them. . . . He's not willing to risk his future on just the politicians. He knows there are good ones and bad ones and so on, but he really does not like them. He's anti-politician."[1]

Downgrading politics in public is not uncommon behavior among presidents, or among other politicians, for that matter. Yet President Carter was severely criticized for his stance, while others have been praised for similar expressions. Why should this be so? What was different about the Carter presidency? Answers are not easily formulated, but these questions must be responded to if one is to understand the special nature of the thirty-ninth presidency.

1. Thomas E. Cronin, *The State of the Presidency* (2nd ed.; Boston, 1980), 216; White Burkett Miller Center of Public Affairs, University of Virginia, Project on the Carter Presidency, Transcripts, XVII, 54. Hereinafter reference will be made to Transcripts, with the appropriate volume and page number.

A natural starting point for this inquiry is simply, What is politics? No one to my knowledge has improved on the definition by Harold D. Lasswell, "who gets what, when, how."[2] In government, these elements are associated with getting elected, organizing to work effectively, and producing policy results. In this broadest sense, one could hardly deny that Jimmy Carter practiced politics. He actively and successfully participated in electoral and governing processes and appeared to enjoy the experience.

What was it, then, that he was against? We find an important clue in the words of the aide quoted earlier. He observed that President Carter "thinks that they [politicians] don't act out of the concern in the best interest for the country, they act out of their best interests."[3] This comment clearly suggests that what is read as President Carter's antipolitical attitude may in fact be a prescription for the behavior of elected public officials. It is conceivable that he believes that politics should be done differently, not that it should be abandoned. After all, politics knows many forms. There is no universal method for selecting "who," determining "what," deciding "when," or establishing "how." It seems reasonable, therefore, to explore another dimension of his antipolitical attitudes, *i.e.*, what it was he favored and why. The concept of the *trusteeship* helps in this regard.

TRUSTEESHIP POLITICS

Often a politician's interpretation of his or her role in acting for others is basic to that person's attitudes toward the political system and how it works. President Carter interpreted his representational role as that of the *trustee*—an official entrusted to represent the public or national interest, downplaying short-term electoral considerations. Almost 202 years to the day before Carter's election, Edmund Burke formulated the classic trustee position. In speaking to his electors in Bristol on November 3, 1774, Burke explained that "your representative owes you, not his industry only, but his judgment; and he betrays, instead of serving you, if he sacrifices it to your opinion."[4] Of course, Burke was speaking as a

2. Harold D. Lasswell, *Politics: Who Gets What, When, How* (New York, 1958).
3. Transcripts, XVII, 52.
4. Ross J. S. Hoffman and Paul Levack, *Burke's Politics* (New York, 1949), 115.

member of Parliament—one representative seeking to define his relationship to a constituency. When he and his like-minded colleagues in the party constituted a majority, they would then select a leader who became head of the government as prime minister. Therefore, the trusteeship arrangement could be rationalized as suited to constitutional or political conditions.

Trusteeship politics in the American setting is considerably more complex. It must account for a separation of elections (president and Congress), the plurality and strength of interest groups, and political parties' weak integrative capacity. As a representative of the people, a president must compete with 535 members of Congress, even when he wins in a landslide. Thus, a president may declare himself the trustee of the national interest, but he may then be challenged by a Congress of delegates who, as a collectivity, also lay claim to the nation's trust.

It is useful to think of representation as incorporating three dimensions—focus, style, and method.[5] For the trustee, the focus tends to be on national over local interests. The style of the trustee emphasizes independence over strict instructions. And the method is more integrative than segmental, that is, it favors comprehensive approaches rather than issue-by-issue treatments. In popular parlance, the trustee's preference is for "doing what's right, not what's political"—a preference commonly attributed to Jimmy Carter.

A president is relatively free to establish the focus, style, and method of representation as he will, bounded primarily by his previous experience and his interpretation of election results. He is in no position, however, to establish or even much influence the focus, style, and method of representation for members of Congress. Representational roles in Congress are created by individual members. Available research concludes that members adopt various roles and that the same member may change representational behavior over time and across issues.[6]

5. I must acknowledge my debt to Hanna F. Pitkin, *The Concept of Representation* (Berkeley, 1967), and John C. Wahlke, Heinz Eulau, William Buchanan, and LeRoy C. Ferguson, *The Legislative System: Explorations in Legislative Behavior* (New York, 1962). Pitkin speaks of the "independence" position in political representation, which is akin to the trustee role (see pp. 145–47). And Wahlke *et al.* provide a particularly clear review of the focus and style of various representational roles (see Chap. 12, drafted by Eulau). The addition of "method" as a dimension is my own contribution.

6. See Roger H. Davidson, *The Role of the Congressman* (New York, 1969), Chap. 4; and Charles O. Jones, "Representation in Congress: The Case of the House Agriculture Committee," *American Political Science Review*, LV (June, 1961), 358–67.

Unquestionably, what David R. Mayhew refers to as "the electoral connection" is an important, though not the sole, determinant of how members of Congress represent. Mayhew found it convenient to "conjure up a vision of United States congressmen as single-minded seekers of reelection."[7] Whether or not one accepts Mayhew's premise, there is little doubt that the electoral connection is important for many, possibly most, members of Congress. And, like other observers of Congress, presidents may be expected to express varied reactions to a preoccupation on the part of legislators with reelection. A president who views his political experience as congruent with that of legislators (for example, Lyndon B. Johnson and Gerald R. Ford) may display a high degree of tolerance for the electoral connection, as well as for changing representational roles (as associated with different issues or different political circumstances). Presidents with extensive legislative experience are not likely either to identify consistency as a necessary virtue in the policy process or to be optimistic about achieving comprehensiveness. Such presidents may be expected to forge a partnership with Congress.

However, a president who views his background and electoral record as incongruent with those of legislators may be expected to establish and protect his independence. Further, he will be less tolerant of the electoral connection and of inconsistencies in representational roles. Unflattering judgments about legislative behavior by a president who then keeps his distance contribute understandably to tense congressional relations. A partnership is inconceivable under these circumstances.

Not surprisingly, I place President Carter in the second category. By his own analysis, the president must stand fast on major national issues because Congress is unlikely to do so. This point is important, since it clearly shows that the trusteeship presidency carries with it assumptions about the congressional capacity to govern. Indeed, the parochial and electoral orientation of members of Congress, serving as delegates for their states and districts, defines the responsibilities of the trustee. As Woodrow Wilson put it: "*Somebody must be trusted.*"[8] In 1977, Jimmy Carter was, in his view, that somebody.

Jimmy Carter expressed himself rather forcefully on these matters before, during, and after his presidency. Here is a sample of what he had to say. *In an interview before being elected* (1976):

7. David R. Mayhew, *Congress: The Electoral Connection* (New Haven, 1974), 5.
8. Woodrow Wilson, *Congressional Government* (Boston, 1885), 283.

Congress is inherently incapable of unified leadership. That leadership has got to come from the White House. . . .

. . . Congress is looking for strong leadership in the White House to make major comprehensive proposals. . . .

. . . I want them [members of Congress] to know that we represent the same people. There's no one in any congressional district in the nation that won't be my constituent if I become President. . . . I want to do a good job for them.

In the famous "crisis of confidence" speech (1979):

What you see too often in Washington and elsewhere around the country is a system of government that seems incapable of action.

You see a Congress twisted and pulled in every direction by hundreds of well-financed and powerful special interests.

You see every extreme position defended to the last vote, almost to the last breath by one unyielding group or another.

You often see a balanced and fair approach that demands sacrifice, a little sacrifice from everyone, abandoned like an orphan without support and without friends. . . .

What I do promise you is that I will lead our fight and I will enforce fairness in our struggle and I will ensure honesty. And above all, I will act. . . .

I will continue to travel this country, to hear the people of America. You can help me to develop a national agenda for the 1980s. I will listen and I will act. We will act together. These were promises I made three years ago and I intend to keep them. Little by little we can and we must rebuild our confidence.

On evaluating his relationships with Congress after leaving the White House (1982):

On most issues, the lawmakers treated me well, sometimes under politically difficult circumstances. However, when the interests of powerful lobbyists were at stake, a majority of the members often yielded to a combination of political threats and the blandishments of heavy campaign contributions.

Members of Congress, buffeted from all sides, are much more vulnerable to these groups than is the President. *One branch of government must stand fast on a particular issue to prevent the triumph of self-interest at the expense of the public.* Even when the system of checks and balances works, a price must sometimes be paid: beneficial legislation may be blocked by the threat of unacceptable amendments that cannot be stomached on both ends of Pennsylvania Avenue at the same time. When Congress and the President succumb to the same pressures and bad legislation is passed, the damage to our nation can be very serious.[9]

9. *Congressional Quarterly Weekly Report*, September 4, 1976, pp. 2380–83, July 21, 1979, pp. 1470–72; Jimmy Carter, *Keeping Faith: Memoirs of a President* (New York, 1982), 88 (emphasis added).

These views can be summarized in a number of tenets that define the trusteeship presidency for President Carter.

1. Members of Congress are oriented to reelection (the electoral connection).
2. Powerful and well-financed special interests dominate a reelection-minded Congress.
3. The president is entrusted to represent all the people.
4. Congress and the public depend on the president to provide leadership in setting the agenda and supplying comprehensive policy proposals.
5. The president must act as the counterforce to special interests; he must represent the public interest; he must tackle the tough issues.
6. Failure of the president to serve as a trustee undermines confidence in the system.

It seems clear that President Carter judged it important that representatives separate electoral politics from policy making. In fact, this separation appears to be at the heart of the image of the president as antipolitical. To evaluate a policy option primarily from the standpoint of possible electoral consequences was considered wrong by the president. That is not to say that he and his advisers never evaluated such consequences, particularly during an election year when the trusteeship was established or renewed. It is simply to emphasize the tendency and preference of the president as chief executive to perform as a trustee rather than as a constituency-bound, election-oriented delegate. And further, his concept of the president's ideal role naturally led to an unflattering evaluation of the policy behavior of members of Congress, which fortified even more the need to perform as a trustee. Indeed, by selecting certain issues, for example, the elimination of water projects, the president could demonstrate in bold relief his trusteeship and their constituency-bound delegate status.

DOING WHAT IS RIGHT, NOT WHAT IS POLITICAL

It was precisely that behavior as trustee that was widely interpreted as "doing what's right, not what's political." The topic was frequently discussed by the White House staff, particularly those with extensive Washington experience. One aide explained that the president viewed himself as above the system of bargaining. In fact, this person judged that the worst way to convince the president on any point was to argue its political merits. Another recounted how the president issued a rebuke for bringing up politics.

It was a matter of enormous frustration to some of us that the president didn't particularly like to hear . . . that a decision was political. It was one of the first lessons that I learned in the White House. I can recall one of the first meetings attended with the president when I went to the White House in the Cabinet Room with other members of the senior staff about a particular issue. The president went around the room asking each staff member what they thought he should do on this . . . issue. When he got to me I started by saying, "Mr. President, I think that politically . . ." I got about that far when he shut me up. . . . He put me down in front of the whole staff. So I was very careful after that to make my arguments, but in a different way. . . . I could not believe that anybody who operated in an atmosphere where literally everything's political could take such a view.

One aide analyzed the problems that the president encountered with this approach—problems associated with doing business in Washington.

I always had the sense of a man who was an engineer, who truly believed that if he knew enough about details of a subject, he could make a decision that was in the public interest rather than in the interest of particular groups. Therefore, you needed a lot of information; therefore, you needed substance; therefore, don't bother me about the politics.

But then suddenly, he would be forcibly jerked back from this position . . . into a sort of purely political context in which a decision had to be made and I don't think that was ever resolved. I don't think it was ever integrated. I had the feeling of moving between the two [substance and politics] but never of pulling it together.[10]

Each of these aides is judging the president from the perspective of the dominant mode of politics in Washington. It was, perhaps, understandable that the president would take any opportunity (as the rebuke of his aide) to reinforce his trusteeship approach to national problem solving. It was also understandable that the president would seek to impress legislators with his command of issues—indeed, creating such impressions was virtually mandatory for the trustee. "Doing what's right, not what's political" is, therefore, *doing the political in the right way,* based on the president's estimate of his personal advantages and how they contribute to his

10. Transcripts, I, 53, VI, 102.

being in the White House. One might even argue that President Carter's trusteeship approach was pragmatic in the context of his evaluation of who he was and how he came to be in the White House. Put otherwise, might it not have been judged extraordinary for Jimmy Carter to have imitated Lyndon B. Johnson in dealing with Congress? Such behavior would have been not only unexpected—it would have been untimely.

Thus we have a preliminary response to the questions posed earlier: What was different about the Carter presidency? What made him the special target of criticism, even ridicule? President Carter's seemingly antipolitical approach was, in fact, something more than mere criticism of those with whom he disagreed. It was, rather, a method favoring a different style of politics—one closely identified with the independence or trusteeship of representation that encouraged the separation of electoral and policy politics. That President Carter was serious about this approach was demonstrated by the persistence with which he acted on his beliefs. Members of Congress felt threatened, since many of them believed that his persistence could cost them reelection. Thus, President Carter was different—just as he intended to be. And many congressional Democrats were bitterly critical because they believed that following his lead would bring about their defeat. They imagined that trusteeship politics ignored the realities of the electoral connection that kept them in office.

We can also begin to comprehend the challenge undertaken by the president. In a manner of speaking, Jimmy Carter worked against the system. By substantive focus, personal style, and political method, he found himself at odds with the Washington community. Political party often is available as a resource for presidents who find themselves in this situation. By definition, however, the outsider president serving as a trustee is unlikely to depend on this resource. Thus, "doing what is right" becomes a practical means for getting the job done. And presumably the president's style was well suited to the post-Watergate public mood, which changed attitudes outside Washington but not necessarily the politics inside Washington.

Further, there are tasks to be accomplished here. First, it is essential to inquire into how it was that Jimmy Carter got to the White House so as to understand his perspective on policy politics. Second, we must review what had been going on in Congress prior to Carter's election so as to judge congressional incentives and reactions. Third, attention must be directed to the framework for practicing trusteeship politics—specifically the organization of White House congressional relations. Fourth, it is helpful to provide concrete illustrations of presidential-congressional contact on major issues. And, finally, an effort must be made to evaluate the effectiveness of Carter's effort. We turn now to those several tasks.

☆2☆
How Jimmy Carter Came to Washington

The opening quotation in Jimmy Carter's campaign autobiography, *Why Not the Best?*, is taken from the work of Reinhold Niebuhr: "The sad duty of politics is to establish justice in a sinful world." The book itself is a story of the efforts by a well-intentioned and dedicated Georgian to perform that sad duty. Two questions are posed at the beginning: "Can our government be honest, decent, open, fair and compassionate? Can our government be competent?" In the concluding chapter, Carter answered both questions affirmatively. But changes would have to be made by those representing the best interests of all people. "Recently we have discovered that our trust has been betrayed." Thus, new leadership is required, one not bound to special interests.

> Our people are understandably concerned about this lack of competence and integrity. The root of the problem is not so much that our people have lost confidence in government, but that government has demonstrated time and again its lack of confidence in the people.
>
> Our political leaders have simply underestimated the innate quality and character of our people.
>
> It is time for us to reaffirm and to strengthen our ethical and spiritual and political beliefs.
>
> There must be no lowering of these standards, no acceptance of mediocrity in any aspect of our private or public lives.
>
> It is obvious that the best way for our leaders to restore their credibility is to be credible, and in order for us to be trusted we must be trustworthy.[1]

These themes are repeated frequently throughout Carter's political career —including, of course, the "crisis of confidence" speech in 1979. They form the basis of Carter's own trusteeship in politics. In this chapter I will briefly explore the roots of Carter's beliefs about government and

1. Jimmy Carter, *Why Not the Best?* (Nashville, 1975), vii, 9, 154.

politics, identify those conditions that favored the currency of those beliefs, and describe the impact of the long presidential campaign. The central question to be treated is: Did Jimmy Carter's pre-presidential experience alter his view of politics, with its unflattering image of legislative life? The short response is no. In fact, how Jimmy Carter got to Washington actually reinforced his trusteeship approach.

CARTER'S PRE-NOMINATION POLITICAL EXPERIENCE

In *The Presidential Character,* James David Barber emphasizes the initial political experiences of a president as important in shaping subsequent behavior. Early adulthood is a particularly significant period, since "the person moves from contemplation to responsible action and adopts a style."

> In most biographical accounts this period stands out in stark clarity—the time of emergence, the time the young man found himself. I call it his first independent political success. It was then he moved beyond the detailed guidance of his family; then his self-esteem was dramatically boosted; then he came forth as a person to be reckoned with by other people. The *way* he did that is profoundly important to him. Typically he grasps that style and hangs onto it. Much later, coming into the Presidency, something in him remembers this earlier victory and re-emphasizes the style that made it happen.

Jimmy Carter's early adulthood was spent in the navy, where he admits to being strongly influenced by the "unbelievably hardworking and competent" Admiral Hyman Rickover. "He expected the maximum from us, but he always contributed more."[2] Rickover reinforced Carter's style, providing a model that suited the future president's predispositions and goals. Jimmy Carter emerged from early adulthood as a person who demanded much of himself.

With his experience in the military and his subsequently having to take over the family business, Carter entered active politics somewhat later than is typical for recent presidents (though not for the incumbent at this writing, Ronald Reagan). He was thirty-eight when elected to the Georgia State Senate. His immediate predecessors—Ford, Nixon, Johnson,

2. James David Barber, *The Presidential Character: Predicting Performance in the White House* (Englewood Cliffs, N.J., 1972), 10; Carter, *Why Not the Best?*, 57.

and Kennedy—were thirty-six, thirty-four, twenty-nine, and thirty when first elected, and their first service was in the U.S. House of Representatives. Barber's proposition regarding the impact of the initial political experience seems credible in Carter's case. His race for a state senate seat was marred by vote fraud that initially prevented him from winning. Certainly the experience was not likely to encourage a favorable attitude toward either the legislature or the Democratic party.

Carter observed fraudulent influencing of voters firsthand in Quitman County, but his protests were ignored. He and his supporters were present when the votes were counted in Georgetown, Georgia. They estimated in advance that about three hundred people had voted. "There were 433 ballots in the box, and according to the names listed, 126 of them voted alphabetically! When the ballots were unfolded, there were sometimes four to eight of them folded together. It was obvious that the box had been stuffed, and I had lost the election by a few votes." With the assistance of an Atlanta lawyer, Charles Kirbo, Carter fought to have the decision reversed. After a lengthy and arduous court battle, accompanied by considerable lobbying with Democratic party officials, Carter finally won the election. By his own assessment he "learned a lot from his first experience with politics." He realized "how vulnerable our political system was to an accumulation of unchallenged power." But he also concluded that something could be done to change the situation.[3] Carter gained confidence in this first experience—confidence that he was right and that he could command the political support to make government work better. Further, in Charles Kirbo, he gained an important political confidant.

By his own account, Senator Carter was a diligent representative who promised to read every bill before voting on it—a promise he kept. He pictured himself as "a sometimes lonely opponent of 'sweetheart' bills." He viewed the legislature as primarily representing special interests. "It was interesting to introduce a proposal and see who squealed." He "began to work on comprehensive approaches"—decrying state government's tendency to deal only with segmented issues. He expressed a concept of the "common good" or the "average citizen," neither of which was well served by "lobbyists who fill the halls of Congress, state capitols, county courthouses, and city halls." The following passage summa-

3. Carter, *Why Not the Best?*, 81, 85.

rizes his impressions during this period: "It is difficult for the common good to prevail against the intense concentration of those who have a special interest, especially if the decisions are made behind locked doors. What occurred was not illegal, but it was wrong. The 259 members of the legislature were almost all good honest men and women. A tiny portion were not good or honest. In the absence of clear and comprehensive issues, it is simply not possible to marshal the interest of the general public, and under such circumstances legislators often respond to the quiet and professional pressure of lobbyists."[4]

In this statement, Carter concedes that most legislators intend to do the right thing. But the system itself—the legislative system—is at fault. In his view, he was the exception to the rule. He was able to spot the special interests for what they were *and* he understood the need to offer more comprehensive legislative packages. He also expressed concern that the system was not sufficiently attentive to the "unorganized citizen." At the same time, he established a record as "an advocate of fiscal restraint." In reviewing his term as a state senator, Betty Glad concludes: "Overall, Carter did perform well as a newbreed legislator and made a good record for himself. He worked hard, cooperated with the governor's programs, committed himself to progressive reforms in the area of education, and secured favors in return. He looked after the interests of his constituents, avoided the controversial race issues that were tearing his home territory apart, and secured a good press at home."[5]

Not surprisingly, perhaps, Jimmy Carter did not intend to stay long in the Georgia State Senate. In 1966 he decided to run for the U.S. House of Representatives from his congressional district, then switched and ran for governor instead. He lost. In 1970 he ran again and won, having worked hard between elections to ensure victory. "I did not intend to lose again."[6]

His experience as governor did significantly alter his view of the legislature. Although initially he worked well with the party leaders, they were in "open conflict" later on. Betty Glad describes what became familiar when Carter was in the White House: "He seemed to experience opposi-

4. *Ibid.*, 99, 105, 101.

5. James R. Wagner, "Carter: Outsider at the Threshold of Power," *Congressional Quarterly Weekly Report*, June 24, 1976, p. 1982; Betty Glad, *Jimmy Carter: In Search of the Great White House* (New York, 1980), 99.

6. Carter, *Why Not the Best?*, 112.

tion as a personal affront and as a consequence responded to it with attacks on the integrity of those who blocked his projects. He showed a tendency . . . to equate his political goals with the just and the right and to view his opponents as representative of some selfish or immoral interest." She concludes that he used "above politics" rhetoric to political advantage but that "he created enmity that could rise to haunt him later."[7]

Carter "enjoyed" his tenure as governor "in spite of its being a highly-controversial, aggressive, and combative administration."[8] He was particularly proud of his reorganization efforts, including the introduction of zero-base budgeting. Georgia governors cannot succeed themselves, and thus Carter was relieved of having to seek reelection. One of his closest aides believed that he could not have been reelected even if he had been able to serve a second, consecutive term.

It might be said that Jimmy Carter's pre-nomination political experience prepared him for a post-Watergate destiny. The lessons taught were consistently favorable to the trusteeship model of politics. Opportunities regularly presented themselves for Carter to convince himself that he was fighting the good fight—challenging the special interests and winning.

CONDITIONS FACILITATING A TRUSTEESHIP CANDIDACY

It took an extraordinary coincidence of personal ambition and political events to produce a Carter presidency. In the first place, recent tradition was broken. Between 1900 and 1960, of the thirty presidential candidates from the two parties, seventeen had served as governors. Only five candidates during that period had congressional experience, and only two had served more than six years. The situation changed between 1960 and 1976. Of the ten candidates in those years, nine had congressional experience. Further, several candidates had experience in both houses (Richard M. Nixon, who was a candidate three times during the period; John F. Kennedy; Lyndon B. Johnson; and George S. McGovern), and several had lengthy congressional service at the time of their candidacy (Barry M. Goldwater, twelve years, Senate; Johnson, twenty-four years, both houses; and Ford, twenty-four years, House). The only candidate without congressional experience was Jimmy Carter.

7. Glad, *Jimmy Carter*, 199, 203.
8. Carter, *Why Not the Best?*, 111.

In the second place, selecting a southerner to run for the White House had become most uncommon. In fact, not since 1848 had a major party candidate come from the Deep South (at that time the Whig party nominated Zachary Taylor, who was from Louisiana). Three candidates came from the border South—John W. Davis from West Virginia (1924), Harry S. Truman from Missouri (1948), and Lyndon B. Johnson from Texas (1964). Truman and Johnson ran, after acceding to the presidency upon the death of the incumbent, and Davis was a compromise candidate following the longest Democratic convention in history—103 ballots.

What, then, were the conditions that favored this unusual choice? Surely the tragedy of Watergate is the starting point for answering that question. Few events have had such a profound effect on the American political system. All major political and policy-making institutions came to be preoccupied with the event before it was over. The public developed an almost morbid fascination, encouraged by daily revelations of wrong-doing at the highest levels. Congressional hearings nearly replaced soap operas as the most-watched television fare. Finally, on August 8, 1974, Nixon resigned in disgrace.

> In all the decisions I have made in my public life, I have always tried to do what was best for the Nation. Throughout the long and difficult period of Watergate, I have felt it was my duty to persevere, to make every possible effort to complete the term of office to which you elected me.
>
> In the past few days, however, it has become evident to me that I no longer have a strong enough political base in the Congress to justify continuing that effort. . . . From the discussions I have had with Congressional and other leaders, I have concluded that because of the Watergate matter I might not have the support of the Congress that I would consider necessary to back the very difficult decisions and carry out the duties of this office in the way the interests of the Nation would require.
>
> I have never been a quitter. To leave office before my term is completed is abhorrent to every instinct in my body. But as President, I must put the interest of America first. America needs a full-time President and a full-time Congress. . . .
>
> Therefore, I shall resign the Presidency effective at noon tomorrow. Vice-President Ford will be sworn in as President at that hour in this office.

On August 9, following his inauguration, President Ford announced: "Our long nightmare is over. Our Constitution works. Our great republic is a government of laws and not of men."[9]

9. *Congressional Quarterly Weekly Report*, August 10, 1974, pp. 2193–94, 2071.

The nightmare may have ended, but the repercussions from Watergate were far from over. The event spawned a new generation of investigative journalists who sought to monitor the behavior of public officials at all levels of government. Public attitudes toward national political institutions changed drastically. Survey data collected by the Center for Political Studies, University of Michigan, showed a dramatic decline in public trust of government—from 61 percent in 1964 to 22 percent in 1976—and an equally dramatic rise in public cynicism regarding government and politics—from 19 percent in 1964 to 53 percent in 1976. At various times during the years from 1966 to 1976, the Harris Poll organization asked respondents whether they had a great deal of confidence, only some confidence, or hardly any confidence in nine public and private institutions. The results showed a serious decline in the number expressing a great deal of confidence (from an average of 43 percent in 1966 to an average of 20 percent in 1976). The decline in confidence for the executive branch and Congress exceeded this average—from 41 percent to 11 percent to 9 percent for the latter. The two institutions ranked seventh and ninth, respectively, in the confidence ratings.[10]

These results mask one interesting and important upsurge in positive ratings for the White House and Congress. President Nixon's last approval rating before his resignation was 24 percent (Gallup Poll, July 12–15). Upon assuming the presidency, Ford had an approval rating of 71 percent (Gallup Poll, August 16–19). Then on September 8, President Ford pardoned Richard Nixon and his rating dropped by twenty-one points to 50 percent.[11] It would drop even farther—into the thirties—by mid-January, 1975.

Congress experienced a similar rise and fall. The Gallup Poll approval ratings for April were 30 percent. Following the resignation they increased to 48 percent.[12] Public ratings of Congress tend to track those of the president, though always somewhat lower. Predictably, therefore, the ratings of congressional performance declined when the president's did. A bizarre incident may have been a contributing factor, however.

10. Warren E. Miller, "Misreading the Public Pulse," *Public Opinion*, II (October-November, 1979), 11. See "Opinion Roundup," *Public Opinion*, II (October-November, 1979), 30–31.

11. *Congressional Quarterly Weekly Report*, August 3, 1974, p. 2025, October 19, 1974, p. 2933.

12. *Ibid.*, August 31, 1974, p. 2365.

On October 9, 1974, a leading House Democrat, Wilbur D. Mills of Arkansas (chairman of the Committee on Ways and Means), was stopped by the police for speeding near the Tidal Basin. A striptease dancer bolted from the car and jumped in the water. The widespread publicity eventually resulted in Mills's resigning his chairmanship and being hospitalized for alcoholism.

Once more, public evaluations of the presidency and Congress declined and ethical issues remained high on the agenda in national politics. In the 1974 election, a large group of House Democrats came to Congress believing that they were the post-Watergate class of reformers. The mood clearly was against politics as usual, though it was not clear what type of politics was favored.[13]

Hamilton Jordan, Jimmy Carter's top political aide, had earlier identified public disillusionment with Washington politics as a potentially important issue in the 1976 campaign. He set forth a nomination strategy for Carter based on a national campaign that would turn a presumed weakness (*i.e.*, lack of familiarity) into a strength (*i.e.*, a fresh political approach). With classic understatement and remarkable prescience, Jordan had this to say in his strategy memorandum written in early November, 1972: "Perhaps the strongest feeling in this country today is the general distrust of government and politicians at all levels. The desire and thirst for strong moral leadership in this nation was not satisfied with the election of Richard Nixon. *It is my contention that this desire will grow in four more years of the Nixon administration.*"[14]

There were also policy conditions that favored a trustee candidacy. A review of the national agenda during the 1960s and 1970s shows a shift from the expansionist issues of Johnson's Great Society to the more consolidative issues of the Nixon-Ford era. The latter concerned the effectiveness of government and thus led to reorganization, budgetary reform, and decentralization. Nixon's resignation did not diminish the importance of these issues. It was unlikely that prominent congressional Democrats (for example, Senator Edward M. Kennedy or Senator Walter F. Mondale)

13. The so-called Koreagate incident also contributed to the ethical problems of Congress. Tongsun Park was a lobbyist for the South Korean government. He reportedly gave large sums of money to various members of Congress. Several investigations were launched.

14. Jules Witcover, *Marathon: The Pursuit of the Presidency, 1972–1976* (New York, 1977), 111 (emphasis added).

would be viewed as credible presidential candidates in a consolidative era, since they were identified with the expansionist programs of the past. And as it happened, neither Kennedy nor Mondale sought the nomination in 1976. Again, developments conspired to encourage Democrats to look outside Washington for a candidate.

Who was available? The two most nationally prominent governors were George Wallace of Alabama and Edmund ("Jerry") Brown of California. Each had important limitations. Wallace had become identified with the segregationist South; Brown had developed a reputation for being somewhat unpredictable, possibly even "flaky." And neither could exactly qualify as a new face in American politics. Thus, the advantage was with an unknown—someone with an umblemished record, untainted by Washington politics, yet ready and willing to take on the arduous task of a national campaign.

In summary, political, institutional, and policy conditions combined to produce a favorable situation for a Carter candidacy. And Carter himself was organized early enough to take advantage of the promising circumstances. It is important to understand how this post-Watergate political context encouraged a trusteeship approach to participating in national politics. Suffice it to say at this point that to expect politics as usual from a person who was the product of the demand for unusual politics seemed somewhat inconsistent, to say the least. For his part, Jimmy Carter had no intention of being inconsistent.

THE LONG CAMPAIGN

Another important conditioning factor favored the outside candidacy of Jimmy Carter. Following their tumultuous convention in 1968, the Democrats enacted many democratizing reforms in their presidential nominating process. One major result was the increase in the number of delegates selected by presidential primaries and committed to candidates. In 1952 there were seventeen primaries that selected 46 percent of the delegates and committed 18 percent of them to candidates. Not much had changed by 1968 when the same number of primaries selected 49 percent and committed 36 percent of the delegates. The system was then reformed, and in 1976 there were twenty-nine primaries that selected 75 percent and committed 66 percent of the delegates. Clearly, the advantage in 1976 would go to a candidate whose strategy and resources were directed to an open process of delegate selection that reduced the role of party leaders. Further, as John H. Kessel points out, increasing the number of primaries has the effect of handicapping late entrants. One must get there early to establish front-runner status—a fact that Senator Frank Church and Governor Brown discovered in 1976.[15]

Additionally the matter of which delegates are selected first is important. Iowa has a caucus system, but it is very open—so much so that campaigning by candidates does not differ dramatically from that in primary selection states. Media attention, too, contributes to that openness. Next comes New Hampshire, traditionally the first state to select delegates with a primary. In both states a candidate can practice what James W. Ceaser refers to as "village politics," which takes more time than money. Thus Carter's early announcement was important, as was his organizational thrust. As an unemployed former governor, he could take the time to become acquainted in Iowa and New Hampshire. Later on, candidates must practice mass politics as the campaign shifts to the larger states. According to Ceaser: "The objective to the outsider . . . has been to try to turn his success in village politics into a mass phenomenon. If the outsider can do well in these early contests, that is either win or perform surprisingly well relative to expectation, his candidacy can take off."[16]

"Jimmy who?" became a campaign slogan that neatly encapsuled the effort by Carter's organization to take advantage of the perceived public need for someone new and different. At any one time a list of "presidential aspirants" can be compiled that typically includes people with sufficient name recognition for the media and the pollsters to maintain interest in their candidacy. Jimmy Carter's name was not on anyone's list two years before the 1976 election year. Carter's press secretary, Jody Powell, commented on this situation: "I think it was an asset for us that we didn't have people looking over our shoulders. In 1975 the level of expectations for Jimmy Carter was extremely low. Deciding not to worry about any of the things we couldn't do anything about gave us a certain amount of freedom to concentrate on the things that we could do something about —like beginning to establish organizations, almost on a person-to-person

15. Nelson W. Polsby, *Consequences of Party Reform* (New York, 1983), 64; John H. Kessel, *Presidential Campaign Politics* (2nd ed.; Homewood, Ill., 1984), 308.

16. James W. Ceaser, *Reforming the Reforms: A Critical Analysis of the Presidential Selection Process* (Cambridge, Mass., 1982), 56.

Figure 1
THE LONG CAMPAIGN

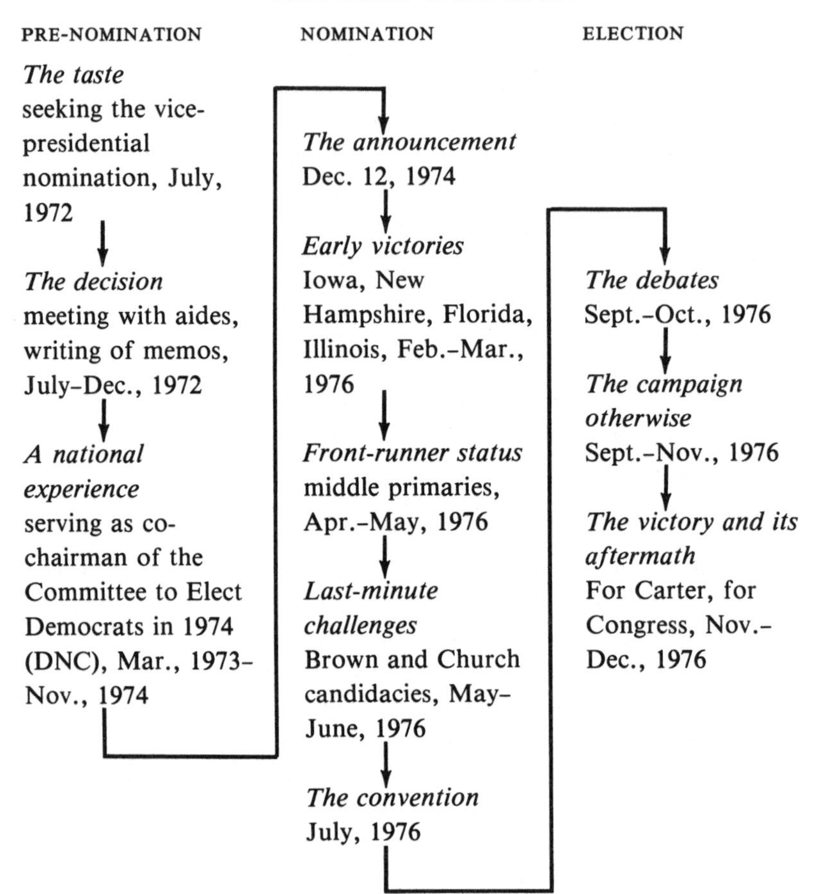

basis, in some of those early states." In essence, Powell was saying that an unknown candidate must prepare an organization so that when "list" status is finally achieved, it can be sustained.[17]

Figure 1 provides an overview of the Carter campaign—from the effort by his aides to have him selected as the vice-presidential nominee in 1972 (to run with McGovern) to the surprising capture of the nomination and the eventual narrow victory at the polls. I do not intend to describe

17. Jonathan Moore and Janet Fraser (eds.), *Campaign for President: The Managers Look at '76* (Cambridge, Mass., 1977), 78–79.

this long campaign in detail; that is done elsewhere.[18] My purpose is to identify the effect of events on Carter's view of politics. Was he likely to be more or less sympathetic toward Capitol Hill politics as a result of his campaign experience? Did the experience of running for president confirm his trusteeship approach to governing?

PRE-NOMINATION ACTIVITIES

I have identified three important activities during this early period—the try for the vice-presidential nomination in 1972, the decision to go after the 1976 presidential nomination, and the experience of working with the national Democratic party in 1974.

The taste. Jimmy Carter was governor of Georgia when he led his delegation to the 1972 Democratic convention. Nothing associated with his role suggested that he would be the nominee in four years' time. Yet the event itself taught Carter and his staff some powerful lessons. Among other things, they came to believe that the nomination was within the reach of a candidate from the outside.

Carter's activities at the 1972 convention were rather limited. His significance as a leader from the South was severely circumscribed by Wallace's presidential candidacy. Carter personally favored Senator Henry Jackson (Washington)—he even nominated Jackson. But the delegation itself was split, and Carter was able to deliver only 14.5 votes for Jackson (McGovern received 14.5 votes; Wallace, 11 votes; Shirley Chisholm, 12 votes; and Terry Sanford, 1 vote). The Georgia delegation was also severely split on the seating of the Illinois and California delegations, issues that were crucial to McGovern's control of the convention.

Carter's limited role did not prevent his aides from trying to promote their man as a vice-presidential candidate. It was an audacious move, but one that contributed to their political education. As one aide described it: "We went to the '72 convention . . . and we had this notion that Carter ought to be McGovern's vice president. [This] was the first time I'd ever been to a national convention, and we found out how naive and foolish

18. See Witcover, *Marathon*; Moore and Fraser (eds.), *Campaign for President*; Glad, *Jimmy Carter*; Gerald Pomper *et al.*, *The Election of 1976* (New York, 1977); and Martin Schram, *Running for President, 1976: The Carter Campaign* (New York, 1977).

we were, and how little we knew about the national scene. But we also came back from the convention in '72 convinced that if we could understand the party structure and understand the process, that Governor Carter could be elected president." As Betty Glad and Jules Witcover state in their respective accounts of this event, Gerald Rafshoon, Peter Bourne, and Hamilton Jordan sought an audience with McGovern's pollster, a Harvard undergraduate named Patrick Caddell. They wanted Caddell to look at polls from Georgia showing that Carter would add strength to the ticket in that state. Caddell "thought we were crazy," Rafshoon said. Perhaps, among other things, Caddell recalled that Carter had been involved in the so-called ABM (Anybody But McGovern) movement.[19]

As it turned out, of course, McGovern would have done well to have selected Carter. His choice of Senator Thomas Eagleton (Missouri) caused embarrassment, and Eagleton eventually withdrew from the ticket. On the other hand, McGovern's crushing defeat would not have contributed to Carter's political future.

In *Why Not the Best?*, Carter explains other lessons of the 1972 presidential campaign.

> I have always looked on the Presidency of the United States with reverence and awe, and I still do. But recently I have begun to realize that the president is just a human being. I can almost remember when I began to change my mind and form this opinion.
>
> Before becoming governor I had never met a president. . . . Then during 1971 and 1972 I met Richard Nixon, Spiro Agnew, George McGovern, Henry Jackson, Hubert Humphrey, Ed Muskie, George Wallace, Ronald Reagan, Nelson Rockefeller, and other presidential hopefuls, and I lost my feeling of awe about presidents. This is not meant as a criticism of them, but it is merely a simple statement of fact.[20]

Carter had an opportunity to observe many senators vying for the nomination at the 1972 Democratic convention—McGovern, Jackson, Humphrey, and Muskie. Only Wallace was from outside the Washington circle. McGovern won the nomination handily, initially selecting another senator (Eagleton) as his vice-presidential candidate. The Democratic ticket suffered one of the most devastating defeats in history.

Jimmy Carter had every reason to consider his own candidacy for president based on his observations of Democratic presidential politics in

19. Transcripts, VII, 17; Glad, *Jimmy Carter*, 207–209; Witcover, *Marathon*, 106–107.
20. Carter, *Why Not the Best?*, 137.

1972. It was evident to Carter and his aides that Washington-based experience was no particular advantage in producing a winning team for the majority party. Nor was McGovern's victory over other candidates from the Senate likely to impress Carter with the high quality and consummate political skill of senators. Thus, the initial foray into national politics fortified the basic attitudes and inclinations of the political outsider-*cum*-trustee.

The decision. After the 1972 convention, Carter and his closest advisers independently concluded that the presidential nomination was not out of reach. Peter Bourne wrote a memorandum outlining how Carter might do it, stressing the need to take risks and rely heavily on "your greatest asset—your personal charm." Bourne, Hamilton Jordan, Jody Powell, Gerald Rafshoon, and Landon Butler met with Carter after he had read Bourne's memo. As reported by Witcover, this group discussed the prospects with the then-governor long into the evening, reviewing strengths and weaknesses. "Rafshoon recalls that Carter was noncommittal after that first meeting, and asked Jordan to incorporate in a memo all the major points raised during the discussion. 'I don't believe he said go,' Rafshoon says. 'I think he took it all in. But we knew. I remember Ham and I walking out and saying, "That son of a bitch, he wants it."'"[21]

Apparently Carter had already discussed the possibility of seeking the nomination with his wife, Rosalynn; his good friend Charles Kirbo; perhaps others. It is a mark of a good staff that they begin to think like the boss. Carter clearly had a good staff.

Hamilton Jordan prepared a detailed memorandum for Carter that was completed by early November, 1972. Over fifty pages long, it outlined the obstacles to the nomination and proposed strategies for overcoming them. The assumption was that George Wallace and Edward Kennedy would be Carter's principal opponents. A strategy designed to defeat these heavyweights was likely to dispose of lesser-known candidates as well. Jordan identified public distrust of government as a major campaign theme. Such a theme was well suited to the record and style of Jimmy Carter and was highly credible with the public. As Betty Glad notes: "Generally, he was advised to run against Washington."[22] By the

21. Witcover, *Marathon*, 110.
22. Glad, *Jimmy Carter*, 211.

end of 1972, he had decided to run, though no announcement was made at that time. Rather, following Jordan's strategy, Carter sought to prepare himself by national and international travel, as well as party service.

In summary, nothing associated with the decision to run was likely to alter Jimmy Carter's view of politics. If anything, the circumstances motivating the effort had the opposite effect. The public was correctly perceived as being troubled about Washington politics. Wallace's capacity to tap this dissatisfaction was limited, because of his past identification with a single issue. Carter, on the other hand, could pose convincingly as an outsider who was to be entrusted with a mandate for change.

A national experience. In what is surely one of the more curious appointments, Jimmy Carter was designated by the chairman of the Democratic National Committee, Robert Strauss, to co-chair (with former governor Terry Sanford of North Carolina) the Committee to Elect Democrats in 1974. Hamilton Jordan joined the headquarters staff to become "Carter's eyes and ears at the national committee."[23]

Why was Jimmy Carter selected? Surely not because of his qualifications as a campaigner for members of Congress or because of his visibility as a national political figure. Apparently he was appointed because he asked for a job. Carter supported Strauss to be Jean Westwood's successor as party chairman, in the aftermath of McGovern's defeat in 1972. Strauss visited Atlanta and, in accordance with Jordan's advice in his memo, Carter asked if he might not play a role in the 1974 elections. He could not succeed himself as governor of Georgia and therefore lacked a political base. Strauss intended to have the national committee more involved in the midterm campaign than had been the case in the past, and so "the job and the man came together."

Under different circumstances, this experience might well have contributed to candidate Carter's understanding of the political life of members of Congress by teaching him of their "home style" and "electoral connection."[24] As it happened, however, members were themselves running against unethical conduct in Washington in 1974. Watergate, the Nixon pardon, and even congressional improprieties encouraged good-government campaigns. Since the Republicans were held responsible for

23. Whitcover, *Marathon*, 117.

24. See Richard F. Fenno, Jr., *Home Style: House Members in Their Districts* (Boston, 1978); and David R. Mayhew, *Congress: The Electoral Connection* (New Haven, 1974).

the low status of politics, the Democrats were favored to increase their margins in Congress, which they did. In fact, these Democrats did not need Jimmy Carter's help to win. Thus he was free to use the experience in a way that was beneficial to his 1976 presidential campaign. It was not demanded that he do otherwise, nor was he so inclined by virtue of the political conditions at the time.

What, then, did Carter and his aides do in fulfilling this national-party responsibility? Witcover concludes: "Carter's new job really was not much, and Strauss didn't think he was giving anything much to him; Carter was not a particular favorite of his. But Carter made the most of it. The post provided an entree for him to labor leaders, political consultants, and liberal special interest representatives in agriculture, education, consumerism, and other areas who met regularly at the national committee to consider political matters." Thus it appears that Carter and his aides used the opportunity to make contacts among those who might well be important in determining delegate selection for the 1976 convention. Given changes in the nominating process, few of these persons were members of Congress. "More important in the long run were Carter's contacts not with local party power-brokers but with the young, experienced party activists in the thirty-two states he visited. These were to become the foot soldiers of his presidential army."[25]

NOMINATION ACTIVITIES

For discussion purposes, the nomination phase is marked here as beginning with the December 12, 1974, announcement by Jimmy Carter that he was a candidate for president. The decision to run had, of course, already been made. The pre-nomination period was characterized by testing the political waters and acquainting the candidate and his staff with the challenge before them. An effort was made to keep Carter's candidacy a secret—a task that was not too difficult, according to Witcover. "The notion of Jimmy Carter running for President was absurd on its face; beyond that, Democrats continued to expect that in the end Kennedy would agree to run and would be nominated routinely." But the Kennedy nomination was not to be. The senator himself made that clear even before the 1974 election. "I will not accept the nomination. I will

25. Witcover, *Marathon*, 117, 118.

not accept a draft. I will oppose any effort to place my name in nomination in any state or at the national convention, and I will oppose any effort to promote my candidacy in any other way."[26]

Two other senators, Henry Jackson and Walter Mondale, appeared to benefit immediately, but Mondale joined Kennedy in declaring himself out of the race. Beyond these men it was literally anyone's guess who might be the nominee. No one of the prospects appeared to have an edge. In fact they were all relative unknowns. In this race, with Kennedy out, Jimmy Carter was no more disadvantaged than was any other candidate by his lack of name recognition. And he had one enormous advantage—he could legitimately conduct an anti-Washington campaign. It is now apparent that the times and the candidate were converging.

Figure 2 shows the sequence of announcements for and withdrawals from the 1976 Democratic presidential race. It was an unusual election year, to say the least. The large number of candidates was spawned in part because of Kennedy's withdrawal. Jackson and Wallace probably would have run anyway. Of the rest, apart from Carter, only Udall emerged as a serious candidate. Governor Brown was a potential threat as an alternative outside candidate but he entered too late. Hubert Humphrey was an unannounced candidate who was viewed as an alternative should no other candidate emerge. He withdrew on April 29, 1976, without even having announced that he would run. Included among the sixteen candidates (announced and unannounced) were nine senators, one member of the House of Representatives, four governors, and one person, Sargent Shriver, who had never been elected to anything but ran as a vice-presidential candidate with McGovern in 1972.

The announcement. As indicated in Figure 2, Jimmy Carter was the second entrant into the 1976 campaign, announcing just days after Representative Morris Udall of Arizona. Carter actively sought support at the Democratic party mini-convention the week before in Kansas City, and thus his candidacy was no surprise to those who followed the politics of obscure candidates. The future president spoke first at the National Press Club in Washington. His speech was entitled "For America's Third Century Why Not the Best?" He then returned home to announce his intentions, appearing in the lobby of the Atlanta Civic Center. These ac-

26. *Ibid.*, 118; *Congressional Quarterly Weekly Report*, September 28, 1974, p. 2609.

Figure 2
THE DEMOCRATIC CANDIDATES' CALENDAR

CANDIDATES	ANNOUNCEMENTS AND WITHDRAWALS (OR SUSPENSIONS)
Edward Kennedy	– – – – Sept. 23
Walter Mondale	– – – – – – – – Nov. 21
Morris Udall	Nov. 23 —— June 14
Jimmy Carter	Dec. 12 ——→
Fred Harris	Jan. 11 —— Apr. 8
Henry Jackson	Feb. 6 —— May 1
Lloyd Bentsen	Feb. 17 —— Feb. 10
Terry Sanford	May 29 —— Jan. 23
Sargent Shriver	Sept. 20 —— Mar. 22
Milton Shapp	Sept. 25 —— Mar. 12
Birch Bayh	Oct. 21 —— Mar. 4
George Wallace	Nov. 12 —— June 9
Robert Byrd	Jan. 9 —— ?
Edmund Brown	Mar. 12 —— July 14
Frank Church	Mar. 18 —— June 14
Hubert Humphrey	– Apr. 29

J A S O N D J F M A M J J A S O N D J F M A M J J — Democratic Convention (July 14)

1974 — 1975 — 1976

SOURCE: Dates taken from Jonathan Moore and Janet Fraser (eds.), *Campaign for President: The Managers Look at '76* (Cambridge, Mass., 1977), 161–66.

NOTE: Kennedy, Mondale, and Humphrey were talked of as candidates, but they never announced and later withdrew.

tions were precisely in line with Hamilton Jordan's August 4, 1974, memorandum on campaign strategy.

> I believe that we have generally agreed that you should announce your candidacy for the Presidency the week following the Charter Conference [the Democratic party mini-convention] in Washington, D.C. It was tentatively agreed that we should pursue the possibility of the press club announcement at least to the point of determining if that is—in fact—one of our options [which it was]. . . . On the same day or next day I believe that it is important that we have some function here in Georgia where you announce your plans to our friends in Georgia. It is terribly important that you "share" your announcement with the Georgia people to avoid [it] being said that Jimmy Carter has gone national and has forgotten his state and people.

Thus, everything up to this point went according to plan. However, Jordan went on to state that "we should never forget that our early announcement is a tactical maneuver which will hopefully result in your receiving inordinate amounts of coverage and publicity."[27] There were not even ordinary amounts of coverage and publicity. Of course, "our early announcement" turned out to be second to Udall's and thus was not as newsworthy as it might have been.[28]

It is hard to say whether the announcement influenced Carter's image of legislative life. A member of the House did upstage him, but it is doubtful that Udall's entry contributed further to Carter's negative view of Congress. Indeed, it is unlikely that the Carter staff judged the Udall candidacy to be a serious one—any more serious than others judged the Carter candidacy to be. Jordan did advise Carter in his memo to inform Democratic members of Congress of his intentions—with "a high-quality, personalized mailing . . . [to] arrive simultaneous with your announcement." But no effort was made to include members of Congress in announcement activities, either in Washington or in Atlanta.

Early victories. In her journal of events in 1976, Elizabeth Drew made the following notes in regard to the upcoming Iowa caucuses: "In May, forty-seven of the Democratic National Convention's three thousand and eight delegates will be chosen by the Iowa Democratic state convention. The precinct caucuses are the first step toward that end. Only about

27. The edited memorandum is printed as an appendix in Schram, *Running for President*, 377.

28. John B. Gabusi, Udall's campaign director, stated that "the Mondale announcement was the real key to the congressman's decision that he would in fact be a candidate" (quoted in Moore and Fraser [eds.], *Campaign for President*, 76).

thirty-five thousand Democrats are expected to vote in the Iowa caucuses next week, but, as with New Hampshire, politicians and the press have already given what happens in Iowa a great deal of importance." The Carter campaign organization was alert to the opportunity in Iowa for gaining an early victory. And, of course, Jimmy Carter was in an excellent position to have "doing well" interpreted as victory. As Donald R. Matthews points out: "Who wins—or loses—a presidential primary is frequently unclear. . . . More often than not, winning a presidential primary means doing better than expected; losing means disappointing expectations."[29]

The expectations about a candidacy are carried from one contest to the next, typically changing along the way. Campaign organizations are forced to accommodate these changes. In Carter's case, expectations were low, and thus the definition of victory could justifiably be minimal. He did not have to destroy his opposition; he just had to rise above the pack. Elizabeth Drew's notes for the week before the Iowa caucus read as follows: "The consensus today . . . is that Jimmy Carter is doing especially well in Iowa. . . . A story by R. W. Apple, Jr., in the *Times* last October saying that Carter was doing well in Iowa was itself a political event, prompting other newspaper stories that Carter was doing well in Iowa. . . . This consensus helps Carter do even better. . . . Perhaps he is qualified for the Presidency, but as of now there is no way of knowing. His ability to organize in Iowa and his attractive looks do not tell us that."[30]

The concept of "doing well" suited the Carter plan and exceeded their goals. Jordan had written in the August, 1974, memorandum:

> Our minimal goal in these early primaries would be to gain acceptance as a serious and viable candidate, demonstrate that Wallace is vulnerable and that Carter can appeal to the "Wallace" constituency, and show through our campaign a contrasting style and appeal. Our minimal goal would dictate at least a second-place showing in New Hampshire and Florida and respectable showings in Wisconsin, Rhode Island, and Illinois. Our national goals (which I think are highly attainable) would be to win New Hampshire and/or Florida outright, make strong showings in the other three early primary states and beat Wallace.[31]

29. Elizabeth Drew, *American Journal: The Events of 1976* (New York, 1976), 5; Donald R. Matthews, "Winnowing: The News Media and the 1976 Presidential Nominations," in James David Barber (ed.), *Race for the Presidency: The Media and the Nominating Process* (Englewood Cliffs, N.J., 1978), 63.

30. Drew, *American Journal*, 6.

31. Schram, *Running for President*, 380.

Figure 3
CARTER AND THE NOMINATING CONTESTS, 1976

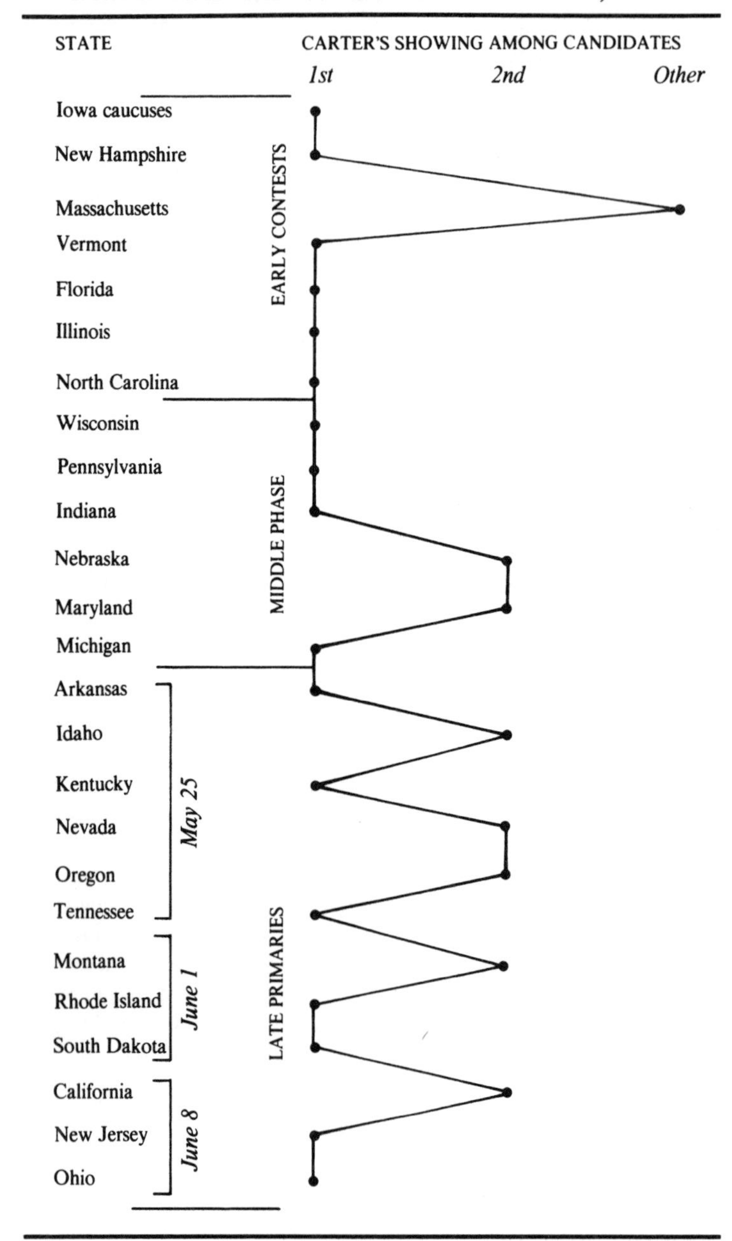

Figure 3 shows the sequence and partial results of the early contests. Carter ran first in six of the nine states and ran first or second in all but one—Massachusetts. He emerged from this period as the consensus front-runner. Equally important, the winnowing process was working well. In matching Figures 2 and 3, one notes that five of the first eleven candidates had withdrawn by the end of March. Fred Harris lasted only until the Wisconsin primary in early April. On the other hand, two new candidates, Brown and Church, joined the contest as late entrants. Still, in consistently performing better than expected, Carter established himself not only as a "serious and viable candidate" but as a credible front-runner. Only Udall, Jackson, Wallace, and the two newcomers remained.

Front-runner status. Another accomplishment of the early contests was the defeat of George Wallace. He remained in the race until June 9 but won no primaries during that period. The Florida and North Carolina primaries had effectively knocked Wallace out of the contest.

As the acknowledged front-runner, Carter had to avoid surprises—that is, unexpected strength from other candidates. He had achieved his status by their having underrated him in the first place. There continued to be doubts that he could still gain the nomination, and yet he won where he needed to win during April and May. The most crucial victories during this middle phase were in Wisconsin, Pennsylvania, and Michigan—three industrial midwestern states in which the doubters might justifiably predict losses. Carter "won" all three, that is, he got higher percentages than did his opponents. Yet in none did he get a majority of the vote: he received 36.6 percent in Wisconsin, 37.0 percent in Pennsylvania, and 43.4 percent in Michigan. In the first two states the combined vote for Udall and Jackson exceeded Carter's (42.0 percent in Wisconsin, 43.3 percent in Pennsylvania, where Jackson actually ran second). The press does not typically count combined votes in declaring winners, however. And the Carter campaign "miracle" moved into its last phase, a prime example of the politics of the reformed nominating process. As Rosalynn Carter observed: "We knew we had reached a turning point in the campaign. . . . Winning is more fun than losing!"[32]

32. Rosalynn Carter, *First Lady From Plains* (Boston, 1984), 132.

Last-minute challenges. Figure 3 indicates clearly that the last three weeks of the primary campaign were not notably successful for Carter. The entry of Brown into the race, followed by that of Church made this last period something less than triumphant. Rosalynn Carter believed that "Democratic party liberals" had launched "a movement known as 'ABC' ('Anybody But Carter')." On this matter of a late announcement Jordan's memorandum turned out to be both right and wrong. "No serious candidate will have the luxury of picking and choosing among the early primaries. To pursue such a strategy would cost that candidate delegate votes and increase the possibility of being lost in the crowd. I think that we have to assume that everybody will be running in the first five or six primaries."[33]

Brown and Church estimated that a front-runner would not emerge from the early primaries and that they would be in a position to attract votes as fresh candidates in a tired field. Unfortunately for them, a front-runner had emerged, and though both performed impressively where entered, neither could command sufficient support to be more than spoilers. They demonstrated what many felt all along—that Carter was vulnerable and that his narrow victories represented electoral weakness. But if Carter's support was questionable, theirs was even more so. Jordan was right in his belief that failure to run in the early primaries would be detrimental. Neither Brown nor Church could claim credible candidacies based on victories in the later primaries. Thus, demonstrating Carter's weakness may have proved a point but it did not produce an alternative candidate.

Never before had there been so many presidential primaries. It was a new era in the politics of selection. The new system was developed in response to criticism of the old method that presumably relied heavily on "insiders"—including members of Congress. A strong anti-politics-as-usual mood during the 1970s gave the Democrats a more open and more participatory means for choosing delegates to their national convention.[34]

33. *Ibid.*; Schram, *Running for President*, 379.

34. For details, see Polsby, *Consequences of Party Reform*; Kessel, *Presidential Campaign Politics*; Ceaser, *Reforming the Reforms*; Herbert Asher, *Presidential Elections and American Politics* (Homewood, Ill., 1980); William J. Crotty, *Political Reform and the American Experiment* (New York, 1977); and particularly Byron E. Shafer, *Quiet Revolution: The Struggle for the Democratic Party and the Shaping of Post-Reform Politics* (New York, 1983).

These developments suited the interests and style of Jimmy Carter. It was possible for him to win the nomination without participating in the politics he disliked, a politics that might well have brought him into contact with legislators and legislative life. Further, he appeared to like the politics he did play—a sort of village or town-meeting politics writ large, through which he gradually defined his trust.

Thus it was that Carter could pursue the presidency with only limited contact with members of Congress and engage in an experience that rather consistently sustained his image of himself as a man for the times. Put otherwise, there was little during this period to alter and a great deal to sustain Carter's trusteeship politics. Further, his own self-confidence and sense of mission were supported by the string of early victories and the failure of a credible alternative candidate to emerge. A man with few self-doubts collected no more during the months before the Democratic convention. This condition alone was unlikely to prepare him well for dealing with an institution designed by doubters to cope with collective insecurities.

The convention. The nomination of Jimmy Carter was a foregone conclusion by the time the Democrats gathered in convention in New York City. As Rosalynn Carter put it: "The Democratic National Convention . . . was a love feast once everyone accepted that Jimmy was going to receive the nomination." The meeting "was the party's most harmonious in 12 years and a stark contrast to the bitter and divisive conventions of 1968 and 1972."[35] Thus, it was not necessary for Carter to negotiate with party leaders from Congress or elsewhere in order to protect his support, select a vice-presidential candidate, manage the convention, or write a platform. His task was to maintain harmony in a conflict-weary party. There were minor skirmishes before the Rules Committee but none of the pitched battles that had characterized the work of committees at other recent conventions.

In a very important sense, the convention reflected the Carter candidacy. More delegates than usual were outsiders. By the design of the post-1968 reforms, fewer national and state party leaders attended as del-

35. Rosalynn Carter, *First Lady From Plains*, 136; Congressional Quarterly, *Guide to 1976 Elections* (Washington, D.C., 1977), 4. It should be noted that the 1976 convention was also more harmonious than was the one in 1980.

egates, though many local party leaders were there. The reformers intended to increase grass-roots participation at the convention, which, of course, was an advantage for Carter. One result was that few members of Congress served as delegates or alternates. The comparative figures for three conventions are as follows:[36]

	1968	*1972*	*1976*
Percentage of Democratic senators serving as delegates or alternates	68	36	18
Percentage of Democratic representatives serving as delegates or alternates	39	15	15

There clearly was less opportunity for the presidential candidate in 1976 to work with members of Congress.

Conventions do offer opportunities for building coalitions of support for candidates and issues. It so happened, however, that the 1976 convention provided fewer such legislative-like experiences than was normal. The platform did require some "negotiating, cajoling, and occasionally strong-arming," but Stuart Eizenstat, Carter's "issues chief," had a relatively easy time of it, and the document was accepted with only minor changes. The platform itself was a "broad statement of party goals rather than a list of legislative programs and controversial stands on issues."[37]

In summary, the convention too was unlikely to change Carter's view of his mission in any important way. His acceptance speech reiterated the themes of his campaign for the nomination.

> 1976 will not be a year of politics as usual. It can be a year of inspiration and hope. And it will be a year of concern, of quiet and sober reassessment of our nation's character and purpose—a year when voters have already confounded the experts.
>
> And I guarantee you that it will be the year when we give the government of this country back to the people of this country.
>
> There's a new mood in America.

His speech also reflected his unusual status within the national Democratic party. "I have never met a Democratic president, but I've always been a Democrat." Jimmy Carter was truly a candidate from the outside who was able to take advantage of a nominating process that had been

36. Nelson W. Polsby and Aaron Wildavsky, *Presidential Elections* (New York, 1980), 110.

37. Witcover, *Marathon*, 357; *Guide to 1976 Elections*, 7.

gradually separated from the governing process. As Nelson W. Polsby and Aaron Wildavsky conclude: "Increasingly, those who do the selecting are not the same as those who live most intimately with the results."[38] Thus, in a sense, two Democratic parties prepared for the 1976 general election—one associated with the new participation of the post-1968 reforms and one associated with the continuity of party traditions and policy stands. The two parties would come together in Washington in January, 1977.

THE GENERAL ELECTION

> Carter 66 percent, Ford 27 percent
> Carter 68 percent, Reagan 26 percent
> Suddenly, Jimmy Carter was the champion of the poll vault. Catapulted by the euphoria of the Democratic Convention, Carter quickly soared to a lead that Louis Harris called "one of the most substantial ever recorded."
> That was in mid-July. Less than two weeks later, on August 1, George Gallup weighed in with figures almost as over-powering.
> Carter 62 percent, Ford 29 percent
> Carter 64 percent, Reagan 27 percent.

Carter's pollster, Patrick Caddell, was cautious, warning that many Carter supporters were unenthusiastic. Still the results were very encouraging at the start of the campaign. The euphoria did not last—as Caddell predicted. Following the Republican convention in mid-August, Carter's lead in the Gallup Poll had slipped to 13 points—50 to 37—and Caddell had it even lower. "The race has tightened with a rush. Later, Caddell figures the bad news might have been good, after all. 'It did wonders for the Carter campaign,' he says. 'It brought everyone back from thinking about where their offices were going to be in the White House.' "[39]

The fall campaign concentrated on winning the number of states necessary for victory, and therefore a strategy had to be devised. Hamilton Jordan understood these facts of political life very well. In his postconvention memorandum, the first-stated strategic premise read: "Our clear and single goal must be to simply win 270 electoral votes." Jordan warned Carter that "we cannot afford initially to become so enamoured

38. *Congressional Quarterly Weekly Report*, July 17, 1976, p. 1933; Polsby and Wildavsky, *Presidential Elections*, 111.

39. Schram, *Running for President*, 218, 238.

with our own survey results and the prospects of a landslide that we lose sight of the 270 electoral votes we will need. To expand our limited resources trying to win 400 electoral votes, we could easily fall short of the 270 we need to win the election.'' The memorandum then analyzed where these votes might be gained. A point system was established, based on the size of the state, the Democratic potential, and the need for that state in order to win. This exercise then led to a determination of how much time was to be spent where.[40]

The Jordan memorandum, devoid of any talk about issues or even themes, concentrated entirely on where, when, and how much time. It is interesting by contrast to read the memorandum prepared for President Ford. The candid and lengthy appraisal of the strengths and weaknesses of both candidates leads up to a set of strategic goals, including themes that should be developed. As expected, Congress receives little attention in either memorandum—none at all in Jordan's. The Ford memo identifies problems with Congress as a possible difficulty for the president. And in speaking of Carter's weaknesses, the memorandum states that "He has the support of the Democratic Party which brought us our current problem of big, unresponsive federal government; he will either have to defend the Congress, or Party, or reject it—either of which will give him problems."[41]

Here, in the Ford memo, was a politically rational reason for Carter to ignore Congress during the campaign. But it seems unlikely that the Carter organization ever drew these conclusions in this way. Rather, their election effort to this point profited, as they saw it, from an anti-Washington mood. Therefore the emphasis was logically concentrated on their man as representing relief from the place. The challenge was to capitalize on a negative public mood, promoting Carter's distance, separation, and independence. What might seem an advantage for many Democratic presidents—the probability of working with a Democratic Congress—could never develop as a major campaign theme for Carter. His task, as correctly outlined by Jordan, was to win 270 electoral votes, and to do so with as few commitments and as much distance from Washington-based Democrats as possible. To campaign without campaigning, to be there to remind voters that they needed someone else—*i.e.*, Carter—appeared to be the strategy. Still it is important to review the fall campaign

40. *Ibid.*, 247.
41. *Ibid.*, 260.

in order to determine whether events were likely to alter Carter's preconceived ideas about Congress and its functions in the policy process. I start with the debates, which put the candidates onstage together.

The debates. The 1976 debates were the first since 1960. The candidates met three times. A fourth debate in 1976 featured the vice-presidential candidates. The presidential debate format is not like that associated with any decision-making experiences of either the president or Congress. In fact, as Harold D. Lasswell pointed out in commenting on the 1960 debates, a "true debate" might well threaten the political system: "Given the presently prevailing institutions of the American polity, we must not overlook the possibility that a true debate between presidential candidates would threaten the genius for ambiguity that is essential to the operation of our complex, semi-responsible, relatively democratic system of multigroup coalition. The implication is that the introduction of 'genuine debate at the top' on TV calls for simultaneous changes elsewhere in the effective practices of American government."[42] I agree with Lasswell. The debate is an unreal political event, yet one that grows out of a desire for a different kind of government—the issues are clearly explicated and the voters are then able to make rational choices. Presidential debates are not the first, nor will they be the last, efforts to get the system to perform better.

My concern in studying the debates is the effects they had on the candidates. Specifically, I am interested in judging whether Jimmy Carter learned something that might have modified his view of the legislature, as influenced by trusteeship politics. Unfortunately, however, the principal study of the 1976 debates offers little on what the candidates got out of the experience, despite the fact that one of them would serve as president. It concentrates on the impact the debates had on the voters.

We can learn something, however, from how Carter was briefed and whether he changed his approach in the later debates. Sidney Kraus, the editor of the volume on the debates, submitted questions to Stuart Eizenstat about this briefing. Eizenstat said that the staff did prepare Carter for the second and possibly the third debate by throwing "a few questions out." These sessions were held in the morning. "Then we'd let him rest in

42. Lasswell's introduction to Sidney Kraus (ed.), *The Great Debates: Kennedy vs. Nixon, 1960* (Bloomington, 1962), 21.

the afternoon and evening so that his mind wasn't cluttered. He, as he currently does as President, likes to work as much as possible by written memorandum, so he relied heavily on the written material that we had given him in those briefing books rather than relying mostly on oral or verbal give and take." Eizenstat emphasized that they were particularly determined to show Carter's "grasp of the issues." In the second and third debates, after having established the capabilities of their man, they wanted Carter to put President Ford on the defensive "by being assertive and direct." Thus, from what little one can glean from this limited amount of material, it does not appear that the basic Carter style was in any way affected by the debate experience. A self-confident candidate first sought to establish his command of the issues, then to show up his opponent. As Eizenstat put it: "The advantages we had were that we had a clearly more intelligent, articulate, photogenic, personable candidate, who was just a better candidate." While it is difficult to measure who won, David O. Sears and Steven H. Chaffee are probably correct in concluding that "Carter, having been ahead before the debates, could well have won the election simply by not losing the debates by very much. And of course Carter did win the election . . . and the end toward which the debates constituted part of the means."[43] Thus the debates did nothing to shake Carter's confidence. He is generally conceded to have lost the first, won the next two, and won the debates overall.

What of the content of the debates? Were there questions or discussions that might have revealed Carter's thinking on the matter of presidential-congressional relations? Surely the most striking aspect of the debates from the present perspective is that *no one of the reporters ever asked Jimmy Carter how he might deal with Congress*. This fact is remarkable, given that Carter had no Washington-based political experience and that Ford had so much. One might have thought that the question would have been asked sometime during the three debates. Carter did make the point in summary statements for each of the debates that he would work well with Congress. In the first debate he said: "It's time to draw ourselves together; to have a president and a Congress that can work together with mutual respect for a change, cooperating for a

43. "Candidate Briefings," in Sidney Kraus (ed.), *The Great Debates: Carter vs. Ford, 1976* (Bloomington, 1979), 106, 107; David O. Sears and Steven H. Chaffee, "Uses and Affects of the 1976 Debates: An Overview of Empirical Studies," *ibid.*, 255.

change, in the open for a change, so the people can understand their own government." In the second debate: "Or will we have . . . Congress, citizens, president, secretary of state working in harmony and unity toward a common future?" And in the third debate: "But I believe that we can now establish in the White House a good relationship with Congress, a good relationship with our people, set very high goals for our country." In the second debate on foreign and defense policy he stressed the need to "restore the involvement of the Congress." He believed that "secrecy . . . has surrounded our foreign policy in the last few years, the American people, the Congress have been excluded."[44]

The only question that elicited a direct discussion of presidential relationships with Congress was asked by Frank Reynolds of ABC News. He wanted to know about the anti-Washington mood in the nation. The question was addressed to President Ford, who responded that the Democratic Congress ought to be the focus of any such mood. Reynolds then asked "whether you can get along with that Congress, or whether we'll have continued confrontation." Ford said that he hoped the ratios would change in the direction of the Republicans but that a Republican president was necessary in any event to check the excesses of a Democratic Congress.

Note that the question of congressional relations was asked of Ford, not of Carter. Carter did have a chance to express himself on the matter, since the format permitted the other candidate to comment. It is important for present purposes, however, that the context for his remark was Ford's relationships with Congress, not his own. As expected, he attacked the president's leadership of Congress, comparing him unfavorably with Eisenhower and Nixon. All he had to say about himself was that "if he insists that I be responsible for the Democratic Congress, of which I'm—have not been a part, then I think it's only fair that he be responsible for the Nixon administration in its entirety, of which he was a part."[45] Thus Carter passed up the opportunity to embrace the Democratic Congress. Rather, he appeared to maintain some distance between himself and the Congress, actually making a debater's point that resulted in an invidious comparison (Nixon for Ford; the Democratic Congress for himself).

44. Kraus (ed.), *The Great Debates, 1976,* pp. 474, 496, 540, 479.
45. *Ibid.,* 471.

The principal conclusion one draws from reviewing the debates is that Congress did not weigh heavily on anyone's mind. My count of references to *Congress* (actually saying the word) for the three debates is as follows:

	Carter	*Ford*	*Total*
First debate	14	41	55
Second debate	12	9	21
Third debate	7	10	17
Totals	33	60	93

The exchange in response to Reynolds' question accounted for twenty-nine of these references (one-third of the total). Of the remainder, President Ford mentioned a program that he had introduced into Congress on several occasions, and Carter noted programs passed and vetoed by Congress or stressed the importance of involving Congress in foreign policy.

In summary, nothing occurred in the debates to force Carter to display or to modify his attitudes toward Congress. He did think that amicable congressional relations were important enough to mention in his closing statements. But no details were provided, and one could gain no insight into how he intended to achieve the results he described.

The campaign otherwise. Nothing matched the debates as a focusing event for the campaign. Hamilton Jordan conceded that "Ford ran a much better campaign than I expected him to run, and we ran a much poorer campaign than we should have." He pointed out that the early polls showed Carter to be very strong when he had just won the nomination and Ford was fighting a strong Reagan challenge for the Republican nomination. "So all of the things that happened to us in the fall were seen in the framework of Carter's slippage; all the news stories were couched in terms of Carter's having blown his lead, and that was a problem almost impossible to handle." The Carter team was also concerned about criticism that Carter was fuzzy on the issues. As Jody Powell observed: "There was no way on God's earth we could shake the fuzziness question in the general election, no matter what Carter did or said. He could have spent the whole campaign doing nothing but reading substantive speeches from morning to night and still have had that image in the national press."[46]

Both Powell and Jordan thought that their candidate was overexposed in the primaries. Powell even thought that "if we could have stayed in Plains until October, as Ford stayed in the White House until October, we would have won by five or ten points." Carter himself was quoted as saying: "One surprise to me was the difficulty of running against an incumbent. The fact that I would be treated as a candidate and he would be treated as a President . . . by the news media was something that we did not anticipate."[47] Therefore Carter was not able to sit back and enjoy his early lead. An active campaign up to election day was a necessity.

Not surprisingly, the campaign relationship with the national Democratic party was something less than intimate. Carter aides worried about being too closely identified with the party. Powell is quoted by Witcover as saying that "it was hard to judge where the balance was between getting the support of Democratic organizations on the one hand and not appearing to be their captive on the other." Hamilton Jordan expanded on this point:

> Carter was an outsider who had rapidly captured the party nomination, so there was a need for him to establish relationships with elements of the party that he had not known before, like labor. Carter developed a relationship with the AFL-CIO which finally resulted in its enthusiastic support in the last three or four weeks of the campaign. But we paid a price with the independent voters: Carter was a guy who wasn't supposed to owe anybody anything, but he kept going to see George Meany, just like politicians have always done. Sometimes the things we had to do over the summer to bring together the elements of the Democratic party helped us with Democrats but hurt us with independent voters.[48]

Clearly, as the Carter people viewed who they were and why they had won, they quite naturally were reluctant to embrace the party (or even know much about it). As one top aide put it: "Certainly Jimmy Carter could not have been elected President of the country twenty or even ten years ago. Only because of the fragmentation that's taken place in the Democratic Party was it possible for him to be elected President." Here was the dilemma. Carter was an outsider, and yet it is the nature of the

46. Moore and Fraser (eds.), *Campaign for President*, 125, 131.
47. *Ibid.*, 131; Schram, *Running for President*, 307–308.
48. Witcover, *Marathon*, 522; Moore and Fraser (eds.), *Campaign for President*, 130.

American party system that such a person can win the nomination. However, victory may come only if that candidate continues to play the more distant role—at least that was how Powell and Jordan sized up the situation. Yet failing to close the distance causes problems of governance, both because party candidates perceive themselves as winning independently of the president's campaign and because the nominee (Carter) may convince himself that once in office, he should maintain that separateness. Nelson W. Polsby discussed this point in his analysis of party reform:

> For the Democratic incumbent, Jimmy Carter, was a President whose conduct in office to a remarkable extent faithfully reflected the learning experiences available along the pathway he followed in order to achieve the Presidency. The argument in brief is that President Carter conducted himself in office in ways that were fully consonant with his personal predilections and his views of public administration but which would have been harder for him to pursue if he had been educated in the course of the nomination process to the need to build a governing coalition.[49]

Polsby argues persuasively that Carter's "pathway . . . to the Presidency" was essentially determined by the new "rules of the game." "His response was to exploit the strategic imperatives these reforms brought into being." This rather permissive pathway was bound to cause difficulties in governance, however. "The institutional constraints upon his personal preferences were weak. . . . And this is the nub of the problem. Nothing in Mr. Carter's prior experience of the nomination process, led him to the view that he needed to come to terms with the rest of the Democratic party."[50]

This analysis suggests another dimension to the separation between the Carter organization and the Democratic party, aside, that is, from worries that too close an identification might repel independent voters. To have moved in and more closely managed the party during the campaign might have displayed the real differences that Jimmy Carter had with major Democratic leaders. The Carter staff believed that their man's reading of the country's mood was different from interpretations

49. Transcripts, VII, 3; Polsby, *Consequences of Party Reform*, 89. For a most intriguing analysis of the effects of nomination process reforms on personality, see Barbara Kellerman, "Introversion in the Oval Office," *Presidential Studies Quarterly*, XIII (Summer, 1983), 383–400.

50. Polsby, *Consequences of Party Reform*, 128, 129.

by such persons as Thomas P. O'Neill (Massachusetts), the new Speaker of the House, and Robert C. Byrd (West Virginia), the new Senate majority leader. Thus, "a basic cleavage" existed that might well have been shown to be irresolvable, had Carter been more aggressive in working with Democrats in the national headquarters or the congressional campaign apparatus on Capitol Hill. Here was a problem that was not, and probably could not be, satisfactorily resolved during the campaign or after.

The campaign was designed to elect Jimmy Carter president of the United States. The organization was basically the one that had won him the nomination. For the most part, the issues were those identified by the candidate, with only occasional commitments being made to special groups. Congress was not an issue. And given Democratic strength in congressional elections, it was not necessary for Jimmy Carter to run a congressionally oriented campaign. In fact, ousting an incumbent president was a serious enough challenge that the Carter organization could rationalize concentrating on that goal to the exclusion of others. Once again (as in 1974), there was little need and less justification for Carter to acquaint himself with the important electoral side of legislative life.

The victory and its aftermath. In an interview before the fall campaign started, Carter was quoted as saying: "I think it is important to win with a broad base of support. I would rather have a six-per-cent victory in all the states than a fifteen-per-cent victory in fifteen states and lose the rest of them." As an outsider, he well understood the need to be convincing when he arrived in Washington from Plains. "He underlined that 'the mandate that's crucial for me' to carry out [my] campaign pledges could come only 'from a wide-ranging success among the electorate' that would impress a recalcitrant Congress."[51] As is evident in Table 1, Carter did not get his wish. His victory falls into a special category in which the winner's share of the two-party vote *and* the Electoral College vote fell below 60 percent. The five cases are noted in the table with an asterisk—Wilson in 1916; Truman in 1948; Kennedy in 1960; Nixon in 1968; and Carter in 1976. Wilson and Nixon were minority-party candidates who were successful primarily because of internal divisions within the majority party. Truman won narrowly, but his victory was considered an upset, thus

51. Witcover, *Marathon*, 529.

TABLE 1
Carter's 1976 Victory in Perspective

Election Year	*Percentage of Two-Party Vote for Winner*	*Percentage of Electoral College Vote for Winner*
1900 (McKinley-R)	53.2	65.3
1904 (Roosevelt-R)	60.0	70.6
1908 (Taft-R)	54.5	66.5
1912 (Wilson-D)	64.4	81.9[a]
*1916 (Wilson-D)	51.7	52.2
1920 (Harding-R)	63.9	76.1
1924 (Coolidge-R)	65.2	71.9
1928 (Hoover-R)	58.8	83.6
1932 (Roosevelt-D)	59.1	88.9
1936 (Roosevelt-D)	62.5	98.5
1940 (Roosevelt-D)	55.0	84.6
1944 (Roosevelt-D)	53.8	81.4
*1948 (Truman-D)	52.4	57.1
1952 (Eisenhower-R)	55.4	83.2
1956 (Eisenhower-R)	57.8	86.1
*1960 (Kennedy-D)	50.1	56.4
1964 (Johnson-D)	61.3	90.3
*1968 (Nixon-R)	50.4	55.9
1972 (Nixon-R)	61.8	96.7
*1976 (Carter-D)	51.1	55.2
1980 (Reagan-R)	55.3	90.9

SOURCE: Compiled from data in *Statistical Abstract of the United States, 1982* (Washington, D.C., 1982).

[a]Theodore Roosevelt was a third-party candidate, garnering more popular and electoral votes than did Taft, the Republican candidate.

strengthening his mandate because he exceeded expectations. Carter's victory comes closest to Kennedy's in 1960—a narrow win in the popular and the electoral votes. They had difficulties with a Congress in which their party had commanding majorities in both houses. Further, their Electoral College maps look very much the same. As Table 2 shows, both combined strong showings in the South and industrial East with a sufficient number of midwestern states to carry the day. Neither did well in the West.

TABLE 2
Kennedy's and Carter's Electoral Vote

Region[1]	Percent of Total Electoral Vote				Percent of Region's Electoral Vote	
	Kennedy		*Carter*		*Kennedy*	*Carter*
Northeast	39.9	73.2 (Northeast + South)	29.0	79.2 (Northeast + South)	91.0	70.5
South	33.3		50.2		60.8	88.2
North Central	23.4		19.5		46.4	40.0
West	3.3		1.3		11.8	4.0

Source: Compiled from data in Congressional Quarterly, *Guide to U.S. Elections* (Washington, D.C., 1975, 1977).

[1]Based on Bureau of the Census definitions.

Thus, in crucial respects, Carter was unable to begin his presidency from a position of electoral strength. His victory was among the slightest for a majority-party candidate in this century. And the win was regionally based, nearly 80 percent of the electoral vote coming from the Northeast and South. How well did he run in relationship to other Democratic candidates? Those results are significant for determining how the members of Congress view the president's political strength within their states and districts. Carter's record did not enhance his standing with Congress, and again the comparison with Kennedy is apt.

One looks first at the total seats gained by the president's party for indications of pulling power. In 1976 the Democrats had a net gain of one seat in the House, none in the Senate. Kennedy's record was less impressive—a loss of twenty seats in the House, two in the Senate. In both cases, the previous midterm elections (1958 for Kennedy, 1974 for Carter) had given the Democrats large majorities in both houses. Thus by this first measure it seems that Carter had performed somewhat better. The Democrats held districts that were normally Republican. The somewhat bloated congressional Democratic majority of 1974 was not reduced in size.

Then one examines the districts and states to determine whether the president's win contributed to congressional victories. The results are displayed in Table 3. Neither Kennedy nor Carter could be convincing that their wins were aiding congressional Democrats. Both ran behind more than 90 percent of the victorious House Democrats and behind all but one victorious Senate candidate.

TABLE 3
Kennedy, Carter, and Congressional Democrats

	Presidential Vote Compared with Successful Congressional Democrats	
	President ran ahead	*President ran behind*
House Races		
1960 (Kennedy)	22	243
1976 (Carter)	22	270
Senate Races		
1960 (Kennedy)	0	20
1976 (Carter)	1	21

SOURCE: John F. Bibby *et al.*, *Vital Statistics on Congress, 1980* (Washington, D.C., 1980), 20; and *Guide to U.S. Elections*; Congressional Quarterly, *Guide to 1976 Elections* (Washington, D.C., 1977).

In summary, the victory itself contained important messages for a politically oriented president. Like Kennedy in 1960, Carter won a narrow victory that was regionally based. He did not get the electoral mandate he judged necessary to "impress a recalcitrant Congress." Further, he ran behind the ticket throughout the country. Thus, like Kennedy, he was faced with having to develop sources of power once in office, sources other than electoral strength. But Jimmy Carter was not a politically oriented president and therefore he had the special problem of creating a positive relationship with Congress outside the accepted political style. It would not be easy.

This brief review of Jimmy Carter's route to the White House reveals that events tended to reinforce his thinking about politics and how it was being practiced in Washington, D.C. Even where a particular experience might have modified his version of trusteeship politics, as when he cochaired the 1974 congressional reelection committee, circumstances allowed Carter to maintain his perspective. This reinforcement contributed to a sense of mission that was wholly consistent with Carter's personal preferences and past political experience in Georgia.

Congressional politics had undergone considerable change during the 1970s. The institution had itself responded to precisely the criticism that made Carter's presidential candidacy credible. In other words, many members of Congress were prepared to resent unflattering presidential evaluations that were based on their pre-reform behavior. Further, new leadership was to be selected in each house, presumably offering a fresh start in 1977. Thus, congressional change must also be examined if one is to understand President Carter's record on Capitol Hill.

☆3☆
A Changing Congress

Members of Congress were not insensitive to political and policy developments during the 1970s. Quite the contrary. They were themselves very much affected by the prolonged war in Vietnam, the landslide reelection of Richard Nixon and his use of presidential power, the Arab oil embargo, and, of course, the Watergate scandal. Congress studied itself more during this period than at any time in its history. It produced its version of change, its response to criticism. And many members were frustrated that their individual and collective reform efforts did not appear to improve the public status of Congress.

The principal theme of this chapter is that the Ninety-fifth Congress was preparing itself to assume an expanded and more effective role in governance. Many of the changes were designed to make Congress more directly competitive with the executive. Spurred in particular by the Vietnam War, Nixon's use of presidential power, and Watergate, the members of both houses supported change. Thus, a more pretentious, confident, and aggressive Congress awaited the new president when he was inaugurated on January 20, 1977.

Attention is directed first to congressional elections and turnover in membership—with special concentration on the 1974 Democratic freshmen. Then the focus shifts to congressional reform and its effects both on the institution itself and on presidential-congressional relations.

CONGRESSIONAL ELECTIONS

In *Keeping Faith*, President Carter observes that "most of the Democratic members had never served with a President of their own political party, and their attitude was one of competition rather than cooperation with the White House." Unquestionably the president spotted a special problem for his administration, yet it was not unique. President Eisenhower said that when he entered the White House, "not a single Republican senator . . . had ever served with a President of his own party. Of the 221 Republicans in the House, only fifteen had served with a Republican President." Congressional Republicans were unfamiliar "with either the techniques or the need of cooperating with the Executive."[1] Similarly, the congressional Republicans in 1953 and the congressional Democrats in 1977 were fresh from confrontations with combative presidents (Truman; Nixon and Ford). There was an important difference, however. In 1952, President Eisenhower's impressive victory seemingly helped Republicans gain majority status in the House and Senate. In 1976, on the other hand, President Carter won a narrow victory and Democratic margins in the House and Senate were unchanged.[2] Thus, Carter faced a substantial challenge in getting on with the sizable Democratic majorities in each house of Congress.

A number of interesting developments in congressional elections during the 1970s affected the functioning of Congress and therefore required special attention from those seeking to have influence there. In the House of Representatives, turnover increased despite members' enjoying, on the average, a higher return rate at the polls. Table 4 shows the average annual turnover of House seats for three recent decades. Two developments in particular are worth noting. Most striking is the increase in the number of members not seeking reelection (those who either retired or ran for another office) during the 1970s. An average of 401 members sought reelection in the 1950s, there were 405 in the 1960s, and 390 in the 1970s. At the same time, fewer members were defeated at the polls during the 1970s—there were 27 per election compared with 36 and 33 during the 1960s and 1950s, respectively. As indicated in Table 4, the consequence of these two trends was a net increase in turnover. Members seeking reelection were returned at higher rates but fewer wanted to return.

1. Jimmy Carter, *Keeping Faith: Memoirs of a President* (New York, 1982), 71; Dwight D. Eisenhower, *White House Years: Mandate for Change, 1953–1956* (Garden City, N.Y., 1963), 192.

2. Democratic margins in both houses were substantial, however: 62 to 38 in the Senate, 292 to 143 in the House. President Carter was the beneficiary of the Democratic landslide in congressional elections following Watergate in 1974.

TABLE 4
Turnover in the House of Representatives

Period	Annual Averages: Not Seeking Reelection	Defeated in Primary	Defeated in General	Turnover	Percentage of Whole House
1950–58	34.4	6.0	26.6	67.0	15.4
1960–68	30.2	7.4	28.4	66.0	15.2
1970–78	45.4	7.6	19.4	72.4	16.6

SOURCE: Calculated from data in John Bibby *et al.*, *Vital Statistics on Congress, 1980* (Washington, D.C., 1980), 14.

Why should House members wish to leave when their jobs seemed to be safer than ever? Joseph Cooper and William West conclude that the principal cause was disaffection with House service. "For a variety of reasons, the personal costs of service have greatly increased." A heavier workload, more complex issues, more travel, strenuous campaigning—these and other problems contributed to the dissatisfaction. "When in Washington, members are confronted by the need to vote on hosts of issues they know little about, frustrated by scheduling conflicts in committee meetings and overlaps in jurisdictions, and debilitated by the need to race continually back and forth from office to committee to floor." The rewards do not balance these costs. Salaries have not kept pace with inflation, outside income is curbed, the prestige of the institution is low, and committee chairmanships are less attractive than they were in the past.[3]

Thus, the president was faced with many new members in the House—those elected in the 1970s to replace many who had served in the Kennedy and Johnson administrations. Table 5 shows the breakdown. The proportions of freshman Democrats elected in 1968, in 1970, and in 1972 were relatively small compared with those in 1974 and 1976. A large number of these members survived, however, and by 1977 more than 65 percent had been elected from 1968 to 1976. Carter's observation that most had not served with a Democratic president was correct. Remarkably, only three Democrats from the large freshman class of 1974 were no longer in the House. In fact, 126 of the 292 Democrats in the Ninety-fifth Congress (43 percent) had been elected in 1974 or later (119 in general and 7 in special elections).

3. Joseph Cooper and William West, "The Congressional Career in the 1970s," in Lawrence C. Dodd and Bruce I. Oppenheimer (eds.), *Congress Reconsidered* (2nd ed.; Washington, D.C., 1981), 87.

TABLE 5
House Democrats Coming to Carter

Year	Democrats Elected	Freshman Democrats	Still There in 1977
1968	243	20 (8.2%)	16 (80.0%)
1970	255	33 (12.9%)	20 (60.6%)
1972	244	29 (11.9%)	21 (72.4%)
1974	291	75 (25.8%)	72 (96.0%)
1976	292	47 (16.1%)	47
			176 Elected in general election
			15 Elected in special elections
Total still in the House in 1977			191 (65.4% of Democrats in 95th Congress)

SOURCE: Calculated from data in various issues of *Congressional Quarterly Weekly Report*.

With the many retirements, young Democrats were replacing older Democrats. The "greening of America" was finally affecting the House. The Democratic Study Group—started in the late 1950s by liberal Democrats—emerged in the 1970s with a majority in the House Democratic caucus. These activist-oriented Democrats were determined to make changes. Cooper and West observe that "the new House that is emerging is more junior, more fragmented, more factious, and more individualistic than its predecessor. . . . What we appear to be returning to is a House that in a number of key respects resembles Houses in the nineteenth century, even though more elaborate or sophisticated in terms of resources, structures, and procedures. These Houses also had problems with the net level of member job satisfaction. These Houses also were highly junior, factious, fragmented, and individualistic."[4]

The specific results of the 1976 election demonstrate the interesting mix of fluidity and continuity that was so characteristic of the period. The number of retirements (or decisions to seek another office) was the highest in the post–World War II period (then to be exceeded in 1978). On the other hand, the number of incumbents defeated in the primary and general elections was the second lowest in that same period. Among those incumbents not seeking reelection in 1977 were several committee chairmen: Robert E. Jones of Alabama, Public Works and Transportation; James A. Haley of Florida, Interior and Insular Affairs; Leonor K. Sullivan of Missouri, Select Aging; David N. Henderson of North Carolina, Post Office and Civil Service; Wayne L. Hays of Ohio, House Ad-

4. *Ibid.*, 97.

ministration; Thomas E. Morgan of Pennsylvania, International Relations; and Joe L. Evins of Tennessee, Small Business. In addition, the Ninety-fifth Congress would be without the services of Speaker Carl Albert of Oklahoma; Wilbur D. Mills of Arkansas, former chairman of the Committee on Ways and Means; and F. Edward Hebert of Louisiana, former chairman of the Committee on Armed Services; Ray Madden of Indiana, chairman of the Committee on Rules; and Otto Passman of Louisiana, chairman of the powerful Subcommittee on Foreign Operations of the Committee on Appropriations. Madden and Passman were defeated in primaries. Among them, these five members had 168 years of House experience—an average of nearly 34 years each.

Note that many of those not returning were from the South. Of the eleven committee chairmen (or former chairmen) just cited, eight were from the South or border South. Only one of these eight was replaced by a southerner—Claude Pepper of Florida became chairman of the Select Aging Committee. In fact, there were only seven standing-committee chairmen from the South and border South in the Ninety-fifth Congress, the lowest number in the post–World War II period. Four of these seven chairmen were from Texas. Only one was from the Deep South. John J. Flynt, Jr., from the president's home state, chaired the Committee on Standards of Official Conduct—not exactly a major decision-making unit for enacting the president's program. Thus, the first president from the South in more than one hundred years was inaugurated at a time when congressional power was slipping away from southern Democrats.

President Carter also had the bad luck to lose three senior Georgians to retirement. Philip Landrum had been in the House for twenty-four years. He was a member of the powerful Ways and Means Committee (fifth ranking Democrat) and the Budget Committee. Robert F. Stephens, Jr., had served for sixteen years and was the seventh ranking Democrat on the Banking, Currency, and Housing Committee and the tenth ranking Democrat on the Interior and Insular Affairs Committee. W. S. ("Bill") Stuckey was a more junior member, with ten years' experience in the House. He was the third ranking Democrat on the District of Columbia Committee and the eleventh ranking Democrat on the powerful Interstate and Foreign Commerce Committee. The new Georgia delegation was one of the weakest ever in terms of committee status and seniority ranking. The average years of House experience for the delegation declined from eight in the Ninety-fourth Congress to five in the Ninety-

TABLE 6
Turnover in the Senate

Period	*Not Seeking Reelection*	*Defeated in Primary*	*Defeated in General*	*Turnover*	*Percentage of Class**
1950–1958	5.2	1.8	6.8	13.8	38.8
1960–1968	4.0	1.8	3.0	8.8	24.9
1970–1978	7.0	1.6	5.8	14.4	42.4

SOURCE: Calculated from data in John Bibby *et al.*, *Vital Statistics on Congress, 1980* (Washington, D.C., 1980), 15.

*Calculated by dividing the average turnover by the average number of Senate seats up for reelection.

fifth Congress. Had Landrum, Stephens, and Stuckey not retired (and been reelected), the average years of experience would have increased to ten, making the Georgia delegation one of the more senior among the large states.

Finally in regard to the House, mention must be made of the party leadership changes. Speaker Albert retired after thirty years of House service. A whole new group took over in the Ninety-fifth Congress. Speaker Thomas P. O'Neill was a strongly partisan liberal Democrat from a traditionally liberal northern state. He had served as majority leader under Albert. Jim Wright of Texas was the surprise winner of the majority leadership spot in a hotly contested race.

What was happening in the Senate during this same period? Table 6 shows that turnover in the 1970s was markedly higher than it was in the 1960s, though only slightly higher than it was in the 1950s. As was the case in the House, however, retirements increased as a proportion of those leaving the Senate. A generational replacement occurred during the 1970s in the Senate. Stalwart Democratic senators like Lister Hill of Alabama, Carl Hayden of Arizona, Ernest Gruening of Alaska, Frank Lausche of Ohio, Mike Monroney of Oklahoma, Wayne Morse of Oregon, Joseph Clark of Pennsylvania, Alan Bible of Nevada, Sam Ervin of North Carolina, William Fulbright of Arkansas, Clinton Anderson of New Mexico, Everett Jordan of North Carolina, Spessard Holland of Florida, Stephen Young of Ohio, Albert Gore of Tennessee, Philip Hart of Michigan, Stuart Symington of Missouri, Mike Mansfield of Montana, and John Pastore of Rhode Island retired or were defeated during this period. The average age in this group was seventy-three when they

TABLE 7
Senate Democrats Coming to Carter

Year	*Democrats Elected*	*Freshmen Democrats*	*Still There in 1977*
1968	18	5 (27.8%)	4
1970	22	5*(22.7%)	4
1972	16	8*(50.0%)	8
1974	23	8*(34.8%)	8
1976	22	9*(40.9%)	9
Total still in the Senate in 1977			33 (53.2% of Democrats in 95th Congress)

SOURCE: Calculated from data in various issues of *Congressional Quarterly Weekly Report*.

*Senators in each of these classes had previously served in Congress with Democratic presidents (as representatives, in most cases).

left the Senate. Their replacements were naturally much younger, and, accordingly, the average age of the institution decreased.

Thus President Carter was also faced with a new Senate—one filled with the individualism, energy, and participatory spirit of the new era. His generalization that most members of Congress had not served with a Democratic president did not exactly apply to the Senate, however. Table 7 shows that thirty-three of the sixty-two Senate Democrats in 1977 were elected during Republican presidential administrations from 1969 to 1977. Four of these thirty-three had served in the House previously with a Democratic president and one (Hubert Humphrey) had served in the Senate (having interrupted his Senate career to be vice-president from 1965 to 1969). Still, President Carter's main point is certainly valid—that he faced a transformed and changing Senate. Whether he might have done better with the old Senate of Hayden, Hill, Hart, Symington, *et al.*, is very hard to know. The implication of his statement is that he would have.

The Senate results in 1976 showed no change in party composition. The Democrats retained their large majority of 62 to 38 (Harry F. Byrd of Virginia is counted as a Democrat for organizational purposes). There were many changes in membership, however. The number of retirements was the second greatest in the post–World War II period, much like the record in the House for this election. But whereas House incumbents seeking reelection were returned at a high rate, their Senate counterparts were not so fortunate. Nine incumbents were defeated—more than a third of those running for reelection. The combined total of those retiring and those defeated was the highest since 1948.

Senate committee leadership changes among Democrats as a result of the election were much less significant than they were in the House. Only four minor committee chairmanships were affected—Aeronautical and Space Sciences, Post Office and Civil Service, Veterans Affairs, and the Joint Committee on Atomic Energy. In fact, all but Veterans Affairs were abolished in the Ninety-fifth Congress. Still, the removal of nine senators does reshape committee and subcommittee operations, given the large number of assignments for each. These nine senators held twenty-three standing-committee positions and ten other committee positions (special, select, joint). Further, they held seventeen subcommittee chairmanships, several of which were on major committees (Appropriations, Armed Services, Commerce, Foreign Relations, and Judiciary).

Those Democratic senators not returning in the Ninety-fifth Congress had served an accumulated 164 years—an average of just over 18 years or three terms. The range of service was from one term for John Tunney of California to over four terms (26 years) for John Pastore. Southern representation in the Senate was little affected by these many retirements and defeats. In fact, this particular class of senators included only eight members from the South, and just three were from the Deep South.[5] Stuart Symington from the border state of Missouri was the only Democratic senator from the region to retire, and no Democratic incumbents from the South were defeated. The Democrats gained two seats from Maryland and Tennessee. Thus, President Carter was not disadvantaged by reason of the loss of southern representation in the Senate.

The most notable retiree in 1976 was Mike Mansfield, who was first elected to the House in 1943. After ten years of service there, he was elected to the Senate. He served as majority leader for sixteen years—longer than anyone in the history of the Senate. As in the House with the retirement of Speaker Albert, Mansfield's leaving resulted in completely new leaders for the Senate Democrats.

The 1976 congressional elections brought more than the normal amount of change to both the House and the Senate. Although House Democratic incumbents were returned at very high rates, a record number of retirements produced major alterations in committee and party

5. Senators are elected by classes in accordance with the initial drawing of lots for two-, four-, or six-year terms. This 1976 group is Class 1—those who drew the two-year terms in the first Senate. The other two classes have more southerners—thirteen (eight from the Deep South) and eleven (seven from the Deep South), respectively.

leadership. These changes contributed further to the South's reduced role in the House. In the Senate, the high turnover had less dramatic effects within the committee structure, but the sheer number of changes plus the selection of new party leaders as well as a revised committee system produced significantly new circumstances for presidential-congressional relations. Whether all these changes amounted to an advantage or disadvantage for the new president was not immediately evident. What is apparent, at least in hindsight, is that these developments invited careful analysis by the White House in order to judge how they might affect the programs of a trustee president.

CONGRESSIONAL REFORM

Congress enacted more reforms during the 1970s than at any other period in its history, indeed, more than in all its history to that time. Counted among the major reforms before the 1970s are the following:

1. The so-called Reed Rules (1890), by which Speaker of the House Thomas B. Reed invoked authority to prevent dilatory tactics on the floor.
2. The reform of the speakership (1910–1911), by which the House removed the Speaker from the Committee on Rules and took away his power to appoint committees (the Cannon reforms).
3. The Legislative Reorganization Act (1946), which reduced the number of standing committees and streamlined procedures.
4. The enlargement of the House Committee on Rules (1961; made permanent in 1963).

The Reed, Cannon, and 1961 Rules Committee changes were essentially internal power struggles. In each case, the practices at issue had existed for some time. And the changes were made when the proponents of reform estimated that they had sufficient support. The 1946 act came about quite differently. First of all, the motivation for reform was the external threat of a powerful executive. Congressional committees had proliferated to the point of interfering with the functioning of the institution. As Roland Young observed: "At the end of the war strong voices demanded that 'Congress regain its power' as the phrase went." No one doubted that structural changes would be required. Second, the reforms themselves were the result of careful study leading to recommendations, not an individual or group waiting to strike. The Joint Committee on the Organization of Congress was created in 1945, and this group prepared a report. Their recommendations were accepted with few changes in both houses. The most striking change to be effected was the reduction in the number of standing committees—from forty-eight to nineteen in the House, from thirty-three to fifteen in the Senate.[6]

Like the 1946 act, the reforms in the 1970s resulted from study and recommendation by congressional groups. The difference was in the number and types of study groups created to produce the avalanche of reform during the 1970s. The more important of these groups are:

1. The Joint Committee on the Organization of Congress (1965). Its recommendations led to the Legislative Reorganization Act (1970).
2. The Democratic Caucus Committee on Organization, Study, and Review—the Hansen Committee (1970).
3. The Republican Conference Task Force on Seniority (1970).
4. The Joint Committee on Congressional Operations (1970). It was created to conduct continuous study of congressional organization and procedure (abolished in 1976).
5. The Joint Study Committee on Budget Control (1972).
6. The House Select Committee on Committees—the Bolling Committee (1973).
7. The Senate Commission on the Operation of the Senate (1975).
8. The House Commission on Administrative Review—the Obey Commission (1976).
9. The Senate Temporary Select Committee to Study the Senate Committee System—the Stevenson Committee (1976; counterpart to the Bolling Committee).
10. The House Select Committee on Committees—the Patterson Committee (1979).

In all, there were three joint committees, two major party groups in the

6. Roland Young, *Congressional Politics in the Second World War* (New York, 1956), 234. For details, see George B. Galloway, *The Legislative Process in Congress* (New York, 1955), Chap. 23.

House (also several minor ones), three House committees or commissions, and two Senate committees or commissions.[7]

The sheer number of these units spread over nearly fifteen years illustrates the continuous pressure for change. Until 1976 the desire for self-examination and reform seemed insatiable. At that time the House stopped making changes, rejecting the Obey Commission recommendations for improved administrative procedures in 1977 and the Patterson Committee recommendation for a new energy committee in 1980.

Why was there so much reform? Only Congress can reform Congress. Thus conditions must be right, and the most important appears to be the perception among members that institutional authority is threatened. The source of threats may be from outside Congress but inside the government (*e.g.*, an aggressive president); from inside Congress itself (*e.g.*, the arbitrary exercise of power by the Speaker, other party leaders, or committee chairmen; or perhaps cumbersome procedures that interfere with law making); or from outside the government (*e.g.*, criticism from public interest groups, or low standing in the polls).

All these conditions existed during the 1970s. The aggressive president was, of course, Nixon. In particular, his reelection by a landslide in 1972 led to direct confrontations with Congress over the budget, the direction of domestic programs, the use of executive privilege, the impoundment of appropriated funds, the use of intelligence services, and the president's war powers. The War Powers Act (1973) and the Budget and Impoundment Control Act (1974) were among the results. Members also became concerned about the distribution of power within the institution itself—particularly in the House. Many of the reforms listed in Table 8 were a direct attack on the power of committee chairmen, as were the seniority system modifications, for example, and the so-called subcommittee bill of rights. But members of both chambers also sought to improve their institutional and individual capacities for coping with complex policy issues. Committee and personal staffs were increased, new policy-analysis units were created, existing units were given expanded responsibilities.

7. For details, see Charles O. Jones, *The United States Congress: People, Place, and Policy* (Homewood, Ill., 1982), Chap. 15; and Leroy Rieselbach, *Congressional Reform in the Seventies* (Morristown, N.J., 1977).

TABLE 8
Congressional Reform, 1970–1979

Year	*Reform Approved*
1970	Legislative Reorganization Act (organizational and procedural changes)
	Provision for nonvoting delegate in the House of Representatives, District of Columbia
	House Democratic Caucus reform committee appointed (Hansen Committee).
1971	Seniority system modifications (House Democrats and Republicans)
	Authorization of computer services for the House
1972	Federal Election Campaign Act
	Office of Technology Assessment (OTA) established.
	House electronic voting system approved.
1973	War Powers Act
	Seniority system modifications (House Democrats, Senate Republicans)
	Steering and Policy Committee activated (House Democrats).
	House Select Committee on Committees established (Bolling Committee).
	House subcommittee bill of rights
	Open House committee meetings (mark-up sessions)
	Closed rule modified (House).
	House staff increases.
1974	Federal Election Campaign Act
	Congressional Budget and Impoundment Control Act
	Congressional Budget Office (CBO) created.
	Steering and Policy Committee to assign committees (House Democrats)
	Hansen Plan adopted in House (organizational, leadership, party, committee changes).
	Speaker nominates Democrats to House Committee on Rules.
1975	Senate filibuster reform (three-fifths of the Senate)
	Conference proceedings open to the public
	Seniority system modifications (House and Senate Democrats)
	Open Senate committee meetings (mark-up sessions)
	House Committee on Internal Security abolished.
	House staff increases.
	Open House party caucuses
	Commission on the Operation of the Senate established.
	Junior senators' staff assistance
1976	House Commission on Administrative Review created (Obey Commission).
	Senate Temporary Select Committee to Study the Senate Committee System created (Stevenson Committee).
	House perquisites revised.

Continued on next page

TABLE 8—*Continued*

Year	*Reform Approved*
1977	Senate Committee system revised (names, membership appointments, limits on chairmanships, staffing).
	Ethics Codes adopted (House and Senate).
1978	Congressional approval of constitutional amendment giving the District of Columbia full representation in Congress (sent to states for ratification).
1979	Senate filibuster reform (post-cloture)
	Reduction of dilatory floor votes (House)
	Second House Select Committee on Committees established (Patterson Committee).

SOURCE: Charles O. Jones, *The United States Congress: People, Place, and Policy* (Homewood, Ill., 1982), 429.

Finally, Congress reacted to criticism from the outside by enacting campaign finance reforms, adopting an ethics code, and opening up committee meetings to the public. Many of these changes were the result of pressure from citizens' groups led by Common Cause.

As is evident in Table 8, most of these reforms were in place by 1977, when Jimmy Carter entered the White House. Profound changes had occurred, changes that affected both institutions. Even those knowledgeable about Capitol Hill were uncertain about the precise policy and political effects. It was apparent, however, that many, perhaps most, members of Congress felt that the institution had been strengthened as a result of these changes. Thus they were prepared to resent those who underestimated congressional capacities to participate meaningfully in the national policy process.

Changes in attitudes. Members of Congress thought differently about themselves and about the presidency. Several complementary developments contributed to their being more interventionist in the policy process: Republican control of the executive branch, the decline in status of the White House during Watergate, conflict over foreign and domestic issues, media attention to Congress during Watergate and as a consequence of policy battles, and the expansion of analytical capabilities on Capitol Hill. Democrats (and some Republicans) came to think of themselves as an alternative government during Nixon's second administration.

This more positive mood did not change with Nixon's resignation. Ford was the first unelected vice-president. In fact, his selection had to be approved by Congress. Perhaps because of this, but possibly also because of a growing sense of need and capability, congressional Democrats actually sought to produce comprehensive programs as alternatives to those offered by the administration, notably the energy and budget proposals.

Those who follow Washington politics comprehended the improved self-image on Capitol Hill. But there is considerable question whether Jimmy Carter and his staff fully registered what had happened. Little or no evidence is available from campaign days to suggest that Carter appreciated this significant development. During the debates, he avoided any detailed discussion of congressional relations. Later, of course, those in the Carter White House came to understand the importance of the changes that had occurred—after many months of difficult congressional relations.

Changes in personnel. I call the increase in turnover in the House and the Senate the "greening of Congress." David S. Broder observed that "America is changing hands."[8] New faces were appearing on Capitol Hill. These younger members were not content to sit back and wait their turn. They were anxious to participate directly in the work of the committees and subcommittees. Soon their numbers were large enough to have an important impact within the party (see Table 5).

It is not possible to produce exactly comparable figures in the Senate, for the terms are longer as well as staggered. As indicated in Table 7, however, 41 percent of Democratic senators in 1977 were serving their first term (*i.e.*, were elected in 1972, 1974, and 1976). These new representatives and senators were socialized during the era of participation, many of them having been educated and/or having become politically active during the 1960s. They were natural allies for an anti-politics-as-usual president, but study of their behavior in Congress suggests that they were unlikely to be passive partners. They were anxious, even demanding, to be involved, not just called upon. "They were activists who had been mobilized by concerns over Vietnam, the environment,

8. David S. Broder, *Changing of the Guard: Power and Leadership in America* (New York, 1980), 11.

TABLE 9
Committee Reorganization and New Chairmen

1975	*House*	*Senate*	*Total*
Committee reorganizations*	12	8	20
New committee chairmen	8	4	12
New subcommittee chairmen	42	18	60
1977			
Committee reorganizations	6	13	19
New committee chairmen	9	1[a]	10
New subcommittee chairmen	56[b]	34	90

SOURCE: Compiled from committee and subcommittee memberships, *Congressional Quarterly Weekly Report*, April 28, 1973, May 17, 1975, April 30, 1977.

*Includes only major reshuffling of subcommittees. There were several other slight changes in each house for each year.

[a]It should be noted that three committees were dropped in 1977.

[b]Includes eight new "task force" chairmen for the Budget Committee.

consumer affairs or some other cause, and the Watergate climate permitted them to win."[9]

The large influx of new members combined with the reform fervor in the early 1970s produced many new committee and subcommittee leaders. Table 9 shows what happened in 1975 and 1977 in each house. One sees the effects of committee reforms in the turnover of subcommittee chairmen. House changes were made before 1975; the major overhaul of Senate committees occurred in 1977. Electoral defeats, limitations on the number of committee and subcommittee chairmanships, and internal committee reorganizations all contributed to these changes. It should be noted that Table 9 includes only those persons who did not serve as a subcommittee chairman on that committee in the previous Congress. Nor does the table record the many shifts among subcommittee chairmanships that may have resulted from reorganization, new methods of selection, or changes in preference among senior members.

The implications of the data in Table 9 for the new president are obvious. He and his staff were faced with the extraordinary task of acquainting themselves with dozens of new committee and subcommittee leaders. Advice that was two or three years old was less valuable for this president than it had been for others. Congressional liaison personnel

9. *Ibid.*, 34.

from previous eras (the Johnson administration, for example) could not be much help, even were they willing. Everyone had to "go back to school" in working with the new Congress. But some experience was better than none in adjusting to the changes on Capitol Hill.

Finally, there were many new faces in the party leadership for both houses. Senator Robert C. Byrd, the new majority leader, had served previously as Democratic whip. His new responsibilities were much more extensive, however, and thus a period of adjustment was to be expected. Presidential support could help Byrd establish his authority with new and old Democratic senators. Likewise, Thomas P. O'Neill had served as majority floor leader in the House. As the new Speaker, however, he assumed what many consider the most important elected post next to that of the president himself. As with Byrd, the new president was in a position to make the Speaker look good. Of the other Democratic leaders in the House—Jim Wright as floor leader, John Brademas (Indiana) as whip, and Thomas Foley (Washington) as caucus chairman—only Brademas had served in a major post, that of chief deputy whip. The Republicans, too, made major changes in the Senate with the retirement of floor leader Hugh Scott (Pennsylvania) and the defeat of Robert Griffin (Michigan) in his bid for reelection as whip.

Taken together, these changes in personnel demanded *special attention* from the White House. Politics was not "as usual" among these many new faces. But it did not follow that the president's new politics would automatically mesh with Congress' new politics.[10]

Changes in capabilities. President Nixon's use and abuse of presidential power and congressional worries about loss of legislative power contributed to a quantum increase in staff during the reform era of the 1970s. Practically every reform measure included additional staff allocations. The results were dramatic. In the mid-1960s, there were approximately 1,100 total staff for Senate and House committees; by the mid-1970s, there were 2,700, and more than 3,000 by the end of the decade. Personal staffs, too, increased dramatically—from less than 6,000 in the

10. For a fuller discussion of the many developments in Congress during this era, see Thomas E. Mann and Norman J. Ornstein (eds.), *The New Congress* (Washington, D.C., 1981).

TABLE 10
Staff Growth Since 1947

	Percentage growth from 1947 to:			
	1957	*1967*	*1972*	*1979*
Personal staff				
House	+69.5	+181.6	+226.7	+390.8
Senate	+89.0	+196.4	+311.2	+512.2
	1955	*1965*	*1975*	*1979*
Committee staff				
House	+97.0	+241.9	+758.1	+1,073.1
Senate	+66.4	+119.4	+450.4	+373.3

SOURCE: Charles O. Jones, *The United States Congress: People, Place, and Policy* (Homewood, Ill., 1982), 58.

mid-1960s to more than 10,000 in the late 1970s. Table 10 shows the percentage increases from 1947 through 1979.

This huge increase permitted senators and representatives personally and in their committee and subcommittee work to expand their horizons. In the past, House members in particular tended to limit their substantive policy work to that of their committee and subcommittee assignments. With staff increases they were able to get involved in other topics as well. Further, additional staff allowed, perhaps even encouraged, all members to venture into activities not normally associated with the legislative process—policy research and initiation, for example, and program implementation and evaluation.

Possibly even more significant were the changes designed to provide Congress with more independent policy analysis. The Legislative Reference Service (located in the Library of Congress) was reorganized into the Congressional Research Service (CRS) and given more staff, funds, and research responsibilities. The General Accounting Office (GAO) was also given more support and directed to work with the committees in evaluating executive implementation of programs. The Office of Technology Assessment (OTA) and the Congressional Budget Office (CBO) were newly created units that were designed to serve the committees and offered the potential for in-house analyses of comprehensive proposals sent down by the executive. OTA's work on the energy plans in 1976 and CBO's on presidential budgets represented an impressive new congressional capability.

In late 1972, then senator Walter F. Mondale (D-Minnesota) observed:

> I have been in many debates, for example on the Education Committee, that dealt with complicated formulas and distributions. And I have found that whenever I am on the side of the Administration, I am surfeited with computer print-outs and data that comes within seconds, whenever I need it to prove how right I am. But if I am opposed to the Administration, computer print-outs always come late, prove the opposite point or always are on some other topic. So I think one of the rules is that he who controls the computers controls the Congress, and I believe that there is utterly no reason why the Congress does not develop its own computer capability, its own technicians, its own pool of information.[11]

By 1977, Mondale's wish had been granted. Congress was by then able to generate its own data for policy analysis. This independence, and the greater legislative-staff population that produced it, brought a new dimension to presidential-congressional relations. There was all the more reason in 1977 for congressional leaders to make a special effort to understand their own institution and for the new White House to comprehend the effects for presidential leadership.

Changes in process. The reforms and changes discussed thus far were clearly associated with new ways of doing business on Capitol Hill. We can identify at least two types of changes in process—those specific to policy areas, and those more generally applicable to law making on Capitol Hill.

Making taxation policy, for example, was altered by reforms directed at the House Committee on Ways and Means. The powerful and resourceful Wilbur D. Mills served as chairman for sixteen years, stepping down in 1974. Mills typically did not rely on subcommittees.[12] Committee Democrats also served as that party's committee on committees, appointing Democrats to all the other standing committees. Ways and Means, one of the smallest committees in the House, had powerful advantages in its use of the closed rule to prevent floor amendments. The target of extensive reform in 1973 and 1974, it was enlarged from twenty-five to thirty-seven members, its appointive authority was transferred to

11. These remarks were made at a conference sponsored by Time, Inc., on The Role of Congress, Chicago, December 5, 1972.

12. See John F. Manley, *The Politics of Finance* (Boston, 1970), esp. Chap. 4.

the Steering and Policy Committee, the closed-rule procedures were modified, and it was forced to create subcommittees. Mills's successor, Al Ullman (Oregon), inherited a committee with quite a different role in the policy process.[13]

No less dramatic was the creation of a new budgetary process for Congress. Before the implementation of the Budget and Impoundment Control Act (1974), it strained credulity to suggest that Congress had any such process at all. There were numerous separate ways for acting on the executive budget but no overarching method for even minimally integrating those actions. Budget committees for each house, working with the CBO to meet specific deadlines, gave Congress a means for setting budget limits and therefore responding in a much more coherent fashion to the president's taxing and spending plans. The first complete process occurred in 1976 for fiscal year 1977. House Budget Committee Chairman Brock Adams (D-Washington) concluded: "Perhaps the most important aspect of the final budget resolution of fiscal year 1977 is the fact that it contains the budget of Congress and not that of the President."[14]

Other important alterations occurred in energy policy and in regard to the exercise of the war powers. There were numerous jurisdictional changes in House and Senate committees for coping with the many energy issues that developed following the Arab oil embargo in 1973. Although the process of decision making remained decentralized in both chambers, many efforts were made to coordinate policy. In the Senate, the Interior and Insular Affairs Committee became the principal energy committee (renamed Energy and Natural Resources). The House fashioned what might be referred to as *decentralized coordination*. Major jurisdiction was divided among three committees. There were ad hoc committees and sequential referral to coordinate action among the three. A new energy-policy process was emerging in Congress, and it took special congressional know-how to comprehend what was going on.[15]

The War Powers Act (1973) was specifically designed to put Congress back into the decision-making process for committing troops abroad.

13. For details, see Congressional Quarterly, *Congress and the Nation, 1973–1976*, IV (Washington, D.C., 1977), 745–65; Catherine E. Rudder, "Tax Policy: Structure and Choice," in Allen Schick (ed.), *Making Economic Policy in Congress* (Washington, D.C., 1983), 196–220.

14. *Congress and the Nation*, IV, 71.

15. For details, see Charles O. Jones and Randall Strahan, "Energy Politics and Organizational Change," *Legislative Studies Quarterly*, X (May, 1985), 151–79.

Concerned about the nation having backed into the Korean and Vietnam wars, Congress was determined to restore its role in foreign and defense policy. Among other things, the act required the president to report in writing to congressional leaders within forty-eight hours of committing or substantially expanding combat forces. Such commitments were to be terminated within sixty days unless Congress either declared war or authorized continuation.

Other reforms were more general, changing the conduct of business. The so-called subcommittee bill of rights signaled a shift of power away from the committee chairmen to the subcommittees, a development that was bound to cause problems for the White House. However difficult it was to negotiate with the sometimes arbitrary committee chairmen, coping with scores of subcommittee chairmen was not exactly a happy substitute. One could at least learn what was required for getting along with a single chairman who was likely to be there year after year. Having to deal with six or seven or more leaders within a committee compounded the problems of getting the president's program passed. Further, an individual could hold only a limited number of subcommittee chairmanships, so members shopped around for the best post after each election, thus increasing turnover.

Another general reform affecting decision making was opening up committee meetings. The House acted first in 1973, followed later by the Senate and conference committees. Hearings and mark-up sessions were to be open unless specific action was taken by a majority of the committee or subcommittee. Whereas 30 to 40 percent of committee meetings were closed before the reform, fewer than 10 percent were closed afterward. This change must be evaluated in the context of other reforms that expanded participation in the legislative process. The sheer number of people on Capitol Hill increased markedly in recent years, and so has the competition for a member's time and support. The White House remains the principal actor, but it must share the stage with many others.

More provision for the legislative veto is another change affecting process. In fact, this development represented a serious restructuring of executive-legislative relations. Having authorized the executive to implement a program, the legislature retains the right to approve or disapprove of a particular action. This technique has been used for decades, but sparingly. In recent years, however, distrust of the executive has injected Congress directly into what are normally judged administrative practices—again, an important change in process. In 1983, the Supreme Court, in *Immigration and Naturalization Service* v. *Chadha*, ruled that the legislative veto in its most common form was unconstitutional.

CONGRESS MEETS CARTER—A SUMMARY

There were new energy and drive on Capitol Hill after a decade of reform and turnover. The new president faced a new Congress, one with changed attitudes about itself, fresh faces and new leaders, improved capabilities, and different ways of doing business. Many of these changes were born out of conflicts with presidents, thus making relations between the two institutions more intricate and adversarial. Still other changes were the consequence of dissatisfaction with the way members were doing business among themselves, as well as concern about the public's view of Congress.

It is a commonplace criticism of President Carter and his closest associates that they did not understand Congress. A review of how the Ninety-fifth Congress came to Jimmy Carter suggests that Congress did not altogether understand itself or the new president. Events, people, and processes changed dramatically. Congress was trying hard to be different. It undoubtedly succeeded, but few understood either the full measure of the changes or their effects.

The dramatic events of the late 1960s and early 1970s had profound effects on both Congress and the presidency. Each institution, in a sense, monitored those events and made adjustments. The results in 1976 produced a president from outside Washington determined to change policy politics and a Congress prepared to participate more actively than before in the full range of policy activities. Both President Carter and the new Congress had cause to believe that each was meeting the policy challenges of the times. Yet neither was sufficiently appreciative, or possibly even aware, of the other's response. Institutional adjustments to changing issues need not necessarily produce an adversarial relationship. In this case, however, misunderstanding and antagonism were apparently assured from the very start.

☆4☆ The Carter Approach to Congress

The transition to a new president is a fascinating, important ritual. Laurin L. Henry describes what happens in the initial months after the election:

> The new President and the associates he brings into the government now must begin to learn their jobs, fulfill their commitments, and re-cast governmental policies in light of their own objectives. This process will require adjustments in the relations of the President with Congress, foreign nations, domestic interest groups, political parties, the federal bureaucracy, and other institutions impinging on the Presidency. *The arrival of a new administration is a crisis for all of these groups, as well as for the Presidency itself.*[1]

The members of Congress are among the more active participants in the ritual of acquaintanceship that accompanies the arrival of a new president. They naturally move toward the president in order to take his measure on matters of direct interest to them. Party leaders are anxious to know and understand the person with whom they must work for the ensuing four years. Committee and subcommittee chairmen want to know what the agenda will look like, testing for effects on issues within their jurisdiction. And individual members are interested in presidential policy proposals for the effects on the states and districts they represent.

This chapter begins with a brief review of the constitutional influences on the institutional relationships between the president and Congress. Attention is then directed to the variations among presidents in regard to the political and personal aspects of their being in the White House. I then turn to the trusteeship presidency of Jimmy Carter and its special "outside-in" methods for building congressional support.

1. Laurin L. Henry, *Presidential Transitions* (Washington, D.C., 1960), 4 (emphasis added).

SEPARATED INSTITUTIONS: THE CONTINUING CHALLENGE

By constitutional design, the president and members of Congress are encouraged to believe they got to Washington on their own. Presidential candidates now endure two long and arduous national campaigns, one for the nomination, the other to get elected. They have every right to think that they have a message to deliver to the nation's capital. But members of Congress, too, have strenuous campaigns. Individually they are convinced that no one knows their particular geographical area as they do. Collectively they believe they understand and represent national issues. Thus, trusteeship can be claimed at both ends of Pennsylvania Avenue.

What an utterly fascinating, if slightly perverse, system. As Nelson W. Polsby describes them, Congress and the presidency "are like two gears, each whirling at its own rate of speed." To gain the full benefits of the diverse means of selection, each elected official is encouraged to believe that he or she knows what is best for those represented. *The Federalist* states that "ambition must be made to counteract ambition."[2] But the participants must have reason to be convinced that they are right and that there are rewards for their persistence. The organizational and electoral separation of the institutions achieves this end, without, at the same time, permitting complete fulfillment for the ambitious. Policy achievements typically require acquiescence among or cooperation between the branches. Thus, participation alone can be rewarding, but mastering the means of institutional and policy compromise can yield an even greater return. For the true constitutional politician, satisfaction arises from the purity of representation secured by independent election and escalates with the blending of ideas and presentments in policy making.

The president is the central figure in this contest of countervailing ambitions. Typically, he has the strongest motivation to make contact since he wants his program approved. But Congress, too, has need for stimulus from the president. Stephen J. Wayne explains: "The president has become a driving force within the legislative system much of the time. This force works to produce policy output, which is why Congress looks to the president for new initiatives and why it tolerates his influence. As

2. Nelson W. Polsby, *Congress and the Presidency* (Englewood Cliffs, N.J., 1976), 191; *The Federalist*, No. 51 (New York, 1937), 337.

an institution Congress realizes benefits from a presidential presence on Capitol Hill. It gains a national perspective, policy leadership, and, in some cases, help in mobilizing partisan support."[3] In this process most presidents seek to accomplish the following tasks associated with improving communication and gaining support:

1. Inform Congress of the details of specific programs.
2. Clarify the effects of and linkages among programs.
3. Provide rationales for supporting programs.
4. Participate actively in the negotiations required to build majorities for programs.

For their part, members of Congress may be expected to react to presidential initiatives in a way consistent with how they interpret their responsibilities. Therefore, they are likely to:

1. Protect constituency interests.
2. Protect committee and subcommittee jurisdictional claims (and the group interests represented by these claims).
3. Display personal expertise and staff capabilities in reviewing presidential policy proposals.
4. Produce alternatives for and refinements of presidential proposals.

Here we witness the practical policy consequences of having separated the election systems for the two institutions. The members of Congress are normally confident and assertive because their claim to independence is convincing—to them and to others. In fact, collectively their claim is usually greater than is the president's. Even a president who wins by a landslide soon discovers just how independent Congress is. E. Pendleton Herring put it this way: "The people elect the president, but they are not organized to support him in office; it is to Congress that he must constantly turn for the fulfillment of his objectives."[4] Thus, all presidents must develop lines of communication and sources of support on Capitol Hill, and how they accomplish those ends varies considerably.

3. Stephen J. Wayne, *The Legislative Presidency* (New York, 1978), 23.
4. E. Pendleton Herring, *Presidential Leadership* (New York, 1940), 1.

PRESIDENTS AND CONGRESSES: RECENT EXPERIENCE

It is interesting to compare treatments of Congress in recent presidential memoirs. President Johnson's congressional experience shows throughout his book. What he provides is more than a simple description of his dealings with the institution. He also analyzes Congress, including observations on its differences with the president. His accounts of struggles to enact his domestic program clearly show a president intimately involved in the politics of congressional majority building. "I understood and respected men who dedicated their lives to elective office. . . . I believed that I, as President, had the responsibility to appeal to that dedication."[5]

Ford's respect for Congress also emanated from his long service there. "These were my friends," he noted when describing his first speech to Congress after becoming president. But his political position was very different from Johnson's. He was an unelected president taking over for his disgraced predecessor and having to deal with a Congress controlled by the Democrats. He believed that "Congress was beginning to disintegrate as an organized legislative body." The institution was "too fragmented"; it "responded too often to single-issue special interest groups." One can understand Ford's change in perspective—he had been House minority leader and became president. Like Johnson, however, Ford appeared to think conceptually about the role of Congress in the political system. In a statement after leaving office, he said:

> I want to emphasize the importance of these personal relationships between the White House and the Congress. I think the President has to accept the fact that he must spend more time personally with members of Congress, and he must work with the leaders of both parties to *enhance their strength and influence. Members of Congress are important*. The President cannot spend too much time with them. . . . I think a President has to give the leaders in the Congress and influential members of both parties an open door to come and take part in policy decisions. He doesn't have to guarantee that he will do what they say, but at least they have to have the feeling that their views are considered before the fact, not after. I think that the President cannot make a decision and then call up the Congress and say, "Give me help." That is unfair. He has got to ask their advice. Even if he does not agree with it, he can then go back and ask for their help, and he would be in a much better position to get results. By strengthening the leadership the President would make the Congress more effective.[6]

5. See Lyndon B. Johnson, *The Vantage Point: Perspectives of the Presidency, 1963–1969* (New York, 1971), 440–41, 459.

6. Gerald R. Ford, *A Time to Heal* (New York, 1979), 133, 150; Gerald R. Ford, "Imperiled, Not Imperial," *Time*, November 10, 1980, p. 30.

By sharp contrast to Johnson and Ford, Nixon tended to stress the importance of the office of president itself in decision making. His memoirs are considerably longer than either Johnson's or Ford's—two volumes and nearly fourteen hundred pages. Yet he has almost nothing analytical to say about Congress. His books are personal—about his leadership, the problems he faced, and how he dealt with them. There is good reason to believe that he doubted the legitimacy of Congress.[7] And it is quite likely that John Ehrlichman spoke for Nixon when he wrote:

> The Nixon White House and the Congress were different worlds. We went to work every day—often on Sundays. We operated on schedule. . . .
>
> . . . Congress is a huge committee of individuals, only slightly interdependent, each answering to a small, discrete political constituency. Each Member is politically cautious, suspicious of his Congressional leaders and incapable of commanding much television time. Any President is therefore capable of acting and forcing the Members to react.
>
> The Members consume time in enormous quantities in their quaint Congressional processes. They recess; they junket; they arrive late and leave early; they attend conferences out of town, fly off to give speeches, sip and chat and endlessly party. And only sometimes do they focus on legislation.[8]

Some years after leaving office, Nixon summarized his approach to Congress: "Many analysts . . . have argued that the separation of powers has itself become a formula for stalemate between President and Congress. Stalemate often results, but it does not have to. *If a President is sufficiently forceful, sufficiently sound in his policies and sure of his purpose, and able to take his argument persuasively to the people, Congress will go along a good deal of the time.*" For Nixon, "there are three keys to an effective presidency. . . . He must 1) analyze, 2) decide and 3) persuade."[9]

President Carter's principal discussion of Congress in his memoirs occurs in a chapter entitled "My One-Week Honeymoon With Congress." He acknowledges that after his election, "we [the president and Congress] needed to get acquainted." Much of Carter's review expresses his disappointment that members of his own party did not give more support

7. Richard M. Nixon, *The Memoirs of Richard Nixon* (2 vols.; New York, 1978). See, for example, Charles O. Jones, "Congress and the Presidency," in Thomas E. Mann and Norman J. Ornstein (eds.), *The New Congress* (Washington, D.C., 1981), 223–49.

8. John Ehrlichman, *Witness to Power: The Nixon Years* (New York, 1982), 196, 195.

9. Richard M. Nixon, "Needed: Clarity of Purpose," *Time*, November 10, 1980, p. 32 (emphasis added).

to him and his program. "I had to seek votes wherever they could be found." As did Johnson and Ford, Carter offers a concept of Congress' role in the policy process, but his analysis is basically unflattering, though somewhat sympathetic. Congress, for Carter, is an institution "buffeted" by special interests, and the members find it difficult to resist the pressures because of their need to be reelected.[10]

These differences among presidential interpretations of the role of Congress encourage one to identify those factors that may help to explain the variations. Stephen J. Wayne states that objectives, approach (of liaison staffs), and presidential style are associated with the ways presidents organize congressional liaison activities. I modify these categories somewhat, incorporating differences cited by Wayne and Eric L. Davis.[11]

1. Congressional Experience
    - Extensive (including leadership posts)
    - Moderate
    - Limited
    - No experience
2. Domestic Policy Objectives
    - Large-scale program
    - Moderate program
    - Limited, or no major initiatives
    - Cut back existing programs
3. Involvement in Lobbying
    - Active and personal
    - Moderate personal
    - On call
    - Restricted
4. Partisan Support in Congress
    - Large majorities
    - Moderate majorities
    - Narrow majorities
    - Party in the minority

10. Jimmy Carter, *Keeping Faith: Memoirs of a President* (New York, 1982), 66, 69.

11. Wayne, *The Legislative Presidency,* 165–66; Eric L. Davis, "Congressional Liaison: The People and the Institutions," in Anthony King (ed.), *Both Ends of the Avenue: The Presidency, the Executive Branch, and Congress in the 1980s* (Washington, D.C., 1983), 60.

5. Initial Electoral Support
   - Landslide
   - Moderately large
   - Narrow victory
6. Subsequent Public Support (measured by polls)
   - Steady and high (over 60%)
   - Steady and moderate (over 50%)
   - Steady and low (below 50%)
   - Variable from high to low
   - Variable from low to lower

Table 11 provides a profile of presidents as tested by these several criteria. From the point of view of the congressional liaison personnel, the variation is in the president's working knowledge of Congress, the job they have to do (the policy objectives), the extent to which they can expect their president to take an active role in lobbying, and the various sources of support upon which they can expect to rely (their party's margin in Congress, the electoral results, and the president's approval ratings).

The first formal liaison office was created during the initial Eisenhower administration. He named "one of his closest personal friends and a longtime military associate," Major General Wilton B. Persons, as head of the office. Later, General Persons was appointed to succeed Sherman Adams as assistant to the president and Bryce Harlow replaced Persons. Both Persons and Harlow were credible liaison chiefs—the former because of his close association with Eisenhower, the latter because of his previous experience in liaison work and on Capitol Hill. According to Davis: "Members of Congress soon came to see that a commitment on the part of either of these men was the equivalent of a commitment from the president himself. By establishing a formal, professional, and politically experienced congressional relations staff, which was able to speak for the president and which worked closely with the legislative leadership of the president's party, Eisenhower set in motion the process that led to further development of the liaison effort under his successors."[12]

As is suggested by Table 11, President Eisenhower's liaison staff had the easiest task of those serving the three Republican presidents: a very

12. Abraham Holtzman, *Legislative Liaison: Executive Leadership in Congress* (Chicago, 1970), 234; Davis, "Congressional Liaison," in King (ed.), *Both Ends of the Avenue*, 61. See also Wayne, *The Legislative Presidency*, 141–46.

TABLE 11
Comparing Presidents

Presidents	Congressional Experience	Policy Objectives	Involvement	Partisan Support	Electoral Support	Subsequent Public Support
Eisenhower (1)	None	Limited	Moderate	Narrow to no majority	Landslide	Steady and high
Eisenhower (2)	None	Limited	Moderate	No majority	Landslide	Steady and high
Kennedy	Moderate	Moderate	Moderate	Large	Narrow	Steady and high
Johnson	Extensive	Large-scale	Active	Large (moderate in House, 1967)	Landslide	Variable—high to low
Nixon (1)	Moderate	Limited	Restricted	No majority (but increase in seats)	Narrow	Steady and moderate
Nixon (2)	Moderate	Limited	Restricted	No majority	Landslide	Variable—low to lower
Ford	Extensive	Limited	Active	No majority	None	Variable—high to low
Carter	None	Moderate to ambitious	On call	Large	Narrow	Variable—high to low

popular personality offered a rather limited program. Although the liaison office had to cope with a Democratic Congress for six of the eight years, the margin was not great for four of those years and the president's image remained strongly positive throughout. Thus, congressional liaison as a formal White House organizational activity got off to a good start under Eisenhower.

The liaison staffs of the other Republican presidents were less fortunate. During Nixon's first term, the Republicans did not have a majority in either house of Congress but they did increase their numbers in both the 1966 and 1968 elections. Thus the trend, at least, was in a positive direction. And the staff could rely on rather consistent presidential approval ratings—not as high as Eisenhower's but not, on the average, as low as Johnson's during his last three years. But, of course, the second term was a disaster. The landslide for Nixon did not translate into sizable victories for congressional Republicans, and the approval ratings soon declined with the series of Watergate revelations. Nixon did not favor a close working relationship with either his liaison staff or with individual members of Congress (see Table 11). Wayne observes that "there was considerable doubt as to whether it was possible to reach Nixon at all" and he quotes a House Republican as saying: "I pretty well concluded that there was almost no way to contact him except if you had a personal relationship. You'd write letters and send telegrams and be as emphatic as you could. You'd normally get back the polite reply that your letter would be brought to the president's attention and you knew very well that it would never be." This situation was not the result of some failure of the liaison office, which was professional, political, and generally respected on the Hill. Rather, the president himself enforced the separation. In the Watergate debacle, that distance at least protected the liaison office. Nixon's liaison chief during this period, William Timmons, concluded: "I don't think that the hearings by the Ervin Committee first, and later, by the House Judiciary Committee, in any way affected the president's legislative program. I can't cite one bill that should have been passed or could have been passed or defeated because of the Watergate issue." As Davis observes: "The Congressional Relations Office was one of the few components of the Nixon White House that never became entangled in the net of Watergate."[13]

13. Wayne, *The Legislative Presidency*, 161, 163; Davis, "Congressional Liaison," in King (ed.), *Both Ends of the Avenue*, 64.

Ford entered the White House with fewer advantages than did any president in this century. He was unelected even as a vice-president—the first congressionally approved vice-president under the provisions of the Twenty-fifth Amendment. His one source of support was as a politician untainted by Watergate, and his initial approval rating after being sworn in was 73 percent. Withing a month, however, this rating had dropped twenty-two points after the pardon of Richard Nixon. Ford had dealt away his principal advantage. Further, the 1974 congressional elections produced huge Democratic majorities in Congress—67 percent in the House, 62 percent in the Senate. Circumstances forced him frequently to rely on the veto, and its threat, in trying to get his way with Congress. President Ford was knowledgeable about Congress, however, and an active and willing participant in lobbying for his program on Capitol Hill.

The two Democratic presidents in Table 11 who preceded Carter had different political and policy conditions. President Kennedy was moving cautiously on a moderate program, in part it seems, because of his youth and his narrow victory in 1960. Although the Democrats maintained large majorities in both the House and the Senate, they actually had their House margin reduced by twenty seats in 1960. Thus, the liaison staff faced a number of challenges in trying to enact the president's program. President Johnson, on the other hand, had more advantages than had any president since Franklin D. Roosevelt. His huge personal victory in 1964 was bolstered by House Democrats' significant gains and by the continuance of a sizable Democratic majority in the Senate. And the president himself developed a reputation as a master legislative politician during his service in Congress. Thus, the liaison staff was given a big job to do—gaining congressional approval for the Great Society—but they could rely initially on impressive sources of support.

A number of lessons from Table 11 suggest that, at a minimum, contemporary presidents must be particularly attentive to their relations with Congress. First, landslide elections clearly do not translate into continuing public support. Often, in fact, they seem to be a consequence of so-called retrospective voting, *i.e.*, more "a referendum on the incumbent" than a mandate for the winner.[14] Second, Johnson's experience suggests that a full set of advantages is required for enacting a large-scale pro-

14. Paul Abrahamson *et al.*, *Change and Continuity in the 1980 Elections* (Washington, D.C., 1982), 142.

gram, including a president willing to work closely with his liaison staff. Third, just as President Carter himself noted in his book, Congress had accommodated itself to frequent anti-executive behavior. Nixon and Ford had to deal with Congresses controlled by the Democrats. But by the end of his term, Johnson too faced frequent and strong criticism from Congress, including members of his own party.

The obvious conclusion is that any Democratic president taking office in 1977 would have been well advised to devote special attention to establishing congressional liaison. President Carter's profile in Table 11 suggests that it was especially important for him to do so. He had no direct experience on Capitol Hill and, as he observes, even had to "get acquainted" with congressional leaders after his election. He had an ambitious program, not on the scale of Johnson's Great Society, but one designed to make a huge government more effective, offering few "goodies for the members to take home."[15] His party had large margins in both the House and the Senate, but they weren't Carter Democrats. His electoral margin was extremely narrow. And while his initial public support was quite high, the experiences of Johnson, Nixon, and Ford demonstrated how quickly that could disappear.

One other point should be emphasized. From the variables in Table 11, presidents are implicitly expected to get Congresses to work for them, not the other way around. Presidents have "policy objectives," and they are expected to use the partisan, electoral, and public support to achieve them. It is true, of course, that many Congresses are difficult to work with. It is also true that congressional structure under the best of circumstances is not well designed for ensuring harmonious and effective relations between the two institutions. Yet even Republican presidents are somehow expected to "lead" Democratic Congresses. Presidents try to shift the burden of responsibility but are seldom successful: the public and the press continue to hold them accountable. And if that is the case for Republican presidents with Democratic Congresses, then Democratic presidents will find the situation doubly difficult with a Democratic Congress. That would be a source of great frustration for the trustee president who favors a separation between how he is evaluated and how Congress is evaluated. Yet, ironically, it is the nature of the trusteeship that

15. Carter, *Keeping Faith*, 88.

such a president will likely be held even more accountable by the media, since his administration will tend to take on difficult problems and establish lofty goals.

WORKING WITH CONGRESS: THE TRUSTEE'S APPROACH

I earlier proposed that the trustee president will adopt an independence style, a national focus, and an integrative method. And I identified a number of tenets that, taken together, set the president apart from the dominant style, focus, and method of the members of Congress. That previous discussion bears on my purpose here, to specify a set of expectations for how the trustee president will work with Congress. I have organized the expectations into several functions associated with presidential-congressional interaction. Together they constitute a model of the trustee president's management of congressional relations.

In *agenda setting*, the trustee president can be expected to identify particularly thorny issues and insist that they be handled whatever the political cost. This approach displays the superiority of the trustee role (at least to the person playing it) and places the constituency-bound delegates at a disadvantage. Second, the trustee president will concentrate *program development* in the White House to an even greater degree than do other presidents. Expect only limited consultation with members of Congress, for they are preoccupied with reelection and the president has a clear sense of knowing "what is right." A third expectation has to do with *program support*. By his choice of issues, as well as the focus, style, and methods associated with the role, the trustee president is forced outside Congress to build coalitions for each program. The support-building mechanisms are not available, since they are excessively sensitive to electoral considerations and therefore compromise both the agenda and the directness of policy proposals. Fourth, expect less intimate participation in *congressional liaison* by the trustee president than was the case with other presidents—particularly those who had congressional experience. The liaison personnel will have to mediate, as delicately as possible, between role players in the White House and on Capitol Hill. Fifth, the *evaluation* of the trustee president will depend on criteria drawn from the ideal role he has chosen to play. Therefore, when incongruities appear, he is likely to be judged more harshly than were other presidents. Sixth, expect a trustee presidency to make *adaptations* over time to preserve the trusteeship while accommodating political realities. Further, expect greater attentiveness to electoral considerations as the first term ends, justified by the need to renew the trusteeship.

Taken together, these expectations illustrate the challenges and the risks for the trustee president. By the nature of his preferences and assumptions, he inevitably tends to take on tremendous responsibilities—those related to the social agenda and to the decision-making processes in Washington. And the trustee elevates the standards by which his performance will be assessed.

ORGANIZING TO WORK WITH CONGRESS

What kind of organization was suited to Carter's style and the issues that were important to him? It involved establishing confidence in and support for the right solutions to issues designated by the president as deserving priority status. Thus, organizing to work with Congress for the Carter administration incorporated many White House units, including:

1. President Carter himself, as the chief interpreter of national needs and chief designator of top-priority matters
2. The Domestic Affairs and Policy Staff, to develop viable policy options
3. The Office of Management and Budget, to provide information on the cost of major programmatic initiatives and to designate the fiscal and other effects of various options
4. The Public Liaison staff, to channel feedback on proposals and to build support among affected interest groups
5. The Congressional Liaison staff, to present congressional reactions to presidential proposals and to create a favorable climate on Capitol Hill
6. Congressional liaison staff of departments and agencies, to lobby for proposals of direct relevance to their parent units.

The order in which these resources are listed is important. What it suggests is a sequence, if not necessarily a designation of importance. One is reminded that we are speaking here of *an approach to Congress*, and, for

Carter, the approach begins with doing what is right. That is the context for evaluating the Congressional Liaison operation. One cannot limit analysis of Carter's relations with Congress to the activities of that office, since Carter himself did not view it that way. *His trusteeship approach was from the outside in, not from the inside out.* It reconstructed the agenda and sought to revise the dominant mode of politics in Washington, at least by example. Such grand purposes naturally relocated and changed the functions of the Congressional Liaison staff, as compared with those of other administrations.

It is not the purpose here to describe and analyze each of these components in detail. The major focus is the Office of Congressional Liaison and its relationship to the president. The other components do require some elaboration, however, to identify the organizational and procedural requirements of their respective roles. They will be treated here, and liaison will be saved for Chapter 5.

JIMMY CARTER BEING JIMMY CARTER: A COMMON CAUSE MONARCH

"He believed 97 percent of the words that he uttered in those campaign speeches. . . . The man that believed those speeches believed . . . that there's something kind of fundamentally corrupt about the governmental process in Washington. . . . *He was a common cause monarch.* He believed in procedural reform, he believed that we ought to be discussing the issues."[16] As with other administrations, the analysis of congressional relations must begin with the president. In the case of Carter, his trusteeship approach tended to exclude congressional input in the early stages of program development. After all, he had won the nomination by stressing that he was an outsider. He had few, if any, obligations to members of Congress. And, in fact, he viewed them as outside the process (his own election) that conveyed his trusteeship. President Carter saw himself as offering a different way of governing, a way that had the approval of the American public. It was not even logical for him to depend on members of Congress in formulating his program. Doing so would, in his opinion, violate the trust placed in him by the public.

16. Transcripts, XIV, 57.

What, then, was the source of his personal agenda? Certainly the campaign itself produced the bulk of the issues. The staff kept a record of campaign promises, which was actually published. The president was very serious about keeping these promises, though many were likely to cause problems on Capitol Hill. Adverse political consequences were not always carefully evaluated, but the president judged that the essential correctness of the proposals themselves would eventually be recognized and would justify his reelection. In other words, the president turned to what he saw as his mandate—his trusteeship, if you will—in setting his agenda. He acknowledged the unpopularity of many issues, as well as the fact that he was asking Congress to do a lot. But he entered the White House with a strong determination to carry out the mandate he interpreted as his.

Although a "detail man" who, by his own admission, "liked the administrative work," Carter had a concept of presidential issues and of what the president should know about these and other issues and government programs. In other words, his penchant for detail was not the result of compulsiveness. Where he judged an issue to be his (such as the budget, or energy, or the Panama Canal treaties), he considered it his duty to master the details. He wanted to understand the issue as well as any member of Congress did. Clearly he viewed such knowledge and awareness as a source of strength in meeting and working with Congress. Relying on his electoral legitimacy to bring different government to Washington, combined with his capacity for mastering details of complex national issues, produced a confidence, perhaps even stubbornness, about what to do and how to do it. One of his close aides explained: "A lot of folks . . . used to . . . say, 'Look, he's not doing that right,' and I'd say, 'Look, there's no sense you being concerned about that. He's going to do it his way. That's the way he's going to do it.' "[17]

There are certain organizational and personal requirements associated with the Carter approach. First, the president must have the time and the isolation to read. The White House is not an especially good place for having either; Carter found the early morning hours and the weekends at Camp David useful. Second, contact with the people—Carter's constituents—must be maintained. As a newcomer presuming to set a different agenda, the president had to reassure others of his legitimacy. Town

17. Transcripts, XVII, 65.

meetings, in which the president would respond to questions from the audience; the Caddell polls; various White House communications operations, by the offices of Anne Wexler and Jody Powell; and occasional visits to homes of ordinary Americans were all important means to this end. Third, any judgment about a decision's electoral effects had to come from those close enough to be trusted implicitly. Among those Carter relied on were his wife, Rosalynn, and Hamilton Jordan. One aide went so far as to say: "I do not think he [Carter] ever made any basic decisions [on issues] where he factored in the political." But Rosalynn and Jordan were "very political": "Now I think that when he listened to Rosalynn that he's no dummy by any means. He knows full well that Rosalynn has factored in the political aspects of it or Hamilton has factored in the political pluses and minuses. And frankly that's an awfully good position for somebody to be in. Because then he's true to his own being but he knows full well that [the political is] not being overlooked."[18]

In *First Lady From Plains*, Rosalynn Carter confirms that the president listened to her in regard to political matters. But she doubted her influence when his mind was set on doing what was right.

> Our most common argument centered on political timing, a question of strategy more than substance. The best things to do are not always the most popular things, and on more than one occasion I pleaded with Jimmy to postpone certain controversies . . . until his second term. My pleas always fell on deaf ears. "If securing a second term was more important to me than doing what needs to be done, then I'd wait," he would snap at me. But I didn't always give up. . . . His standard answer when I talked about political expediency was a seemingly pompous: 'I'll never do anything to hurt my country." But he meant it, and I meant it too when I appealed to him, loudly sometimes when I was very concerned: "The thing you can do to hurt your country most is not get re-elected." I believed it then. I believe it now.
>
> Though I could seldom sway him when his mind was made up, he always listened. I am much more political than Jimmy and was more concerned about popularity and winning re-election, but I have to say that he had the courage to tackle the important issues, no matter how controversial—or politicaly damaging—they might be.[19]

Fourth, since the outside-in method of dealing with Congress stresses personal control, it is important that things do not get out of hand. There must be time, contact, and continual reassurance that the right choices

18. *Ibid.*, 63.
19. Rosalynn Carter, *First Lady From Plains* (Boston, 1984), 164–71.

are made. If the presidential agenda gets overloaded, then real problems develop. It is particularly troublesome if the overload includes items that the president does not define as deserving attention. The whole schedule is then disrupted. Further, the failure to treat issues that others define as presidential may lead to a charge of incompetence—a particularly harsh criticism for one who prides himself on a capacity to maintain control. It is in this context that one can comprehend the adverse effects of personnel problems—such as the independence of certain cabinet secretaries (notably Joseph A. Califano, Jr., secretary of health, education, and welfare, and W. Michael Blumenthal, secretary of the treasury)—or of the Iranian hostage crisis, which came to dominate the president's schedule during his last year in office. In the latter case, the president had no doubts that the issue was his to resolve. But that meant he had less time for other situations that deserved his attention. More than that, the crisis in Iran was one of those persistent problems that, according to Carter, ought to have been susceptible to solution but were not. This most irritating overlay on the regular order of business in the White House was destructive of the president's strategy for setting and justifying his priority list. Thus was damaged a major source of Americans' confidence in the president.

Carter thought Congress should support the president because he spent time on an issue, demonstrated public support, and personally avoided the strictly political (by his definition). Unfortunately for the president, this approach created a distance between him and Congress. Since Congress is an institution that depends heavily on personal communication and trust, a more impersonal style causes perplexity, even suspicion. A common cause monarch is bound to make the members uncomfortable.

PROVIDING THE OPTIONS

The Domestic Affairs and Policy Staff, headed by Stuart Eizenstat, was charged with the responsibility of identifying major domestic policy issues and providing the president options for dealing with them. Modern presidents have all required some mechanism for planning domestic policy. It was not until the first Nixon administration, however, that a formally structured domestic-policy unit was created in the White House. Roy L. Ash headed a study group appointed by Nixon to make recommendations for reorganizing the executive branch. The Ash Council suggested such a unit to coordinate proposals forwarded by various agencies.[20] Nixon established the Domestic Council, with John Ehrlichman as its executive director.

Subsequent presidents retained a coordinating mechanism with functions similar to the Domestic Council's. The unit came to have a very important role in the Carter administration and successfully avoided the "incompetent" label that was pinned on so many other White House operations. Much of that success is attributed to Eizenstat's intelligence and organizational ability. As Dom Bonafede reported in 1979: "Throughout his White House tenure, Eizenstat has risen steadily in stature, and is recognized today within the departments and in Congress as a fair and able presidential emissary."[21]

This brief history of the Domestic Affairs and Policy Staff (typically referred to as the DPS) reminds one that the unit operates within a context of ongoing policy activity. Many departments, agencies, and congressional committees are involved in domestic policy on a continuing basis. In fact, Nixon's effort to control this continuous activity led to the unit's creation in the White House. Members of the DPS, the president's people, of course, must keep abreast of what else is happening in government. That is, the DPS has to maintain lines of communication beyond the president's appointees into the permanent bureaucracy if it is to provide credible and feasible policy options.

For President Carter, the DPS performed vital functions in preparing the legislative program. The president arrived in Washington with a full agenda derived from the campaign. Eizenstat had been intimately and continuously involved in producing that agenda. He had been assigned by Carter to develop issue papers for the Democratic National Committee during the 1974 congressional election (when Carter co-chaired the campaign.) Then he served as issues director during the 1976 presidential campaign. This experience was essential, for Eizenstat's difficult job was to coordinate the president's domestic policy with the program initiatives from departments and agencies. When he became director of the DPS, Eizenstat knew the president very well both in terms of substantive policy preferences and political style.

20. For details, see Wayne, *The Legislative Presidency*, 114–19.

21. Dom Bonafede, "Stuart Eizenstat—Carter's Right-Hand Man," *National Journal*, June 9, 1979, p. 944.

The primary function of the DPS was to manage program development (and, by implication, agenda setting) within the White House—a vital task in Carter's approach to working with Congress. Legislation sent to the Hill by the trustee president had to be well conceived and well integrated. To this end, the DPS often had to broker disagreements among the agencies while, of course, representing the president's preferences on an issue. When settlement was not possible, the DPS would analyze possible bases for agreement and forward that analysis to the president.

As one can see, the DPS was strategically well placed to influence the shape and direction of the president's domestic legislative requests. Yet DPS members emphasized that their influence was a consequence primarily of becoming familiar with what the president wanted rather than of giving him direct advice on an issue. That is to say, it was more as savvy managers of the paper flow and interagency conflicts that the DPS had impact. As one staff member put it: "We were the President's fingers out there in the government. . . . We operated on the narrow line between substance and tactics." Another judged that advice giving on specific proposals might actually jeopardize the effectiveness of the DPS, since that would verge on advocacy. It was important that the DPS be seen as a relatively neutral manager of information and options, again within the context of the president's clear preferences. Otherwise, departments and agencies would be encouraged to seek other routes to the Oval Office, and the domestic policy process would break down. This matter of advice giving versus analysis was summarized by a member of the DPS: "Our job, as he defined it, was not to be President but it was to advise him of the considerations which he wanted to take into account and how he wanted to make this decision. Certainly the way we structured the information we got . . . and the way we helped the government decide which issues would go to him . . . were far greater sources I think of real influence and impact on government than the actual advice we gave him in any particular situation."[22]

Of course, not every issue is the subject of settled views on all sides. The DPS also managed a process that produced "presidential review memoranda" (PRM), which Eizenstat adapted from that used by the National Security Council. The purpose was to examine an issue in some detail over time, inviting input from agencies, interested private groups,

22. Transcripts, XIV, 4–5, 5.

even occasionally the public through hearings. The president was involved in the early stages, approving the questions to be answered about the given issue. Subjects included youth employment, solar energy, nonfuels minerals, and Vietnam veterans' benefits.

Much of the DPS's work brought them into direct contact with Congress, which, after all, is also in the business of agenda setting and program development. During the first year of the administration, DPS coordination with Congress was not well developed. By the end of the first year, however, Eizenstat met with the chief counsels of committees that had domestic jurisdiction, trying to synchronize agendas as much as possible.

Once legislation was actually introduced, the DPS was less directly involved since the Congressional Liaison staff took over. Still, as with all high-level White House staff operations, the line among functional units is not always crisply drawn. Thus, members of Congress and committee and subcommittee staff personnel do not necessarily honor the divisions of responsibility established elsewhere. If, for example, a senator believed that Eizenstat could be helpful in regard to some aspect of a presidential proposal, then he or she was likely to call on him for assistance. As a matter of fact, Eizenstat was viewed favorably on Capitol Hill as intelligent and resourceful. In spite of such contact, the DPS tried to avoid being identified as a lobbying unit. A DPS member explained:

> I didn't regard [lobbying] as a domestic policy staff function. It was just something that we did sometimes and that took the burden off. It was always clear between us [Congressional Liaison and DPS] that while we had contacts with the Hill so that we'd know what was going on and be able to make a judgment that we didn't try to lobby. We didn't. Sometimes we would break that rule but we had always considered ourselves as doing it at their request. It's fairly important for those two functions to be separated because the lobbyist has to have somebody back at the ranch they can blame. They've got to be loved [on the Hill]. . . . It's a very bad idea to mix those functions. If you send your substantive people up there to lobby on one issue you're just inviting people to log roll on other issues. We tried to avoid that.[23]

The specific role of the DPS in advising the president changed during the four years because the president himself changed—at least according to some. As the administration moved through the agenda set during the campaign and toward the 1980 election, political (*i.e.*, electoral) considerations became more important. In a sense, the natural rhythm of the

23. *Ibid.*, 32.

four-year term brought the president to the kind of activity that he defined as politics, an election campaign. In addition, according to his domestic policy advisers, the president may have learned that policy politics on Capitol Hill were more important, and less manageable, than he had thought. The president was not prepared either for the fragmentation in Congress or for the Democrats' lack of discipline and loyalty to a Democratic president. Discovering these facts did not enhance the president's image of Congress, to be sure. But it did contribute to his becoming aware of the complex requirements of majority building in the House and Senate. One member of the DPS described the change: "I guess he believed that once he had been elected to get those ideas into being and once he had the substance of a great proposal to Congress he could do the same thing he had done in the campaign. I think he misjudged that. I think towards the last two years of the administration he didn't say that so much. You could get his attention much more on politics."[24]

The combination of a more experienced DPS and the freedom to work on all aspects of issues—including the political—resulted in a more confident operation by 1980. "There was a lot less wasted effort," is the way one staff person put it, describing efforts during the early months of the administration. "It [1980] was the first year in which I think we accurately identified what the problems were. We knew what the legislative problems were, we knew what the political problems were and we had a realistic notion of how you put together a plan to deal with it. We had a sense of who was good at it and who was bad at it. I think we deferred more to OMB [Office of Management and Budget] where they deserved to be deferred to in the budget process for example and told them to sit down and shut up very effectively in some other areas." It is significant that the election itself focused attention. "We finally had a big thing. We could finally agree on what the big thing was." Thus a goal was established for judging what was "right." "Everybody had a common objective from the lowliest deputy secretary to the President."[25]

In summary, the DPS was a vital unit in the Carter approach to congressional relations. The staff members provided the president with the kind of trusted support that he needed in preparing his program for Con-

24. *Ibid.*, 58.
25. *Ibid.*, 70, 71

gress. They were available with the substantive backup later when Congress was taking action on presidential requests. And they were crucial actors in making policy and political adaptations during the life of the administration.

MAKING A BUDGET

There is, of course, another agency close to the president that is intimately involved with domestic policy matters. The Office of Management and Budget (OMB) is in natural competition with the DPS by virtue of its responsibilities for preparing the budget and clearing legislative proposals from departments and agencies. The DPS has the advantage of proximity to the president; the OMB has the advantage of expertise and experience. It is said that the OMB became more politicized when it was reorganized during the Nixon administration. Louis Fisher is very blunt on this point: "Much of the leverage within the OMB shifted from career civil servants to political appointees; objectivity and professionalism lost ground to a politicized operation." A Carter official put it differently: "I don't think OMB is politicized. I think it's there to serve Presidents. When it stops serving Presidents, then presidents will turn to some other entity to serve them." One does not have to resolve that issue to understand the importance of the agency—particularly for a president who wants to impress Congress with his command of the issues. Clearly the OMB has much to give such a president. The functions of the OMB, as described by a staff member, sound like those of the DPS with its "fingers out there in the government."

> It's the link between the President or the White House and the rest of the government. It's the agency that should translate for the agencies what the President has decided, and then be there on a day-to-day basis to see that agencies do what the President has decided to do. OMB is not a green eye shade agency. It makes policy development in some instances. It is a very professional organization, and I believe it should be. It has the institutional memory to know where the pitfalls are in any kind of policy proposal. It also knows where the roadblocks might be both in the agencies and on the Hill. If properly used, it is an invaluable resource for a President.[26]

26. Louis Fisher, *The Politics of Shared Power: Congress and the Executive* (Washington, D.C., 1981), 41; Transcripts, VI, 3.

What is the difference between the OMB and the DPS? In large part it has to do with longevity. One can predict with considerable confidence that the OMB will be there, president after president, performing similar functions, if not exactly the same in every case. A domestic policy staff will vary more in organization and the functions assigned to it. Still, in order to make the OMB work for him, the president must be able to take control of the agency through his appointments. President Carter first appointed one of his closest advisers, Bert Lance, as the OMB director. Lance was forced to resign early in the administration, however, following charges of wrongdoing as a banker in Georgia. The loss of Lance was a serious blow to the president. Lance's successor, James McIntyre, was also part of the Georgia group but his status was considerably below Lance's. He could not expect to override advice on domestic policy from other White House sources. Rather, he was a contestant in the struggle to gain access to the president.

McIntyre's task was, in many ways, more difficult than that of either his predecessor or his competitor in the White House, Stuart Eizenstat. It is in the nature of the job that the OMB director has a great deal to manage. The OMB is a large agency with manifold responsibilities. Lance expected others (mainly McIntyre, who served as his deputy) to cope with these problems. He served primarily as a principal aide to the president, but he happened to hold the position of OMB director. But this arrangement was not particularly beneficial to the agency, according to one aide: "Mr. Lance never worried about OMB's institutional role because as director he always had access to the President. He could weigh in on the important issues. As advisor to the President, he was never left out of those issues. OMB, as an institution, was cut out of the process in the beginning. . . . Most of the career staff at OMB were viewed by non OMB senior people as being holdover Republicans. . . . As a result the domestic policy staff stepped in and filled the void initially."[27] McIntyre did not have Lance's advantage among his peers. His base of influence was as director of an agency whose role had been de-emphasized during the Nixon and Ford administrations. He had to restore OMB's credibility by managing its operations in a way that would impress the president and White House aides. Accomplishing this task was complicated by the opinion of

27. Transcripts, VI, 60.

some White House domestic advisers that the OMB had many "holdover Republicans."

Eizenstat simply had more flexibility organizationally and procedurally to fashion an advisory role for the DPS suited to his interpretation of the president's policy interests. The White House domestic policy apparatus can be adjusted to suit each president's wishes. The OMB is a continuing agency with a formal institutional role. Not surprisingly, the president's people in the OMB were suspicious of the DPS. They were concerned that the DPS had been captured by interest groups and the agencies and therefore was not reflecting what was important to the president (at least as those issues were understood in the OMB). Here is a sample of the OMB perspective:

> There was an implicit policy there [in the DPS] and it was an expansionary policy. Get government more involved in things.
>
> The domestic policy staff oftentimes was the advocate within the White House for the positions taken by various assistant and under secretaries and deputy assistant secretaries. They not only were representatives of interest groups directly, but they also were fighters within the establishment of these positions. This took form . . . during the budget process. They would come and argue their points there.[28]

The OMB staff members believed that they more accurately reflected the president's consolidative approach to government. These differences were displayed in the budget process, but some OMB officials thought that the DPS would lobby on the Hill against OMB decisions if the DPS lost in earlier encounters. This situation allegedly developed when efforts were being made in the OMB to balance the budget.

The variable institutional role of the OMB and the DPS led to important differences in the services provided to the president in his dealings with Congress. As was the case with the DPS, the OMB did the type of front-end policy development that suited the president's penchant for detailed preparation. The OMB's work was associated with the routine and predictable functions of the agency. Despite the alleged de-emphasis of the OMB during the early months of 1977, certain tasks had to be performed with the OMB's assistance. And, in fact, many of the president's hoped-for accomplishments—balancing the budget, establishing zero-base budgeting, and reorganizing government—required active OMB cooperation.

28. *Ibid.*, 108.

At this crucial time, when the Carter administration was in the process of fashioning its way of governing, Bert Lance was forced to resign as OMB director. That event had a profound and lasting effect on the president's approach to Congress. Among other things, the first summer (1977) was very hectic. There was disorganization rather than the efficiency and preparedness that the president would have preferred. An OMB aide explains: "I have to be quite candid with you. There was a great deal of chaos and confusion in the Office of Management and Budget during that summer. [In addition to preparing the budget and office organization] we were trying to get our . . . reorganization plan [of the executive office] finished. . . . There were tremendous turf battles that took place in that reorganization. . . . There were questions about the role of the Domestic Policy staff vis-a-vis OMB. . . . In addition to that, we had made a pledge to cut down the size of the White House staff, which was an agonizing matter."[29]

In addition to assisting the president and other domestic policy advisers in preparing the budget and other policy recommendations, the OMB is expected to have a direct relationship with Congress. As part of the internal reorganization, the Office of Legislative Affairs was upgraded. Hubert L. Harris, another Georgian, was in charge. Again, the institutional role is important in determining how the OMB operates. The agency is naturally viewed as centrally involved in budget making and reorganization. Congress therefore expects to call upon the OMB for assistance. But others in the White House are involved in the budget-making process too. A task force on the budget was created in 1978 to coordinate White House lobbying on the Hill:

We formed the budget task force with a memorandum from Frank [Moore] and Jim [McIntyre] to the President, recommending this as a way to speak with one voice on budget issues . . . to try to use detailees from departments to work with certain functional areas. We had human resources, natural resources, energy and natural resources; we had defense and one other area using these people as shock troops to go to the Hill and represent the issue. They worked with the various OMB people, the White House domestic policy people, and the departmental people to be sure that we talked about the President's budget consistently.[30]

29. *Ibid.*, 5.
30. *Ibid.*, 70.

According to the OMB top staff, this system worked well. There were no "turf problems" with the White House Congressional Liaison Office, in part because McIntyre and Moore knew each other well enough to coordinate their efforts.

Clearly, as we have seen, the OMB had a significant role in shaping Carter's relations with Congress. By reason of institutional position, the OMB was bound to be important in preparing the president's program. However, the agency's work was frequently contested—most notably by the DPS. The OMB staff members were actively involved in supporting presidential proposals on Capitol Hill. Unfortunately, however, Lance's resignation dramatically altered the dynamics of White House policy interaction by enhancing Eizenstat's position. Further, it projected an image exactly contrary to that preferred by the trustee president. Carter would have wanted members of Congress to be persuaded to support him because executive preparation was so thorough. Instead, they were encouraged to participate actively in all phases of policy making, matching their collective competence against that of the White House.

BUILDING OUTSIDE SUPPORT

All modern presidents can be expected to rely on public support in managing their relations with Congress. Even President Johnson found it necessary to go to the public occasionally, though he disliked doing so since he usually had "to pick a fight with Congress [in order to] reach the papers and the people."[31] If a president separates himself from the prevailing policy views of legislators, then demonstrated outside support for his program is imperative. Public and group support is important for all presidents, to be sure, but it is crucial for the trustee. Thus the Office of Public Liaison came to perform a primary function in the Carter scheme. His approach required that proposals have intrinsic merit and that the groups primarily affected acknowledge it. The task of building coalitions for "what is right" was assigned to the Office of Public Liaison.

The Public Liaison staff was initially under the direction of Midge Costanza, an early supporter of Jimmy Carter. Under her direction, the office "had been defined . . . as a much more 'responsive' office than an

31. Johnson, *The Vantage Point*, 450.

'initiative' one. Interest groups based in Washington felt that they could come into the White House with their particular agendas and problems and the door was always open, but there was essentially no follow-up and there was no structure to the operation." In May, 1978, Anne Wexler was appointed director. She brought a very different perspective to the job. The staff's principal responsibility was to build coalitions to support presidential initiatives.

> The problem for the White House was that they had developed a very ambitious and complex legislative agenda, yet, there were no mechanisms to blend that agenda with all the processes and issues with outside support. Such a blend would have made it possible for the White House lobbyist and issue groups to go to the Hill and demonstrate to the members of Congress that not only was the White House in favor of an issue but also that there were armies of people behind the White House lobbyist who could demonstrate strong public support for those issues. . . . The White House had found that without those coalitions it was very, very hard to pass legislation. It was not enough to go to the Hill and say, "The president wants this bill." Support had to be demonstrated and manifested in many ways.[32]

The model for this effort was the building of support for the Panama Canal treaties, an operation directed mainly by Hamilton Jordan. It was generally conceded that his campaign transformed sure defeat into victory. Wexler tried to do the same for other administration programs, seeking as well to have groups participate in policy development. In direct contrast, however, was the energy program sent to Congress in April, 1977. The proposals were, according to one White House aide, "conceived in secret [and] presented to the country as a fait accompli without the consultation of interested parties."[33]

The Public Liaison staff under Wexler organized itself to accomplish legislative-like tasks. Coalition building is a common legislative function —indeed, probably the most important one. In pursuit of this goal, the Public Liaison staff organized task forces. These groups were built around major issues or proposals, and their purpose was to generate support and coordinate activities through the process of policy development and approval. A staff member describes the operation:

32. Transcripts, I, 3, 2–3.
33. *Ibid.*, 3.

The makeup of the task force included at least two people from the relevant agencies, the assistant secretary who was substantively responsible and the Congressional Liaison person. Usually, but not always, the lead press person from the agency was also included. . . . Task forces also included several people from the White House. There was a lead person from the Congressional Liaison office as well as a person from the Media Liaison office. . . . Several other officials in these groups were the Domestic Policy staff, the associate director responsible for the particular substantive area or the equivalent person from the National Security Council. . . . Eventually, when Al McDonald's office was created [in 1979 to reorganize White House staff operations], there was an additional person from his staff. . . . The Chief of Staff's office, when he came, was fully involved. . . . The Intergovernmental Relations office participated when the issue concerned mayors and governors and other local officials, or whenever issues dealt with the other side of their responsibilities, the Cabinet.[34]

A Wexler task force had several responsibilities: to identify the full dimensions of an issue, to develop a strategy for building support, to test proposals for their effect on various interests, to keep groups informed of issues and proposals, to maintain a good working relationship with the media, and, eventually, to promote lobbying for the proposal before Congress. A staff official spoke about the process.

[We would] try to put together an overall strategy that incorporated Congressional Liaison, Media Liaison, and our work with the interest groups. . . . — would draft . . . the strategy by identifying the goal and the possible obstacles, citing the problems that we had to overcome, and proposing a range of possible solutions and activities. Following review . . . [we] discussed implementation such as: identifying the appropriate groups; how to build the relationships by consulting with them on the front side of the issue; timing for the president to announce his policy; development of a time line for inviting interest groups in for briefings and to discuss their concerns and suggestions and finally identifying the appropriate administration people for the purpose of conducting the briefing. From there the Domestic Policy Staff would refine the policy or legislative piece, we would then reassemble the interest groups, and discuss the finished product. We would talk about it, tell them the whys and wherefores, indicate what was and was not included from their suggestions. . . . Our efforts then turned to coordinating the efforts of the Congressional Liaison people, Media Liaison and the others who worked on the Hill. Our goal was to synchronize the resources of the interest groups with the White House efforts.

This same official evaluated the effort: "Obviously, the process did not completely, in some cases even partially, satisfy the people who were in-

34. *Ibid.*, 14–15.

terested in the issue, but it did give them a sense that their participation was important. It also helped in developing a sense of ownership afterward. It generated, I think, a good feeling about the President and a willingness on the part of the participants to use their resources in moving the issue on the Hill."[35]

I stress that this coalition-building process is legislative-like simply to reiterate the requirements of Carter's approach to Congress. Separation was preferred to intimacy in presidential-congressional relations. One can easily imagine that another Democratic president would leave coalition building to his party's leaders in Congress, possibly to develop a "sense of ownership" among them, as well as among interest groups.[36] That was apparently Johnson's approach. George C. Edwards III said: "Johnson consulted with Congress at all stages of the legislative process, from what problems and issues his task forces should consider to the drafting of bills. He appointed members to secret task forces, thus implicating them in the resulting proposals."[37] Johnson's staff also cleared proposals with interest groups and the appropriate agencies. But they were aware that members of Congress, too, had many contacts with both, and they did not for the most part object to the manner in which members relied on these connections.

The Democratic party of 1977 was not that of 1965, however, and Jimmy Carter held unflattering views about those sorts of contact. He was therefore unlikely to rely so heavily on the members of Congress in building support for his program. The matter came up in the Miller Center discussions with Public Liaison personnel. The reactions were revealing.

Question: Why didn't the president rely on the Congress to perform these kinds of services with committees and subcommittees, which have traditionally performed the function of organizing these interests? Why wasn't the Congress thought of as performing those kinds of roles?

Response: Well, I don't believe they [Congress] were strong enough to do that.

35. *Ibid.*, 19.

36. Or, as Polsby puts it, "to bring Congress into the process of formulating proposals before they arrive, fully blown on Capitol Hill" (Nelson W. Polsby, *Consequences of Party Reform* [New York, 1983], 107).

37. George C. Edwards III, *Presidential Influence in Congress* (San Francisco, 1980), 119.

> I don't think they had any interest in doing it. The Congress was saying to the president, "Show me that you have got enough support out there to earn my vote for this issue." And they weren't saying, "I am going to get out there and show that there is enough support for you to earn my vote for this issue." They wanted it proved to them so that they could feel safe and secure in supporting him. That's what happens when you don't have any strong political system. Congress had no particular vested interest in doing that because it wasn't going to help them at home.[38]

This reasoning developed in part because of the view that the issues themselves were not attractive ones for Congress. "They always needed a little help. . . . They wanted us to show them."[39] During the Johnson administration, the president's domestic proposals were primarily positive ones for the members—benefits were distributed to states and districts. President Carter, on the other hand, had consolidative, reorganizational proposals, some of which were designed to reduce benefits. It was unlikely that he would have gone to Congress during the early stages of policy development in any event. But, as it was, his staff was probably correct in believing that the members were not interested in being implicated in programs of dubious benefit to their constituents.

In summary, the Office of Public Liaison came to perform an important, even vital, function. After some early defeats, it became apparent that outside support had to be developed and demonstrated if the president's program was to gain congressional approval. The president's style and, to a certain extent, his program prevented more active cooperation with members of Congress. It fell to the Public Liaison staff to create networks of support in which decision makers would work with those affected by proposals. These networks were very much like the fabled "cozy little triangles" of representatives from executive agencies, congressional subcommittees, and interest groups. The difference was that members of Congress were often left out of the Wexler networks or triangles and White House staff were substituted. In fact, Wexler designed them in part to break the hold of more traditional groupings.

The Carter approach to Congress resulted in an institutional separation of policy functions. Agenda setting and program development were

38. Transcripts, I, 60.
39. *Ibid.*, 61.

regarded as the practically exclusive province of the executive, a view consistent with the expectations of the trusteeship presidency model. It was the function of Congress to approve the proposals that were developed. Having learned, however, that nothing is automatic on Capitol Hill, the Office of Public Liaison sought to manage approval processes as well. This effort, made with only limited congressional participation, is, in some ways, reminiscent of the Nixon White House. Democrats in Congress did not expect to work closely with Nixon, however. Carter, on the other hand, was a Democrat, and therefore members of his party resented the self-imposed distance between the president and Congress. Thus, those in the White House with direct responsibility for congressional liaison had their work cut out for them.

☆5☆

Congressional Liaison in the Carter White House

Carter's approach to Congress was not and could not be limited to the activities of the Office of Congressional Liaison. His method stressed the careful development of policy proposals that would then merit the support of a rational Congress. This emphasis on substance over politics is a matter of degree if one compares the Carter White House with others. All presidents seek to formulate meritorious programs that will then command congressional backing. Carter's image of Congress' ordinary role in the politics of policy making did not encourage him to invite input from the members, however. In *Keeping Faith* he observed that "Congress had an insatiable desire for consultation, which, despite all our efforts, we were never able to meet."[1] From his perspective, he consulted enough—perhaps too much. It is difficult, if not unnatural, for the trustee president to rely heavily on the delegate-legislator.

Members of Congress are naturally anxious when a new president comes from out of town and has campaigned on an anti-Washington, anti-government-as-usual theme. They want to know whether the president meant what he said in the campaign. They may even resent a president who conveys the impression that his actions are justified by public approval and theirs are not—particularly when the president in question wins by a very narrow margin. And when a president fails to consult adequately with members of Congress, they in turn may seek guidance from sources other than the White House, judging that the president's views in effect release them from loyal service to the administration.

The Office of Congressional Liaison had to work in this atmosphere

1. Jimmy Carter, *Keeping Faith: Memoirs of a President* (New York, 1982), 71.

of suspicion and discontent. It was not within their power to resolve all the conflicts that would arise. But the staff did work both ends of the avenue and therefore had important mediating functions to perform. The assignment would not be easy. It was predictable that their performance would receive constant criticism.

THE ORGANIZATION OF CONGRESSIONAL LIAISON

In 1978, Eric L. Davis asked what Carter could learn about Congress from his predecessors. Davis concluded that "in one sense, very little at all. . . . The contemporary Congress is an institution made up of independent-minded members subject to very little central control. If Carter and his associates were to attempt to replicate their predecessors' approaches to legislative relations, they would be using an entirely inappropriate set of strategies and tactics."[2]

Normally, one president would not adopt another's approaches. The conditions noted in Table 11 are changeable, thus encouraging differences in method. Still, this fact does not then suggest that one president has nothing to learn from his predecessors. As noted earlier, Table 11 also contains general lessons about what must be done in a post–Great Society and post-Watergate era in order to work productively with "an institution made up of independent-minded members subject to very little central control." In commenting on the Carter administration at midterm, Davis observed that it "has not yet, after twenty months in office, been able to develop a coherent and consistent strategy for working with Congress. Yet, because of Congress' reassertion of its position in Washington, such a strategy is perhaps more necessary today than at any other time in recent memory."[3] Thus, Davis acknowledged that there was at least one lesson to be learned from previous administrations—that congressional relations required more attention from the White House as a consequence of events in recent decades.

2. Eric L. Davis, "What Can Jimmy Carter Learn About Congress From Previous Presidents?" (Paper delivered at the annual meeting of the American Political Science Association, New York, August 31–September 3, 1978), 25.

3. *Ibid.*

PRESIDENT CARTER'S ROLE

However politically sensible it may have been for Carter to spend time developing a congressional liaison organization suited to Washington standards, he was unlikely by reason of personal inclination, sense of what mattered, and Washington-based experience to do so. As one staff member put it: "The President never really talked about the methodology of congressional liaison to us."[4] Yet a liaison system would emerge whether or not the president participated actively in shaping it. This system could be expected to orient itself to Carter's preferences. Thus the staff would try to give the president what they thought he wanted. And there were signals from the president that were bound to have an effect: first and foremost was the choice of Frank Moore as liaison chief, second was Carter's emphasis on cabinet government (and, as a related point, reducing the White House staff), and third was the president's method of preparing the correct policy response to major issues.

The selection of Frank Moore embodied the president's preference for managing his program rather than coping with any problems that might develop on Capitol Hill. Moore's appointment appeared to be a consequence of three factors: his experience in Georgia as Carter's liaison with the state legislature, his work in 1976 in coordinating the Carter campaign with various House and Senate campaigns, and, of course, his close association with Jimmy Carter personally. The last was apparently the most important. In fact, his most relevant experience—in the 1976 campaign—had already resulted in considerable criticism. *National Journal* reporter Dom Bonafede explains: "Numerous officials come to Washington preceded by their reputations: Moore's arrival, unfortunately, was preceded by criticism 2½ months before he formally became assistant to the President for congressional relations. According to these reports, he was insensitive to the unwritten laws of protocol that help determine the relationship between the executive and legislative branches. It was alleged that he often failed to return phone calls, neglected requests and missed appointments with Members of Congress."[5]

4. Transcripts, IV, 21.

5. Dom Bonafede, "Carter's Relationship with Congress—Making a Mountain Out of a 'Moorehill,'" *National Journal*, March 26, 1977, p. 456.

The president himself viewed Moore's task in management terms more than in political terms: "I needed to recruit knowledgeable people to work on Capitol Hill, keep track of the voluminous legislation being considered, and provide some continuity in our efforts to put my campaign commitments into effect. I chose Frank Moore for this job. A professional management specialist, Frank had been an associate since 1966 when I hired him as executive director of a multi-county planning and development commission, where he demonstrated an ability to recruit good people and deal effectively with the competing and sometimes suspicious officials of the eight counties and twenty-two towns and cities involved."[6] This most interesting statement (made after his term in office) reveals the president's analysis of the job to be done. Political realities did not appear to play an important role in this appointment. It should be noted that his reasoning is consistent with what one would expect from the trustee president. After all, the crucial work is identifying issues and formulating the proper courses of action. Support should follow once these programmatic results are made clear to the public and to Congress.

Presidents, of course, get to choose whomever they wish for such positions to do the job they judge needs to be done. In the case of Carter, however, members of Congress were concerned that he really intended to carry out his campaign promises, many of which threatened programs they supported. Naturally, then, they were anxious to have access to the new president through someone who could act as their emissary. Their experience with Frank Moore during the campaign was not reassuring—nor should it have been, from Carter's perspective. President Carter explained the problems Moore had during this period: "Although he worked prodigiously on his infrequent trips to Washington, Frank was unable to return all the telephone calls or answer the great volume of special requests that flooded to me through him. He had to bear the brunt of criticism from all those who were frustrated in their efforts to reach me."[7] Members would have been reassured if they had known Carter better—if he had been one of their own. Or they might have been less apprehensive and critical if Frank Moore had worked on Capitol Hill or was well known there. Failure to return telephone calls is not an unknown phenomenon in Washington. But many members of Congress

6. Carter, *Keeping Faith*, 44.
7. *Ibid.*

were worried about access to *this* president. Thus the failure to communicate contributed to the doubts they had, and therefore defined the special task facing the president in working with the legislature. As regards the rest of the liaison staff, the message from Moore's appointment was clear enough: it was important for the president to have a close associate in this key position and so it was important for them as well. Had members of Congress understood this president better, they too might have read the Moore selection quite differently.

The president's initial devotion to cabinet government carried with it organizational implications for liaison operations. For example, the president decided that a large staff was not necessary, since departments and agencies would take on much of the lobbying. But members of Congress often want direct contact with the president, particularly if he comes from the outside and is fortified by a trusteeship. One White House aide understood this point:

> The reason we had such a small staff to begin with is because President Carter originally felt he was dedicated to cabinet government. He asked, "Why have a big White House congressional liaison staff?" HEW [the Department of Health, Education, and Welfare] had forty people in congressional liaison; the Defense Department had hundreds. Commerce maybe had thirty people. . . . Our idea was to farm out the stuff; let them do it. What we were doing in the White House was to coordinate this. The reason it didn't work was that every Senator and every Congressman first wants to talk to the President. If they can't talk to the President, they want to talk to the next person and during 1977–78 in our administration, they thought it was Hamilton Jordan. They want the closest person to the President who is making decisions.

Associated with this rationale for a small staff was a campaign promise: "At the height of the Nixon years there were 565 people attributed to the White House, that is, that they admitted being on the White House staff. President Carter arrived at the number 351, which became the magic number, as the maximum number of White House staff." Another person agreed that this limit caused organizational problems. "There was an arbitrary twenty-five percent reduction in the number of staff members without looking to see how much work had to be done. So that's one reason we . . . organized as we did."[8]

8. Transcripts, IV, 1, 12.

The president's strong issue orientation was a third unmistakable signal likely to influence the organization and operation of the liaison office. Initially the office assigned House and Senate liaison personnel on the basis of substantive policy areas rather than assigning them a certain number of members for whom they were responsible. A Senate liaison person explained the system: "There were several organizational options. The Ford and Nixon Administrations had divided the Senate up according to members. . . . We chose instead to divide the work load according to issues, feeling that it would be better for us to have an in-house specialist who understood each particular issue. In addition, it would give each of us the opportunity to get to know all of the senators."[9]

Frank Moore consulted Lawrence F. O'Brien, President Johnson's director of congressional liaison, and O'Brien advised Moore to organize the office "to correspond to the particular regional and partisan blocs that ally to form coalitions in the House." The advantage, according to O'Brien, was that "each Democratic member of Congress would feel that he had a specific contact person in the White House who was sensitive to his concerns and the concerns of members representing similar districts." One of Carter's own liaison officers cited several basic problems with this system.

> I don't think that the issue-based organization of the liaison office was a very good idea. Too many members simply fall through the cracks. You might be assigned an issue, and that issue might never come up during the entire two years of a congressional session. Also, with the issue-based system, you don't get around to talking to many members until it's too late. You won't talk to the lowest ranking member of the Energy Subcommittee until you need his vote, and that's not when we should be talking with him. Our job is to serve the members' needs, to hold their hands, to stroke their egos. We have to do all kinds of little things with them that have nothing to do with issues. It's sort of like we're in the Green Stamps business. But we have to give out a lot of stamps before the members will trade them in.[10]

The system was changed on the House side after William Cable joined the liaison staff as chief House lobbyist in May, 1977, but it was retained on the Senate side. Why was it adopted in the first place? One of the liaison personnel emphasized that "it was our reacting to the lack of

9. *Ibid.*, 12.

10. Eric L. Davis, "Legislative Liaison in the Carter Administration," *Political Science Quarterly*, XCIV (Summer, 1979), 288, 289.

numbers. How can we organize this thing so it makes sense?"[11] But issues as a basis for organization require as many personnel as does organizing to suit Congress' size and complexity. When it came time to decide how to "organize this thing so it makes sense," the logical solution adopted was oriented more toward executive management than toward legislative politics, more toward the issue emphasis of the trustee president. That it was so quickly abandoned in the House illustrated the problems of enforcing Carter's outlook in day-to-day liaison operations there.

In summary, the president did not take a direct role in organizing the congressional liaison system. But his appointment of Moore, his preference for cabinet government and a leaner White House staff, and his emphasis on substantive issues created the context within which that system was structured.

THE CONGRESSIONAL LIAISON OFFICE

One of President Carter's principal congressional aides described the situation immediately after the election and during the early months of 1977. Speaking to another aide, he observed:

> You didn't have a job and I didn't have one. I didn't know I was going to have one. So we didn't have a lot of time to sit back and say, "How are we going to organize the office? Are we going to have these people, or those people?" . . . Democrats had been out of office for eight years. Because of some campaign rhetoric there were some high expectations for a Democratic White House. Pet legislation had been kept on the back burner, and patronage jobs or appointments had not been available to Democratic congressional people. We were absolutely deluged with telephone calls. Somebody put a counter on it, and recorded between two and three thousand calls a day. . . . We fell into the job of doing protocol, making up lists [of possible appointees] during the transition, and making courtesy calls for appointments. If somebody was being considered for the cabinet, [we] would call around, and ask various people, "What do you think about Jim Schlesinger? What do you know about this or other names being mentioned?" We would pass those comments back to Plains. . . . Those were the functions of the congressional liaison at that [early stage]. The point I'm trying to make is that we were not at that time working on legislation. We were not planning strategy, how we were going to get votes or call on committee chairmen. We were doing protocol lists and confirmation calls. [Later] we realized we had a lot of legislation up there. We had overloaded the circuits. We needed more staff.

11. Transcripts, IV, 24.

. . . We started out with thirteen people on the staff. I guess by April or May or June maybe we were up to twenty-three. We ended up, counting detailees and budget task force, with forty-[one] people on the staff.[12]

The aide described a maelstrom. Everything going on at once is the way it is when a new president moves into an empty White House. In this regard, Carter's experience was not extraordinary. There are always jobs to be filled, legislation to be enacted, expectations to be met, telephone calls to be answered. And many people like it—the pace itself is satisfying, even comforting, to them.

Note that the simple matter of *jobs*—who gets what coveted position—constitutes a first, very important test of presidential-congressional relations. The president appoints his government (cabinet, subcabinet, and other important executive positions) and hires a White House staff. Members of Congress want to make certain that friends get some of these positions. Since the size of the staff has increased, members of Congress pay more attention than they have in the past.

This initial emphasis on patronage has to be repulsive to the trustee president. As Frank Moore observed, "every Democrat on the Hill had a backlog of people he wanted jobs for."[13] This statement makes the whole process sound quite crass, and it is often just that. But there is more to it for members of Congress. Getting your people close to the president and the cabinet is a principal means of providing future communication. Every member of Congress—Democrat or Republican—would like to have someone near the centers of executive power. And so the race is on when a new president comes to town—the race for jobs. The results can mean access, information, and advantage for those who successfully get their friends well placed. It was not a race in which the president wanted to participate, either as judge or spectator.

Members of Carter's liaison team were well aware that they faced special problems in working with Congress. Their reviews of the challenges they faced are worth citing.

When I came on board I immediately detected from several [members of Congress] ill disguised hostility toward the administration. . . . Quite frankly, there were probably a number of people who called Jimmy Carter a friend who re-

12. *Ibid.*, 2–3.
13. *Time*, December 12, 1977, p. 15.

sented him as well, but they were no friends of the administration. . . . There were people whose hostility toward the administration was there.

It wasn't just that House members thought they should have been senators, others thought they should have been in the White House either at the staff level or as President. You don't spend a year and a half running against Washington, then come to Washington, and not have to pay for some of that rhetoric. A lot of the things that Jimmy Carter did in his campaign challenged the way things had been done traditionally in the Congress. . . . People described the President as having some sort of feeling toward the Congress that they were all a little bit dirty or tainted or somehow or another less good or less clean.

Let's flip the coin over and talk about Congress. They too had to go through an educational process. First let me make this point. Washington does not revolve around the White House. Washington revolves around Congress. I think a lot of people who came to Washington with President Carter didn't realize that. A lot of people who came to Washington with the President felt that in a sense he was crowned king, not inaugurated President. They learned fairly quickly. But Congress had to go through an educational process which was very painful, not so much for them as it was for us. They had to catch up with the changing times.[14]

These are nice descriptions of two sets of strangers meeting in Washington. The first statement is particularly interesting as an illustration of the transformation that occurred as this person assumed a role in the administration. Hostility was immediately communicated to him as a representative of Carter.

The liaison office had a clear agenda. The principal tasks included:

1. Leadership of the office and liaison with the president
2. Direct liaison with Congress—House and Senate
3. Liaison with departments and agencies, and coordinating their liaison efforts with those of the White House
4. Liaison with other White House units that had business on Capitol Hill
5. Responding to congressional correspondence.

As one can readily see, a liaison office is constantly in danger of flying apart. The personnel of this communications center are pulled in the direction of Capitol Hill, the Oval Office, the departments and agencies, and other White House operations. And in the middle is a huge stack of mail and telephone messages. The demand for coordination is constant; the problems of actually coordinating are insurmountable.

14. Transcripts, IV, 15-16.

Figure 4 should be viewed more as a locater system than as a standard organizational hierarchy. The fact is that Moore's style was not that of a bureau chief but rather that of a team leader. Although devoted to the president, Moore was not in any sense a whip-cracker or an enforcer, nor would Carter himself have expected that behavior from his liaison chief.

Note that I have placed the liaison operation within a set of ongoing associations among the president, his other White House staff, the departments and agencies, and Congress. The liaison office appears to be surrounded, and, in a very important sense, it was. Its functions complemented or fortified relationships among those policy-making bodies. Displaying the office in this way graphically illustrates its dependent role and therefore stresses its importance as a communications center.

Each of the liaison organizational units deserves separate treatment. Of course, they changed over time in function and personnel. The office evolved—not according to some master plan but rather in response to increased awareness of political responsibilities as defined by congressional expectations and presidential style.

Chief of liaison. Frank Moore's role as Carter's chief of liaison has not been well understood. Typically, the accounts of his service are highly critical of the job that he did on Capitol Hill. Dom Bonafede, reporter for the *National Journal*, wrote several stories on Carter's relations with Congress and, no doubt, accurately traced the attitudes of many members of Congress toward Moore. Here is a sample:

> After only two months on the job, Moore, alone of the Carter circle, has come under heavy criticism, a situation that perplexes and disturbs him.[15]

> Carter, even with a congressional majority of his own party, is largely viewed on Capitol Hill as an uncertain commodity, a novitiate in the art of sharing powers. . . . Slightly defensively, Frank B. Moore, assistant to the President for congressional liaison, who bears much of the blame for Carter's rocky relationship with Congress, remarked on a Washington phenomenon: "It's not how things are, but how they are perceived."[16]

> With the 96th Congress scheduled to convene January 15, President Carter may find it easier to normalize relations with 900 million Chinese than to establish har-

15. Bonafede, "Carter's Relationship with Congress," 456.

16. Dom Bonafede, "Carter and Congress—It Seems That 'If Something Can Go Wrong, It Will,'" *National Journal*, November 12, 1977, p. 1756.

Figure 4
CONGRESSIONAL LIAISON IN THE CARTER WHITE HOUSE

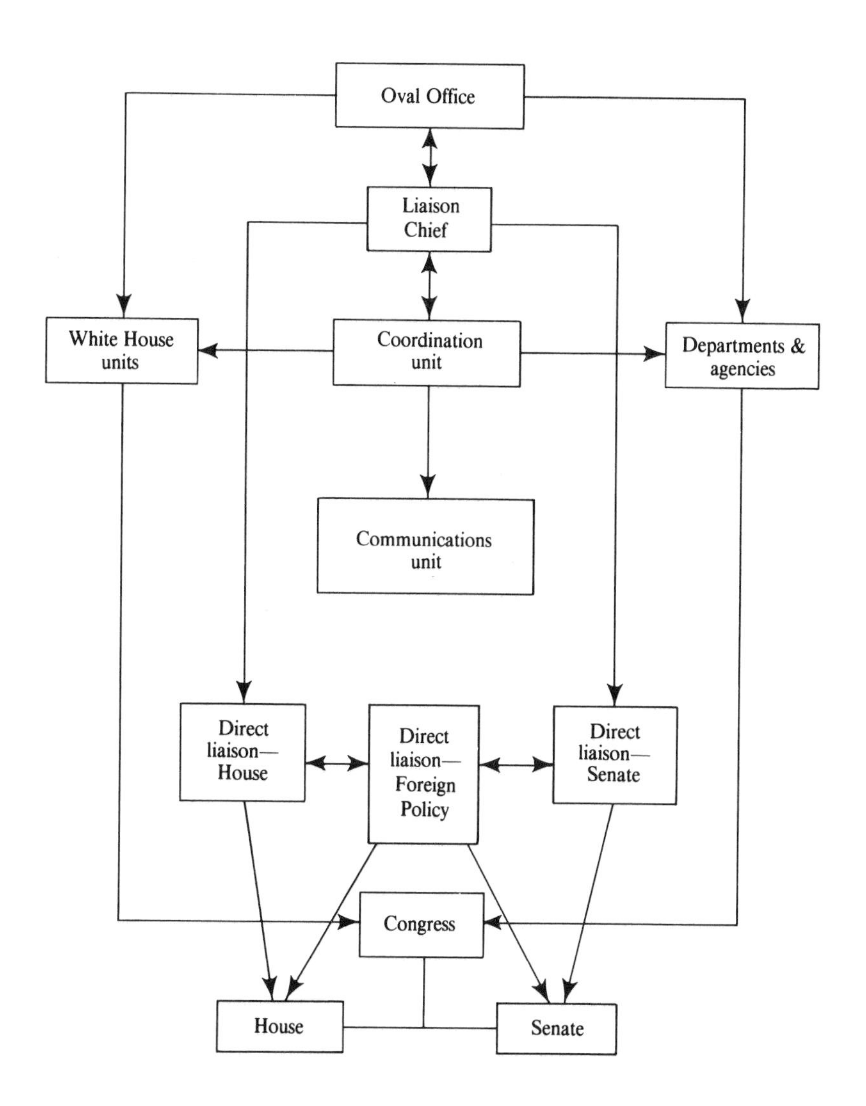

monious operations on Capitol Hill. . . . As Carter's chief emissary to Capitol Hill, Moore has been on the receiving end of a disproportionate share of criticism for the President's erratic relationship with Congress.[17]

A careful reading of Bonafede's reports indicates another significant development. Moore was consistently criticized, but he just as consistently received support from the man who made the difference—the president. "Moore is alive and well . . . meeting frequently with the President, whose confidence he reportedly retains." "Members of Congress who wonder about Moore's closeness and accessibility to the President should have no concern on that score." "Carter, meanwhile, continues to express confidence in Moore. He and Zbigniew Brzezinski . . . are the only two White House aides listed daily on the President's formal appointments schedule." The president's own judgment was that Moore "put together an outstanding staff and worked hard to overcome this original stigma of ineptitude."[18] It is noteworthy that Moore kept his job throughout the administration in spite of heavy criticism from the press and the Hill.

It is this confidence and daily contact that should encourage one to reassess the functions, and therefore the tests of success, of Frank Moore as chief of congressional liaison. The members of his own staff relied on his role in maintaining their access to the president—a role absolutely crucial for the trustee president coping with a Congress of delegates. One staff member described it:

There was no shop in the White House, thanks to Frank, who had better communication and more constant communication with Jimmy Carter on [legislative] issues and on tactics and on strategy than we did. Bill [Cable] and Dan [Tate] were in to see the President virtually every morning when important issues were on the floor. They went in with Frank, and Frank had access to the President any time of the day or night. From the standpoint of when I first came on board, it was staggering. I would be expected to pick up the phone and call Frank if there was a development on the Panama Canal treaties and other issues on the Hill and Frank immediately would call the President with it.[19]

17. Dom Bonafede, "The Tough Job of Normalizing Relations with Capitol Hill," *National Journal*, January 13, 1979, p. 54.

18. Bonafede, "Carter's Relationship with Congress," 456; Bonafede, "Carter and Congress," 1756; Bonafede, "The Tough Job," 57; Carter, *Keeping Faith*, 45.

19. Transcripts, IV, 21. Moore's daily contact with the president was often in the company of other White House staff members with a major interest in congressional strategy—for example, Jordan, Wexler, Eizenstat, and Powell.

Another staff member expressed his surprise and delight at the access Moore's close association with Carter afforded: "Frank had a relationship with Carter whereby he could walk in at night into the Oval Office and literally drop a piece of paper into his in box. I did that one night and I was amazed that I could do it. Frank just wrote it down and I just walked in and put it in his in box."[20]

It seems that most analysts have evaluated Moore's performance according to criteria drawn from a model of presidential-congressional relations that simply was inapt for the Carter administration. It is perfectly understandable that those testing the Carter liaison operations would make reference to the last Democratic president, Lyndon B. Johnson. But criteria established from the Johnson administration are unsuitable for measuring Carter. Political conditions had changed dramatically, and, in any event, Jimmy Carter was no Lyndon Johnson—nor did he have any intention of becoming one. Johnson's style, majority leader as president, was essentially based on a partnership model of presidential-congressional relationships.[21] Carter's style as the trustee president had to do with an independence model of presidential-congressional relations. In the partnership model, it makes good sense to judge the performance of the chief of congressional liaison by analyzing effectiveness on Capitol Hill. After all, this is the criterion the legislator as president is likely to employ. In the independence model, however, the test is whether the liaison chief establishes effective communication between the president and Congress. Vital to this linkage is maintaining access for liaison personnel to the Oval Office. The trustee president will probably not reach out. Nor will he probably work easily with insiders unless they are escorted by someone he trusts. Thus, the effective liaison chief for such a president is one who creates what is not likely to be there naturally. His attention is drawn more to his boss than to Capitol Hill. If he is unsuccessful in keeping the door open to the Oval Office, then whatever good will is established among the members will come to naught. Liaison chiefs act for the president; they have no special policy or political significance in and of themselves.

20. Transcripts, V, 33.

21. For details, see Charles O. Jones, "Presidential Negotiation with Congress," in Anthony King (ed.), *Both Ends of the Avenue: The Presidency, the Executive Branch, and Congress in the 1980s* (Washington, D.C., 1983), 96–130.

Having the president's confidence also permitted the office to develop the capacity to coordinate congressional liaison. Unfortunately, the task was complicated by the president's tolerance of independence among other White House units and the departments and agencies. This permissiveness tended to devalue the coin of presidential confidence. Comparisons with other presidents are too tempting to resist. Speaking for Presidents Johnson or Reagan, for example, afforded a person greater authority than did speaking for President Carter.

Coordination unit. Leslie C. Francis was the first person in charge of this unit. He was appointed after the initial organizational period. Previously Francis had served as administrative assistant to Representative Norman Y. Mineta (D-California). "Les Francis set up a legislative liaison office which principally interfaced with . . . the domestic policy staff and OMB. We found that we didn't have time, being on the Hill, to answer phone calls. We didn't have time to both go to all the meetings with the domestic policy staff and be on the Hill, so we created this other office that coordinated it for us with Les Francis."[22]

Moore was occupied by his relationship with the president and the need for his active presence at meetings and on the Hill. The House and Senate liaison personnel were most effective on site—that is, working the offices, halls, committee rooms, cafeterias, and other hangouts on the Hill. That left certain legislatively oriented tasks as local White House business:

> We had a central coordinating group which worked on several different things. . . . It really had three elements. Number one, there was a two-person element which wrote the weekly legislative report for the President. We had a second element of agency liaison. These were the people that were responsible for communicating with agency congressional liaison people and for organizing our weekly meetings with the agency congressional liaison people. A third element of this central coordinating unit was the congressional correspondence section, which had some of the hardest working people in the White House.[23]

Of course, *coordination* is a term of convenience. In practice, what this function amounted to was an effort to determine who was doing what and where. Anyone who has ever worked at the White House

22. Transcripts, IV, 3.
23. *Ibid.*, 10.

knows that coordination is more attentiveness than "harmonious adjustment," as one dictionary defines the word. Mostly it is important to know what others are doing that might affect your responsibilities. In the case of congressional liaison, everything was relevant. Thus the coordination unit could properly be described as too few people trying to learn too much in too short a time. Yet the effort had to be made—someone had to stay behind, so to speak, to mind the shop. Les Francis was that someone at first; he was followed by Robert Thomson, who initially served as a Senate liaison aide for the White House. The need for a coordination unit was made greater because Carter gave department heads a substantial amount of discretionary power in making subcabinet appointments. The 1979 cabinet shake-up was viewed as having a beneficial effect in this regard. Three departmental secretaries were fired—Joseph A. Califano, Jr. (Health, Education, and Welfare), W. Michael Blumenthal (Treasury), and Brock Adams (Transportation). James R. Schlesinger (Energy) and Griffin B. Bell (attorney general) resigned. As one liaison staff member put it: "I think you saw from the Camp David cabinet reorganization a move that would have taken back some of the discretion that was given almost exclusively to the cabinet. . . . We really got some first rate people . . . in that new cabinet group. I'm thinking particularly of Secretary Miller [Treasury] and Secretary Goldschmidt [Transportation]. They really did make a difference. It was a spirit kind of difference. There was more of a team spirit in the process after that."[24]

The change was a consequence more of new cabinet officials (and the conditions leading to their appointment) than of new departmental and agency liaison personnel. "It was more in the way things worked rather than in the numbers" is the way one staff member put it. Another observed that "we were dealing more directly with the cabinet officers after the change. . . . Any of us could have picked up the phone and called [Secretary of Transportation] Goldschmidt as quickly as we'd call someone at an agency."[25] The same person pointed out that the internal White House reorganization that followed the 1979 Camp David retreat was also eventually beneficial to the congressional liaison staff. At first Hamilton Jordan was appointed chief of staff, with direct responsibility for

24. *Ibid.*, 87.
25. *Ibid.*

congressional relations. Jordan immediately sought to acquaint himself with congressional leaders. His success was limited, since by that time they were wary of working with the White House.[26] In June, 1980, Jordan turned his attention to the reelection of the president, and Jack Watson then became White House chief of staff. The advantage for the liaison team was that the chief of staff provided greater coordination within the White House. Their burden was reduced.

Another staff member reflected that the Carter administration as a whole lacked discipline. "There were clearly blatant examples of disloyalty to the President." Prior to Camp David, however, there was almost no punishment for such behavior. "I never saw Carter or Frank [Moore] discipline anyone."[27] And Carter and Moore were, by nature, less likely than most to call their people to account. Yet failure to do so suggests a lack of direction—and tolerance of disloyalty is as discouraging to the faithful as it is encouraging to the faithless.

Coordinating congressionally related White House activities proved an extremely challenging task in the Carter administration. Not initially appointing a chief of staff certainly contributed to the challenge. The liaison team found they had to create their own coordination unit. As expected, therefore, the Camp David reorganization improved conditions sufficiently that staff members judged their efforts to be much more effective.

Communications unit. This hardworking unit dealt with telephone calls as well as paper correspondence.[28] Still, the major task was managing letters. Incoming mail from members of Congress to the president or to Frank Moore was handled by a small staff of three. Letters were forwarded to the appropriate person or unit for response, or responses were drafted by those in the correspondence unit. All incoming mail was logged in, and a computer-based tracking system was developed to maintain control. The president read the mail log every day, sometimes requesting to see a specific letter.

26. See Larry Light, "Jordan Now Assuming a New and Expanded Role in Congressional Relations," *Congressional Quarterly Weekly Report*, July 28, 1979, p. 1502.

27. Transcripts, V, 62.

28. This section profits considerably from interviews with communications unit personnel conducted by Stephen J. Wayne, George Washington University. I am much indebted to him for permitting me to listen to his tapes of those conversations.

The unit also initiated mailings to Capitol Hill, often to all the members, sometimes to specific members (to just the Democrats, for example, or to a state delegation). The letters, from the president or from Moore, might be primarily informational, serve to clarify the president's position, or represent an effort to make contact with the members (for example, congratulating them on some achievement). It does not take much imagination to realize that the volume of work could lead to mistakes, as the wrong letter being sent to a member. Incoming mail averaged approximately fifty letters a working day to the president, one hundred letters a working day to Moore. The actual number of mistakes was small, though they typically received publicity.

The incoming mail was of various types. The unit staff identified eight different categories. The majority of mail coming to the president dealt with substantive issues, scheduling requests (for a presidential appearance or for a member to see the president), and recommendations for appointments. Other mail included requests for photographs or autographs, requests for proclamations or other such White House actions, messages to be sent to individuals for a special occasion, constituent cases (*i.e.*, requests for assistance regarding a government program), and constituent "substantive" cases (*i.e.*, matters associated with upcoming policy issues).

Clearly this unit was a major source of information about what was going on between Congress and the president. It was appropriately an adjunct to the coordination unit. The communications unit had to have accurate knowledge of White House operations in order to draft an intelligent letter. It performed one of those vital functions upon which the whole liaison system depended.

Direct liaison. Those involved in direct liaison work spent most of their time on Capitol Hill, and so they needed good secretaries back in their White House offices. One of the Senate lobbyists explained: "If Hill lobbyists are doing their job, they are going to be on the Hill most of the day. You simply cannot, if you are a line lobbyist, conduct your business from the White House on the telephone. You've got to have face to face contact and you've got to be up there where the action is. Consequently, you have to have someone down at the White House who is looking out for your interests, someone who can conduct business effectively over the telephone when Senators, administrative assistants, personal secretaries, committee chief counsels and staff directors call.[29]

The Carter lobbyists on Capitol Hill were divided between the House and Senate, as expected. The House lobbyists were initially led by Frederick T. Merrill, Jr., but he left very early in the administration.[30] Merrill had served as legislative coordinator for the Democratic Study Group in the House from 1969 to 1976. William H. Cable then joined the liaison staff as chief House lobbyist in May, 1977. At the time, Cable was serving as staff director of the House Committee on Administration—an excellent post for contact with many members, since it deals with issues associated with the internal management of the House. Earlier he had served on the staff of the House Committee on Education and Labor. He brought a political savvy and experience that were badly needed in the White House liaison operation. Cable had been approached earlier in 1977 by Frank Moore to join the staff. He had said no, partially because he was not pleased with the issue-based organization of the Hill staff. When he agreed to serve, Cable was given the freedom to organize the lobbyists as he thought best.

Eventually, Cable headed a staff of twelve—five lobbyists, five administrative assistants, and two clerical personnel. The other House lobbyists at full complement were: James C. Free (no prior Hill experience; had been chief clerk of the Tennessee House of Representatives), Valerie F. Pinson (previously worked for Senator Christopher J. Dodd, D-Connecticut, and Representative Yvonne B. Burke, D-California), Robert W. Maher (had been on the staff of the House Committee on Interstate and Foreign Commerce), and Terrence D. Straub (was special assistant at the Democratic National Committee and then president of his own consulting firm in Washington).

Cable organized the work load by state delegations. Each lobbyist was allowed to pick a group of states so as to manage one-fifth of the total membership (approximately ninety members for each). Cable took the states that were left. Each staff member could then concentrate on getting to know his or her representatives, and their respective staffs. Cable

29. Transcripts, IV, 61.

30. For Merrill's analysis of Carter's relations with Congress, see "How Carter Stopped Playing Politics and Started Having Trouble With Congress," *Washington Monthly*, July-August, 1977, pp. 28–30.

wanted to develop a close, two-way relationship with the members—he even solicited their ideas on how the White House might be of assistance to them. Of course, by the time Cable arrived, the list of items demanding immediate action was very full. Thus it was not easy for the House lobbyists to find free time to cultivate harmonious working relationships with the representatives, on a "non-need basis," to quote one liaison staff member. Rather, they were pressured to be requesting support for or preventing the dismantlement of the president's program.

Dan C. Tate led the Senate lobbying team from the start. He had served as legislative assistant to Senator Herman E. Talmadge (D-Georgia) for seven years. Robert Thomson joined Tate in April, 1977. Thomson had previously worked with the Senate Democratic Campaign Committee and the unsuccessful presidential campaign in 1975–1976 of Senator Lloyd Bentsen (D-Texas). Tate and Thomson worked together for more than two years, and then Thomson became Moore's deputy for coordination after the Camp David reorganization. Tate favored organizing by issues rather than by members—it was better, he thought, to have follow-through on a particular issue. He also judged that issue-based organization permitted the Senate liaison staff to get acquainted with each senator. Such an approach was unquestionably more adaptable to the smaller Senate than it was to the 435-member House of Representatives.

The liaison team included another lobbyist who was practically independent, concentrating primarily on foreign policy issues. Robert Beckel had served as executive director of the National Committee for an Effective Congress and thus knew his way around Capitol Hill. He first joined the Carter administration as a deputy assistant secretary of state for congressional relations and he worked primarily on the Panama Canal treaties. Beckel was to assist with the more political aspects as they developed domestically. An early memorandum on the political difficulties the treaties encountered in the Senate eventually found its way to Frank Moore, and Moore led Beckel into the Oval Office to brief the president. Following this meeting, Beckel went to work at the White House in congressional relations, dealing initially with the Panama Canal treaties, then with other matters of foreign policy, national security, defense, and intelligence. He was loosely attached to the Senate side, given that chamber's responsibility for foreign policy, but was to treat these issues wherever they arose in both houses.

This unusual arrangement was bound to cause some problems between Beckel and the Departments of State and Defense as well as the national security adviser and the Central Intelligence Agency (CIA). They all had contacts on Capitol Hill. The departments and the CIA had their own liaison staffs, and National Security Adviser Zbigniew Brzezinski added a congressional liaison person after Beckel came to the White House. Beckel, however, was given the responsibility of chairing an interagency legislative group that was to effect some coordination in foreign and defense policy liaison. The situation for Beckel was difficult, but Carter's interest in foreign and defense policy, along with Moore's close connections with the president, provided support for this arrangement.

The Carter liaison team was criticized for its lack of congressional experience, and this criticism persisted through all four years. Why should this be so, *when, in fact, most of the staff had worked on the Hill*? First and foremost was the appointment of Frank Moore. His lack of familiarity with the workings of Congress was taken as a signal of Carter's lack of interest in building harmonious congressional relations. Second, the sheer volume (and some of the content) of the legislative program overwhelmed Congress. The poor scheduling of legislative requests suggested the liaison staff's inexperience. Third, the office initially was understaffed and preoccupied with nonlegislative work, such as appointments, which were not handled well. Fourth, the initial organization suited the president's orientation toward issues rather than Congress' way of doing its business. By 1978, changes had been made in staff (there were more experienced Hill lobbyists—*e.g.*, Cable, Thomson, Beckel), in scheduling the legislative program, and in organization (a coordinating unit set in place, and the issue-based approach dropped for the House). Still the continued criticism perhaps reflected more the basically negative attitudes toward the president himself among some Democrats on the Hill, and press reports critical of the congressional liaison system likely reinforced those attitudes.

THE CHANGING LIAISON SYSTEM

Changes in liaison staff, organization, and working relationships during the Carter administration were associated with a kind of learning curve, one that indicated the staff members' understanding of their location within a complex web of political interactions. Basically their tasks were defined by others—the president, other presidential staff, the departments and agencies, the members of Congress (see Figure 4). Thus, they had to determine how to serve these several sets of decision makers in order to facilitate policy action. Although the staff could not resolve incompatibilities among these sets, liaison personnel could be effective in reducing conflict and capitalizing on whatever agreements existed. Much depended on their success as a communications center. If the liaison staff could provide reliable political and policy information, then they would be indispensable. Their record on this score was mixed, but organizational changes were consistently in the direction of achieving this goal.

The staff members themselves describe the various changes as basically marking improvements. I quote them here at some length to illustrate their satisfaction with an operation heavily criticized elsewhere, as well as to display their understanding of their role.

I'd measure [the improvement] from inauguration day to the time Bill [Cable] and Bob [Thomson] came on the staff, in April and May respectively. We constantly improved from there. We had the thing running by that fall. The same Congress. From there we had Les [Francis] and Jim Copeland setting up the legislative coordination.

There were really two thrusts of development. Number one, you had the increase in the number of people and we staffed up both the House lobbyists and the Senate lobbyists. Number two was a sort of a significant change in the way the headquarters group [those located in the White House] responded to what was going on in the White House. Les Francis [as the first director of coordination] was a key person to that development. . . . Les built a system during 1977 where he gradually inserted himself more and more into the loose decision making process in the White House. It enabled him to get intelligence to [the rest of us] earlier and earlier about the decision making process [in the White House]. We became more and more aware of how these decisions were being made and where they were going. Formerly we had to rely almost entirely on Frank [Moore] and his attendance at senior staff meetings for our intelligence about what was happening in OMB and DPS. It was an impossible job for Frank to do, although he did it quite well to begin with.[31]

This intelligence function within the White House was viewed as a two-way operation—just as would be expected from carriers of reliable knowledge.

31. Transcripts, IV, 91, 92.

> Another thing . . . bears repeating relates to the larger question of when we got our act together. I would agree . . . that it was by Christmas of the next year [1978]. But important to that was an education of the rest of the White House staff to the importance of Congress and how you treated it. You just couldn't leave it exclusively to the congressional liaison to handle it. We could do a lot of good work and one person at a party or [social] function could blow it. A vote or a carefully cultivated friendship could be undermined, just in terms of attitude. . . . It really began with the seven o'clock [morning] meeting, as a means of educating the rest of the White House. All of the people who did the work at the deputy level below stressed the importance of Congress and how it affected us and how it affected the President's popularity.[32]

It is a reasonable interpretation of events to suggest a process by which the liaison staff first learned how members of Congress defined the job of congressional liaison. This knowledge led to an understanding of the staff's many roles within the White House and the administration. In essence they learned how members viewed President Carter, giving them a larger sense of the challenge that faced them within the White House. Unfortunately for them, much damage had been done, and so their task in later years was extremely difficult, if not impossible.They had to reshape their own image while managing a sizable program for the administration.

AN ANALYSIS IN SUMMARY

The organization and operation of the congressional liaison staff reflected Carter's trusteeship style in several respects. First, the president's own association with liaison activities was based on his personal motivations. He was available as a resource but was unlikely very often to manage those activities directly. Second, he selected a person to head the unit more on the basis of his needs than on the basis of congressional needs. Any president would do so—but Carter viewed his purposes as strikingly different from those of Congress. Third, he permitted the liaison unit to organize as it saw fit, which was initially a reaction to his issue orientation. Later, but not much later, the House lobbyists organized to accommodate the members' district orientation. Fourth, Moore's position developed as that of intermediary between his staff and the Oval Office, thereby facilitating access that might not have existed had the liaison

32. *Ibid.*, 93–94.

chief been more congressionally directed. Fifth, there was a special foreign and defense policy lobbyist, which suited the president's emerging interest in these areas.

How should a trustee president organize his congressional relations staff? There may not be a definitive answer to that question. What I do believe is that the apparatus that developed during the Carter administration was apparently a response to Carter's perspective on Washington, Congress, and public policy. *This perspective, it so happens, was not predominant in the president's party in Congress.* It is hard to fault the liaison unit for these circumstances. The president was Jimmy Carter, and the liaison team was in no position to change that fundamental fact of political life. In that important regard, by the way, this team was very like others—that is, they were doing their work in the context of the president's values.

As is evident, the liaison staff was in a difficult position for moving the Carter administration forward inside the existing national policy process. The lobbyists functioned as a bridge to the type of Washington politics their boss had campaigned against. Yet they faced a strategic problem of some magnitude. It was their responsibility to get members of Congress to cooperate, but the president was not their natural ally in this effort. He was willing to do his part in telephone calls and meetings with members. In fact, the liaison staff estimated that they probably brought more members to the White House for such meetings than had been the case in any administration. But they had to manage how the president would be utilized in order to promote cooperation. That was a sensitive and difficult task, since Carter was not inclined by his nature or personal preferences to like this kind of work. The liaison staff had daily contact with those whose business it was to strike bargains and make compromises rather than, in the president's words, to do "what is right." They were, in effect, white-flag bearers trudging up and down Pennsylvania Avenue. True understanding between the principal leaders of the contending forces was not likely to occur, and it did not.

Change the metaphor and picture a sort of two-way transmission apparatus. At one end the gears whir away in one direction and do so in the vertical mode. At the other end the gears work in the opposite direction and do so in the horizontal mode. Each set must somehow function to move the whole machine. Yet each set is independently powered. Now transfer this imagery to the Carter White House and the Democratic majorities in Congress. The congressional liaison personnel, located at the center of the transmission, are responsible for creating a series of wheels and belts to achieve forward motion on policy. The task challenged even the most adept facilitator. And, of course, it was unlikely that all staff members would be equally good at transmission at both ends of the avenue. What was needed, therefore, were personnel who were effective at each end and some in the middle to hold the system together. There were some such persons, to be sure, but the nature of their work was such that it would go unrecognized. Put otherwise, few in Washington were prepared to understand or appreciate the complications of working according to the Carter model of presidential-congressional relations.

☆6☆

Jimmy Carter and the Ninety-fifth Congress

Let us now consider relationships between President Carter and Congress in regard to specific policy proposals. Presidents set congressional agendas. What should one expect in agenda setting from a trustee president? He is likely to identify issues that are particularly nettlesome, ones that others might avoid as politically costly. Similarly, he is attracted to issues that are highly complex and, possibly for that reason, have not been acted on. He is also encouraged to propose comprehensive solutions, which presumably contribute to greater integration among policy makers. Included in the latter may be reorganization proposals designed to integrate future programs. These preferences are consistent with the trustee's independent style, focus on national over local interests, and comprehensive method.

These expectations provide the proper setting for analyzing President Carter's relation with Congress. As will be described, he had rather explicit intentions that were consistent with the changing agenda in national policy making. I will begin by identifying that agenda and Carter's understanding of it, as expressed during the 1976 campaign. This discussion will lead directly into a review of the president's legislative agenda. Finally, I will illustrate some of his initiatives and describe an incident (the Bert Lance matter) that diverted attention from the president's program during the first, crucial months of the new administration.

THE CHANGING AGENDA AND THE CARTER CANDIDACY

Historically one can identify periods in which the national policy agenda is dominated by calls for an expanded government role. Typically, such times are followed by periods of consolidation in which there are efforts to reorganize, adjust, or even terminate programs in order to achieve effectiveness. Expansionist periods are associated with Democratic presidents, the consolidative ones with Republican presidents. After Wilson came Harding, Coolidge, and Hoover; after Roosevelt and Truman, Eisenhower; after Johnson, Nixon. Seldom has there been actual contraction, though Ronald Reagan sounded that call.

The Great Society programs of the Johnson administration were, by any measure, among the most expansionist in American history. The many entitlements and defense needs produced an escalation of expenditures that many thought uncontrollable. Nixon's victory in 1968 can hardly be attributed to demands for consolidation of existing programs, but it surely had that effect. The Nixon administration made an effort to reorganize the government, to cut back on programs judged to be wasteful or ineffective, and to identify those that might be better allocated to state and local levels of government. Yet the Great Society had strong support in Congress, and government expenditures continued to rise dramatically. The Nixon administration also introduced a number of new regulatory programs that were consolidative in intent but that contributed to the intrusiveness of the federal government.

Whatever long-range plans President Nixon had for the eventual contraction of government were interrupted by Watergate. That event introduced a pause in political leadership from the White House. But government growth during an administration devoted to curbing it seemed to emphasize even more the need for new approaches to policy making in Washington. That freshness was unlikely to come from Ford, an unelected president serving out Nixon's last two years. Thus, the 1976 election promised to be a contest that would reestablish White House ascendancy in coping with the consolidative agenda of the post–Great Society era.

As it happened, both presidential candidates in 1976 campaigned on similar themes—that is, making government work better, not necessarily more. One might have expected that from the Republican candidate. But Jimmy Carter, the outsider from Georgia, the governor proud of having reorganized his state's government, also announced a basically consolidative program for the nation's government. There was frequent criticism during the campaign that Carter lacked a clear and consistent theme. Yet a reading of his acceptance speech reveals his observations on the politics of the time, his view of government's role, and his policy intentions—and these themes dominated his presidency:

1. "1976 will not be a year of politics as usual."
2. "Our people are searching for new voices and new ideas and new leaders."
3. "We've seen a wall go up that separates us from our government."
4. "It is time for the people to run the government, and not the other way around."
5. "As President, I want you to help me evolve an efficient, economical, purposeful and manageable government for our nation."
6. "We must strengthen the government closest to the people."
7. "We Democrats believe that competition is better than regulation."[1]

And in his inaugural address, the new president stressed that "we have learned that 'more' is not necessarily 'better,' that even our great nation has its recognized limits, and that we can neither answer all questions nor solve all problems. We cannot afford to do everything, nor can we afford to lack boldness as we meet the future. So together, in a spirit of individual sacrifice for the common good, we must simply do our best."[2]

These were consolidative messages, suggesting that Carter was reflecting the shift in agenda that characterized the post-Johnson era. In accepting the nomination of his party, Carter was moved to say: "I have never met a Democratic president, but I've always been a Democrat." He promised to "work in harmony" and "mutual respect" with the Democratic Congress. Yet it was by no means certain that congressional Democrats were prepared to accommodate the changes in politics and the agenda that Carter had identified in his campaign. After all, they had won huge majorities in the House and Senate in 1974 and were successful in retaining those majorities in 1976 while Carter eked out a narrow win over Ford. Political conditions allowed congressional Democrats to bring their own message to Washington in 1976—or at least to be in a position to resist the new president's message if it was not to their liking.

1. The speech is reprinted in *Congressional Quarterly Weekly Report*, July 17, 1976, pp. 1933–35.

2. The address is reprinted in *Congressional Quarterly Weekly Report*, January 22, 1977, p. 106.

THE PRESIDENT'S LEGISLATIVE PRIORITIES

Despite the clarity of Carter's message during the campaign and after, his administration received heavy criticism for failing to establish clear priorities. Even his own staff judged that priorities were not that clear beyond two or three major requests. There was so much to do, and this president was anxious to get it done on his watch. This situation may not be endemic to the trusteeship presidency, but it is surely consonant with the trustee's motivations to solve the nation's problems, many of which are interrelated.

Now it happens that the American system poses special difficulties for a new president. Victory is not followed immediately by position—the president-elect does not take office until January 20. The government continues under the incumbent even when that person has been defeated. The newly elected Congress begins its business before the new president takes office. He is nevertheless expected to give policy direction, to set the legislative agenda. Yet the budget process, which is so critical for agenda setting, is continuous. It does not pause for presidential elections or inaugurations. The outgoing administration provides a budget for the new fiscal year. The State of the Union address is delivered by the outgoing president.[3] Here are two major agenda-setting occasions that occur early in the congressional year, and neither one is available to the new administration. Yet the winner is expected to "hit the ground running," as the phrase has it.[4]

Jimmy Carter's dilemma was that he had to know Washington politics without appearing to have accommodated those politics in his first days in office. What he faced, of course, were the special problems of the outsider, trustee president. Moving inside was not, and could not be, that easy. The president-elect met with many congressional leaders both in Georgia and in Washington. What was lacking was any single opportunity to present a concise policy agenda to the nation. And in Carter's case such an occasion was important since his anti-Washington campaign resulted in uncertainty among members of Congress about his true inten-

3. It is relevant that the State of the Union address in 1977 was by one of Congress' own, Gerald R. Ford. The parting was both tearful and joyful as members loudly applauded their friend and former colleague.

4. The inaugural address is an occasion for expressing a theme for a new administration. Most presidents do not use it to announce a legislative program, however.

tions. The president was frustrated by the failure of the Washington community to comprehend his intentions: "Throughout the 1976 campaign, the most persistent question of the news reporters was, 'Are you a liberal or a conservative?' When forced to answer, I would say that I was a fiscal conservative but quite liberal on such issues as civil rights, environmental quality, and helping people overcome handicaps to lead fruitful lives. My reply did not satisfy them, and sometimes they accused me of being evasive, but it was the most accurate answer I could give in a few words."[5]

In fact, his policy agenda was principally consolidative. Just as he had done in Georgia as governor, Jimmy Carter wanted to reform many government functions and programs, and to reduce the deficit and balance the budget. Having this intent does not in and of itself settle the matter of legislative priorities. What is to be reorganized? Which programs are to be reduced or made more effective? What is the preferred order of action? The president had many answers: Messages on a wide range of issues poured forth during the early months of 1977. Frank Moore was quoted as saying: "We've got a full plate. We're going to heap it up before June and eat on it the rest of the year."[6]

This volume of legislation naturally caused problems for the administration on Capitol Hill. There simply was neither time enough nor the resources to do everything. Various members of the White House staff acknowledged that priorities were not well set during the first year. And the president appointed the vice-president to head a group to offer legislative priorities at the beginning of each year.[7] Two staff members said:

> We recognized when we first went there the first year that we had too much legislation up there. We overloaded the circuits. We also realized that the White House wasn't unlimited. We had limited resources.

> One of the most painful things that a president has to do is choose among his children, so to speak, and President Carter was like most presidents in that respect. If given a choice he would want to do it all. It wasn't that we didn't have priorities during the first year. Obviously economic stimulus and energy were the two highest priorities. After those, the congressional leadership would come to us and say,

5. Jimmy Carter, *Keeping Faith: Memoirs of a President* (New York, 1982,), 73–74.

6. Judy Gardner, "Rebates Dropped As Honeymoon Spirit Ebbs," *Congressional Quarterly Weekly Report*, April 16, 1977, p. 723.

7. Legislative issues were categorized by presidential or cabinet-level involvement in order to coordinate contact with members of Congress.

"OK, we've spent half the year on these things, now we've got three months left. Now what do you want us to spend that on? You've got a hundred items up here and we've got time to do ten."[8]

A profile of agenda setting does emerge from these comments. President Carter had identified many issues that required his attention and subsequent congressional action. All were important, and it appeared to be his judgment that Congress should act more quickly. He seemed truly perplexed, and frustrated, by the complexity of the legislative process and the Democrats' lack of loyalty to his leadership. When he learned that major bills moved slowly in Congress, he sought to create a mechanism by which priorities were set among the many issues that he thought needed action. There was not only the group chaired by Vice-President Mondale, there was also the president's contact with his congressional liaison staff. That process was a continuing one and developed from the feedback that the staff was getting on Capitol Hill. As a liaison staff member put it: "We said, 'We've got to have some kind of priority setting.'" Another recalled that a weekly "prioritizing process in terms of congressional legislation" was begun in November, 1977: "It was a culmination, a realization that there was not somebody who just would say, 'Hey you've got to set some priorities.' The president set a bunch of priorities. He sent them all to the Congress. He would have liked to have had the Congress do all of those things. There was a realization that we had to look at that again, that we couldn't get them all, and that there wasn't time for all of them."[9]

THE CARTER PROGRAM AND CONGRESS, 1977

What were these many programs that were requested the first year? The list truly is long. Stuart Eizenstat prepared a hundred-page draft of the "nucleus" of the domestic program to be circulated among cabinet appointees. It included: reauthorization of the clean air program, creation of a Department of Energy, a comprehensive energy program, strip-mining controls, increase in the minimum wage, an omnibus farm and food program (including food stamps), creation of an Agency for Consumer Protection, restoring the president's reorganization authority,

8. Transcripts, IV, 49, 54.
9. *Ibid.*, 53–54.

welfare reform, hospital cost containment, Social Security financing, an economic stimulus program, reduction in water projects, reauthorization of the water pollution control program, and housing and urban aid proposals. As is evident, there were not many new initiatives for government involvement in social and economic life. The program was designed to make government work better in providing necessary services and protections, and to stimulate action within the private sphere to resolve such problems as hospital costs, for example. Eizenstat identified the economic stimulus package, renewal of presidential authority to reorganize the executive branch, a Department of Energy, an energy and environmental program, and welfare reform as top priorities for 1977.[10]

I have chosen three proposals and one event to illustrate presidential-congressional relations in 1977. First is the economic stimulus package, which was part of Carter's campaign pledge. Its development reveals early consultation with the Democrats in Congress and mismanagement of relations later on. Second is the energy program, which is indicative of a comprehensive approach to enormously complex issues, as well as very limited discussions with members of Congress. Third is reducing the number of water projects, a proposal bound to cause problems on Capitol Hill. Perhaps more than any other issue, this one illustrates the trustee president's determination to do "what is right, not what is political." The event is the resignation of Bert Lance and the circumstances that led up to it. The Lance matter had significant effects on Carter's relations with Congress.

THE ECONOMIC STIMULUS PACKAGE

"When the Carter administration took office in January 1977, the performance of the economy was clearly unsatisfactory."[11] Quite understandably the president-elect was anxious to develop a program that could be introduced into Congress early in his administration. An economic task force headed by Lawrence R. Klein, Nobel Prize–winning economist from the University of Pennsylvania, advised Carter during the campaign and the transition period. Although not on the task force

10. Mercer Cross, "Carter Aide Lists Domestic Priorities," *Congressional Quarterly Weekly Report*, January 15, 1977, p. 85.

11. Joseph J. Minarik, "Fiscal Policy," in Joseph A. Pechman (ed.), *The 1978 Budget: Setting National Priorities* (Washington, D.C., 1977), 55.

early in the campaign, Charles Schultze from the Brookings Institution was also active in advising Carter, primarily through his contacts with Stuart Eizenstat, Carter's domestic adviser. It was Schultze who was asked by Carter to be chairman of the Council of Economic Advisers (possibly following Klein's declining the job), and he then took on the major responsibility for formulating an economic stimulus package.

Much of the work was done in Georgia during the transition period. Those being appointed to the principal jobs related to economic planning—the secretary of the treasury, Michael Blumenthal; the assistant secretary of the treasury for tax policy, Laurence Woodworth; the OMB director, Bert Lance; the secretary of labor, Ray Marshall; the DPS director, Stuart Eizenstat—were among the participants in the early discussions of what should be done.

The group was well aware of the dangers of providing too much stimulus. As Schultze later told a House committee: "This package has been designed to tread prudently between the twin risks of over- and understimulation."[12] It was the group's view that the economy would recover in time. They simply wanted to give it a boost and create greater confidence in continued growth.

The proposals were a package with several components. Included were a temporary, one-shot tax cut (eventually developed as a tax rebate), certain other tax adjustments for individuals and corporations, a public works program, and additional public service employment and job training. Given this range of legislative goals, it was essential that members of Congress be consulted. And, in fact, many were. The president and his economic advisers met with the Democratic leadership (including the relevant committee chairmen) at the Pond House in Plains. Reportedly, congressional Democrats were less enthusiastic about the tax cut than about public works programs. But they were willing to support the package. The new majority leader, Jim Wright of Texas, was quoted as saying: "There wasn't a person in the room who did not add something to the composite thinking. The package belongs to all of us."[13] It was obvious to White House aides who attended the meeting and to the press afterward that Democratic congressional leaders were very pleased to have been consulted.

12. Judy Gardner, "Congress Weighs Changes in Stimulus Plan," *Congressional Quarterly Weekly Report*, January 29, 1977, p. 181.

13. Judy Gardner and Mary E. Eccles, "Carter Stimulus Plan: Some Questions Remain," *Congressional Quarterly Weekly Report*, January 15, 1977, p. 95.

TABLE 12

The Economic Stimulus Program

Date	*President*	*House*	*Senate*	*Conference*
Jan. 7	Program outlined			
Jan. 11–13			Budget Committee holds hearings on economy	
Jan. 27	Program presented to Congress	Budget Committee hearings		
Jan. 27–Feb. 4		Various committee hearings	Various committee hearings	
Feb. 3		Budget Committee approves alternative (doubles job, public works spending)		
Feb. 9			Budget Committee approves alternative (doubles job, public works spending)	
Feb. 16		Public Works Committee approves larger program		
Feb. 17		Ways & Means approves tax cuts		
Feb. 22			Approves FY 1977 budget changes	
Feb. 23		Approves FY 1977 budget changes		

Continued on next page

Table 12—*Continued*

Date	*President*	*House*	*Senate*	*Conference*
Feb. 24		Approves larger public works program		
Feb. 28				Agreement on FY 1977 budget changes
Mar. 2			Approves conference report on budget changes	
Mar. 3		Approves conference report on budget changes		
Mar. 8		Approves tax cuts		
Mar. 8–11			Finance Committee holds hearings	
Mar. 10			Approves larger public works program	
Mar. 21			Finance Committee approves tax cuts	
Apr. 14	Drops $50-rebate proposal			
		Easter work period (Apr. 1–18)		
Apr. 15	Announces anti-inflation program			
Apr. 28				Agreement on larger public works program

Continued on next page

Table 12—*Continued*

Date	*President*	*House*	*Senate*	*Conference*
Apr. 29			Approves tax cuts and larger public works program (conference report)	
May 3		Approves conference report on larger public works program		
May 4		Approves conference report on supplemental appropriations		
May 5			Approves conference report on supplemental appropriations	
May 6				Report on tax cuts
May 13	Signs bill for larger public works program			
May 16		Approves conference report on tax cuts	Approves conference report on tax cuts	
May 23	Signs bill on tax cuts			

SOURCE: Various issues of *Congressional Quarterly Weekly Report*, 1977.

The package was formally presented to Congress on January 27. Table 12 shows the bare outlines of congressional action. The principal committees with jurisdiction were the two Budget committees, the House Ways and Means and Senate Finance committees, and the House Public Works and Transportation and Senate Environment and Public Works committees. Congress disassembles presidential legislative packages, sending individual proposals to those committees and subcommittees with jurisdiction. The president found this allocation to be somewhat frustrating, since it was then difficult to hold the proposals together as an overall plan.

It did not take Congress long to approve a larger public works and jobs program. The Budget committees endorsed an alternative that doubled the amount of spending for these purposes. Both authorizing committees also acted well before the Easter work period (the label members now use for their April recess). The tax changes moved almost as fast, but while the members were away, the president decided to withdraw his proposal for a fifty-dollar tax rebate, even though many congressional Democratic leaders reluctantly had agreed to support it and had made an effort to get other Democrats to go along. In fact, the House had already approved it. The economy had been improving, and the president became concerned that the rebate might trigger greater inflation. Unfortunately, key members of Congress were notified almost at the last moment. They had not particularly liked the proposal at the start, decided that the president should be given what he wanted, "stuck their necks out" (as one White House aide put it), and then were not properly informed of the change. According to one aide: "There was where we first got the reputation—'you can't trust these people.'" As it happened, the president's decision was made so quickly that even Secretary of the Treasury Blumenthal was caught off guard. He was asked about the rebate at a National Press Club talk: "And he danced and danced but he had to be assuming we hadn't changed policy. Five hours later the president pulled the switch and poor Mike had a credibility problem."[14]

The case of the economic stimulus package is especially interesting because the new administration's instinct to consult with members of Congress on an important issue was politically correct. And the response from the members was positive—they enjoyed being consulted. The pres-

14. Transcripts, XI, 30, 29.

ident was able to use that enthusiasm to good purpose when he announced his program on January 7 and got Democrats to support even those aspects they did not like. Why, then, did consultation not become accepted practice for other parts of the president's plan? First and possibly most important, the economic stimulus program was very much in the tradition of the New Deal and the Great Society. Being able to offer reduced taxes, public works projects, and government-sponsored jobs is more attractive to members of Congress than is having to reduce benefits or regulate consumers' behavior. Thus, consultation was predictably satisfying to both the president and his Democratic colleagues in Congress. Second, in the end the experience led to disappointments at both ends of Pennsylvania Avenue. The president saw the committee system separate his program into parts, as well as the positive congressional response to an increase in public works programs that benefit constituents. There was, for Congress, less participation in formulating programs as the president turned to other, less politically attractive issues (regulating energy use, for example, and reducing the number of water projects) and little, if any, consultation in regard to one major controversial proposal in the economic stimulus package (the fifty-dollar rebate).

THE ENERGY PLAN

Neither President Nixon nor President Ford was successful in developing a good working relationship with Congress on energy questions. Organizational changes were made in the energy bureaucracy immediately following the Arab oil embargo—the creation of the Energy Research and Development Administration and the Nuclear Regulatory Commission; the abolition of the Atomic Energy Commission. But the two branches could not agree on anything approaching national energy policy. Nixon's resignation and Ford's weak political position help to account for the insufficient efforts. The decentralized nature of Congress made it unlikely that a broad-scale plan could be produced on Capitol Hill. House Speaker O'Neill explained that "it is extremely difficult to write an energy bill. This, perhaps, has been the most parochial issue that could ever hit the floor." In 1976, Jim Wright, who headed a House Democratic task force to produce an energy program as an alternative to President Ford's, summarized Congress' record as follows: "Since the Arab oil embargo three years ago, we have tried to do a few timid things to reduce consumption. . . . We have dabbled with oil and gas pricing. We have made more money available for long-range research, for things like solar energy, that may help us 30 or 40 years from now. But as far as doing anything practical to increase the supply of energy and reduce our dependence upon foreign sources in the foreseeable future, we have done nothing."[15]

The energy issue was tailor-made for the trustee president. In the first place, Carter acknowledged the low level of awareness of the problem, stating that "the energy question had rarely come up during the 1976 campaign."[16] Second, it was a matter of great concern to constituency-minded members of Congress. Here was an issue that was obviously national in scope but one in which local, regional, and private interests could act to obscure or thwart identification of and policy action on more general concerns. And third, the fractionalization of interests and issues invited an integrative response because of the interrelatedness of energy resources (oil, natural gas, coal, nuclear power, etc.) at the point of crisis. In summary, it was all there—a need for independent judgment to overcome selfish constituency interests (defined earlier as the trustee's style), the identification of the national interest (focus), and the demand for a comprehensive solution (method). Further, recent evidence clearly demonstrated that neither a Republican president and a Democratic Congress nor a Democratic Congress working alone could do what was necessary. Thus, it was a reasonable judgment that ordinary politics was not equal to the task at hand.

As it happened, there was an additional stimulus for a national energy policy in the early months of 1977. A record cold wave depleted fuel supplies and caused schools and factories to close. Therefore the president's first request of Congress was for authorization to act in such an emergency, specifically to allocate on a temporary basis interstate natural gas to areas of greatest need. In less than a week Congress passed the Emergency Natural Gas Act. In the Senate, majority leader Robert C. Byrd even bypassed the committees, bringing the bill directly to the floor. By

15. O'Neill and Wright quoted in Congressional Quarterly, *Congress and the Nation, 1973–1976*, IV (Washington, D.C., 1977), 202.

16. Carter, *Keeping Faith*, 93. The issue was discussed in the first debate.

February 1 the president had the authority he had asked for, an encouraging sign for future dealings on this topic. "Unfortunately," President Carter wrote, "the almost unbelievable speed of Congress in enacting this legislation was not a harbinger of things to come."[17]

Although the president had not anticipated the need for emergency powers to transport natural gas, he did have proposals for reorganizing the energy bureaucracy. A plan for creating a Department of Energy was proposed to Congress, with the expectation that James R. Schlesinger would be appointed its first secretary. Schlesinger joined the Carter campaign before the first debate in September as an adviser on energy issues (Schlesinger had served Nixon and Ford as secretary of defense from 1973 to 1975). The new department was authorized by Congress before the August recess. Again, the president was pleased with how Congress acted, though there had been some conflict with Jack Brooks (D-Texas), chairman of the House Committee on Government Operations, who was reluctant to restore the president's reorganizational authority.[18] And Carter had reason to be encouraged that his efforts in this area could result in positive action on Capitol Hill.

Unfortunately, things did not go so smoothly in Congress when it came to the president's comprehensive energy plan. He likened the experience to "chewing on a rock that lasted the whole four years." He was not prepared for the intricacy of congressional and interest-group response: "When I declared the energy effort to be the moral equivalent of war . . . it was impossible for me to imagine the bloody legislative battles we would have to win before the major campaign was over. Throughout my entire term, Congress and I struggled with energy legislation. Despite my frustration, there was never a moment when I did not consider the creation of a national energy policy equal in importance to any other goal we had."[19]

Much of the criticism leveled at the program had to do with how it was formulated and presented to Congress. Whereas members were involved in developing the economic stimulus program, they had almost no role in preparing the national energy plan. In large part this lack of consultation

17. Carter, *Keeping Faith*, 93.
18. For Carter's account of this conflict, see *Keeping Faith*, 70–71.
19. Carter, *Keeping Faith*, 91.

arose from the administration's self-imposed time limit. The president set a deadline of ninety days after his inauguration for producing a plan. He thus demonstrated his sense of urgency and his commitment to acting on an issue that had great currency. But the timing also dictated a procedure that was bound to be denounced later. Broad consultation with members of Congress was simply not possible if Schlesinger and his staff were to develop a comprehensive energy program by April 20. Indeed, they would likely not have been able even to confer extensively with the relevant departments and agencies. The failure to consult prescribed, in turn, a virtually covert operation. The details of proposals could not be revealed during the process of development or those not consulted would naturally react in public. Therefore, the Schlesinger team worked under severe constraints. They were charged to develop a program with widespread consequences, do so quickly, and prevent leaks. Schlesinger himself also was involved in the emergency natural gas legislation and the Department of Energy reorganization proposal.[20] This extraordinary procedure produced an enormously complex set of energy proposals that included a gasoline tax, a tax on vehicles that burned too much fuel, conservation measures, a crude-oil tax, federal regulation of intrastate natural gas, inducements for industry to use more coal, and tax credits for solar installations. There were 113 interlocking provisions. The president wanted Congress to consider the program as a whole—not dismantle it and pass individual parts. That was asking a lot from those who had not been involved in developing the program and yet would be subject to intense lobbying by the many interests affected by the proposals. It is relevant here to mention that Anne Wexler had not yet moved to the White House to direct the Office of Public Liaison. So the coalition-building process, which characterized later administration efforts of this type, did not exist. Nor was there a Department of Energy congressional liaison staff to lobby for the program.

One of the president's closest aides reviewed the formulation of the energy program and concluded that it was consistent with the policy-making style of this president.

20. The oral history sessions indicate that the White House staff had considerable sympathy for Schlesinger's difficult task.

> [Congress should support the proposals] because this [the energy issue] was a national problem that deserved the highest priority . . . and here was the man [Schlesinger] who was going to deal with the problem. We're going to come to you [Congress], we've thought this through, we know what the answer is and we're going to present it to you and we're not going to try to cajole you into saying that this is the thing that needs to be done. It's very evident to you and everybody else that it has to be done, we don't have any choice about it and here's what we're going to do. . . . That was vintage Jimmy Carter in my opinion.[21]

As suggested earlier, "vintage Jimmy Carter" happens to coincide in most respects with classic trusteeship politics.

The program was announced during the week of April 18—right on the president's schedule of ninety days after taking office. As it happened, he spoke first to the American public on television on April 18. One White House aide referred to the speech as Carter's "the-sky-is-falling" message. The president admonished the people about their energy use and explained that "our decision about energy will test the character of the American people and the ability of the President and the Congress to govern this nation. This difficult effort will be the 'moral equivalent of war'—except that we will be uniting our efforts to build and not to destroy."[22]

The president went to Capitol Hill next. In a nationally televised joint session of Congress on April 20, he presented his program. Finally the members knew the details. The highlights of the elaborate program were:

1. A gasoline tax of five cents per gallon beginning in 1979 for every year that national gasoline consumption exceeds the previous year's target level
2. A gasoline "guzzler" tax on vehicles burning more fuel than standards allow (starting with 1978 models)
3. A variety of conservation measures—home insulation installation by utility companies (financed by loans repaid in the monthly utility bills), tax credits for conservation expenses, efficiency standards for new buildings and appliances, etc.
4. Taxation of domestic crude oil at the wellhead to raise prices by 1980 to world levels; revenues would be rebated to the public

21. Transcripts, XVII, 54.
22. The speech is reprinted in *Congressional Quarterly Weekly Report*, April 23, 1977, pp. 753–55.

5. Federal control of intrastate natural gas sales; set the price of new gas; reserve cheaper gas for homes and commercial users and higher-priced gas for industry

6. Encourage industries and utilities to shift to coal by taxing those using gas or oil, allowing tax credits for conversion

7. Expansion of enriched-uranium production, speeding up licensing of conventional reactors, strengthening safety standards

8. Encourage installation of solar equipment; end gasoline price controls.[23]

Initial congressional reaction to this complex package was cautious and mixed, with no one expressing enthusiasm. Some members were upset that the president chose to go to the public first, then to Congress. Predictions of a lengthy congressional struggle proved to be correct despite the speed with which the program passed in the House.

Table 13 offers an abbreviated sequence of congressional action on the energy program in 1977. In the House of Representatives, Speaker O'Neill used an extraordinary Ad Hoc Select Committee on Energy to facilitate coordination among the five standing committees that had jurisdiction over various sections of the bill. This tight management of legislation reduced the effectiveness of the energy lobbies. They were to have their day in the Senate, however. In striking contrast to what had happened in the House, the program was disassembled in the Senate. Five bills were reported from two committees, and floor action was spread over a period of a month. The natural gas bill was the most controversial. Initially the issue deadlocked the Committee on Energy and Natural Resources, then a lengthy filibuster ensued once the bill got to the floor. The natural gas controversy was also a major reason that the conference failed to reach agreement before the end of the session.[24]

In his review of the energy policy imbroglio, Bob Rankin identifies five basic problems and five complicating factors. The problems were: (1) The manner in which the program was drafted (limited time period,

23. For details, see Bob Rankin, "Carter's Energy Plan: A Test of Leadership," *Congressional Quarterly Weekly Report*, April 23, 1977, pp. 727–32.

24. For more details, see Charles O. Jones, "Congress and the Making of Energy Policy," and Alfred R. Light, "The National Energy Plan and Congress," both in Robert Lawrence (ed.), *New Dimensions to Energy Policy* (Lexington, Mass., 1979), 161–78, 179–90.

TABLE 13

Energy Proposals, 1977

Date	*President*	*House*	*Senate*	*Conference*
Apr. 20	Program announced			
Apr. 21		Ad Hoc Select Committee on Energy created		
May 2		Bill introduced; referred to 5 committees		
May 5			Program introduced as 5 bills; referred to 2 committees	
June 9		Ways & Means rejects gas tax		
July 14		Last of 5 committees completes work		
July 23		Ad Hoc Committee completes work		
July 29		Modified closed rule approved for debate		
August 5		Bill passed, 244–177		
Sept.–Oct.			Committees report out bills	
Sept. 23–Oct. 3			Filibuster on natural gas deregulation	
Oct. 18				Begins work
Nov. 1			Last of 5 bills passed	
Oct.–Dec.				Intermittent work on House-Senate differences

SOURCE: Various issues of *Congressional Quarterly Weekly Report*, 1977.

limited consultation, closed sessions); (2) technical flaws ("With embarrassing frequency, the administration's numbers conflicted with each other"); (3) lobbying ("The Capitol was crawling with lobbyists"); (4) poor salesmanship from the White House ("Key energy legislators . . . felt disregarded, left out, and most importantly, in the dark"); (5) lack of constituency (as Schlesinger said, "There is no constituency for an energy program"). There were, in addition, several complicating factors. They were associated with either the nature of the legislative process in a bicameral system or the failure of the administration to comprehend or appreciate the intricacies of congressional politics. (1) The loss of momentum following House passage of the bill in August (attributed by Rankin to the August recess and the Bert Lance "fiasco"); (2) contrasting committee traditions and styles in the House and Senate; (3) different leadership in the two chambers (Speaker O'Neill was determined to demonstrate to the president that he could deliver; Senator Byrd was just as determined to permit the Senate to work its will); (4) administration misreading (swift House passage did not mean that the Senate would eventually support the program); (5) conference proceedings (primarily the wide differences between the House and Senate bills and the unusual procedure of negotiating while the Senate was still acting).[25]

The president acknowledged many of these problems and complications when he wrote about the energy program in his memoirs. He expressed his exasperation with the Senate and "the influence of the special interest lobbies," which he labeled "unbelievable." In the Senate, his program was subject to forces beyond his control. It seemed that a miracle might be in the making after House approval, but there was to be no such event in the Senate in 1977. There were conflicts among headstrong committee chairmen about legislation that "bore little resemblance to our proposals." At one point the president met with congressional leaders, including the committee chairmen who were at odds on the natural gas provisions—Senator Russell Long, chairman of the Committee on Finance, and Senator Henry ("Scoop") Jackson, chairman of the Committee on Energy and Natural Resources, who, it will be recalled, was one of his opponents for the nomination. He described the meeting: "Met with the congressional leaders for breakfast. . . . I particularly

25. Bob Rankin, "Many Factors Led to Energy Stalemate," *Congressional Quarterly Weekly Report*, December 24, 1977, pp. 2631–35.

wanted Scoop Jackson and Russell Long there, so that we could have it out among a group of Democrats concerning their differences, which are very deep and personal. I thought Russell acted very moderately and like a gentleman, but Scoop . . . was at his worst. . . . At the same time, he is supporting my positions much more closely than Russell is." The president and his aides were forced into defensive positions. Sometimes they were mere bystanders. "It was a truly awful mess" is the way Senator Spark M. Matsunaga (D-Hawaii) put it. At one point, Senator Abraham Ribicoff (D-Connecticut) wondered "if the President shouldn't admit that his energy program is a shambles."[26] Unquestionably, much was learned from this experience with the energy program, but the lessons were costly ones in terms of the administration's reputation on Capitol Hill.

THE WATER PROJECTS

The energy program shows the trustee president "doing what is right" in regard to highly complex national issues. Proposing cuts in water projects is an example of "doing what is right" in regard to decision making. When conditions are appropriate, as they were for energy issues throughout much of Carter's term, the president is expected to act on large-scale domestic issues. There never is a perfect time for challenging an accepted policy qua political practice such as distributing public works projects among constituencies. The president must himself decide to take on this task. It does not necessarily come with the territory for a trustee president, though it is indeed consistent with the style, focus, and method of that role.

For President Carter, the "unnecessary dams and water projects" represented the "worst examples" of the "pork-barrel." Members of Congress were spending government money to win votes. Often the projects themselves did "more harm than good." The trustee politician finds this practice odious—the electoral connection in its rawest form. The president believed that he had sent clear signals about his intentions before

26. Carter, *Keeping Faith*, 99, 100; Matsunaga quoted in Rankin, "Many Factors," 2633; Ribicoff quoted in Bob Rankin, "Senate Continues Dismantling Energy Plan," *Congressional Quarterly Weekly Report*, October 8, 1977, p. 2121.

coming to Washington: "As governor and during my campaign, I had repeatedly emphasized the need to eliminate waste and pork-barrel projects in the federal government. Some of the people had heard and understood what I was saying. The members of Congress had not. They were amazed when I moved to cut out the worst examples of this abuse."[27]

It was unquestionably true that many members of Congress reacted negatively to the president's actions. And as one liaison staff person noted: "There was a residual effect that carried on. There was kind of a lack of trust."[28] As was the case with the energy program, the administration did not notify or consult the members, which contributed mightily to the problems that developed. But having decided to make reductions the first year, the White House had to act quickly. Once again, timing made consultation difficult—though one cannot imagine consultation proceeding very smoothly on this issue regardless of when it took place or the amount of time available.

The quick action was dictated by the budgetary process. New presidents must submit a budget very soon after being inaugurated. Carter's budget, presented to Congress on February 22, provided for the elimination of 19 water projects affecting 17 states. The projects were to be deleted so that they might be examined further for environmental impact and cost effectiveness. Morris K. Udall, chairman of the House Committee on Interior and Insular Affairs, and another of Carter's opponents for the nomination, concluded: "It's like pronouncing a verdict of guilty before the trial."[29]

In spite of the early negative reaction on Capitol Hill, the Carter administration soon announced 13 more projects for review, for a grand total of 32. The second list affected an additional 6 states. An effort was made to reassure the members that 307 projects would *not* for the present undergo further review. And 3 projects, slated for elimination in the first round, were reinstated.

The final decision was announced on April 18. There were 18 project deletions and substantial modifications in 5 others. Table 14 shows the 23 projects, their location, and the number of congressional Democrats

27. Carter, *Keeping Faith*, 78.

28. Transcripts, IV, 119.

29. James R. Wagner, "Congress Protests Water Projects Cuts," *Congressional Quarterly Weekly Report*, February 26, 1977, p. 379.

TABLE 14
The Politics of Water Projects

State	Project	Percent Complete	*Democrats Affected (no.)* H	S	*Committee Chairmen* H	S
Arizona	Central Arizona Project**	25	2	1	1	–
Arkansas	Cache River Basin	5	3	2	–	1
California	Auburn Dam-Folsom South Unit*	20	29	1	1	1
Colorado	Fruitland Mesa Dam	6	3	2	–	–
	Savery and Pot Hook Dams	5				
	Narrows Unit Dam*	5				
Georgia	Russell Lake	8	10	2	–	1
Kansas	Grove Lake	2	2	–	–	–
	Hillsdale Lake	30				
Kentucky	Yatesville Dam	19	5	2	1	–
Louisiana	Atchafalaya Navigation Project	50	6	2	–	1
	Bayou Bodcau	27				
	Mississippi River–Gulf Outlet**	1				
	Tensas Basin**	31				
Mississippi	Tallahala Creek Dam	7	3	2	–	2
Missouri	Meramec Park Lake	28	8	1	–	–
North Dakota	Garrison Diversion Project**	29	–	1	–	–
Oklahoma	Lukfata Lake	6	5	–	–	–
Oregon	Applegate Lake	9	4	–	1	–
South Carolina	Russell Lake	8	5	1	–	–
South Dakota	Oahe Diversion Project*	18	–	2	–	–
Utah	Bonneville Unit, Central Utah Project**	19	1	–	–	–
Wisconsin	LaFarge Lake	33	7	2	2	1
Wyoming	Savery and Pot Hook Dams	5	1	–	–	–
	Totals		94	21	6	7
	(Total Democrats)		(289)	(62)	(22)	(16)

SOURCE: Projects (with percentage of completion) are listed in *Congressional Quarterly Weekly Report,* April 23, 1977, p. 735. Other data compiled by author.

*Projects to be deleted pending reevaluation. **Projects to be modified, not deleted.

affected. Nearly a third of the Democrats in each chamber were from the states where there were to be deletions or modifications (though not all representatives were from the districts that were affected). In addition, several chairmen were from those states. In the Senate, the committees were Agriculture, Nutrition, and Forestry; Appropriations; Armed Services; Banking, Housing, and Urban Affairs; Finance; Judiciary; and Veterans Affairs. In the House they were Banking, Housing, and Urban Affairs; Education and Labor; Interior and Insular Affairs; International Relations; Public Works and Transportation; and Ways and Means. That is an impressive group of members to have upset within the first ninety days of a new administration.

President Carter was not willing to make just one symbolic foray into this political hornet's nest, however. For the remainder of his term he persisted in his efforts to delete projects. And he intended more than a simple cutting out. He sought as well to change the process of selection. He hoped to institute policy reforms by establishing economic and environmental criteria for new projects. Further, the president wanted to have *full funding* for a project once it met the criteria. The standard practice was for Congress to appropriate funds for a project each year, thereby reminding constituents annually of the member's support. The proposed changes would remove such projects from the classic pork-barrel style of decision making and establish a national bureaucratic procedure for determining the utility of a project.

Table 15 portrays this unresolved conflict. The first two years were the most difficult. The president intended to demonstrate his authority and to change the decision-making process. His patience was tested by Congress in 1978 when members tried to restore projects that had been deleted in 1977 (a year in which the president reluctantly agreed to a compromise). Carter vetoed the bill. He also threatened to veto the appropriations bill in 1979 when two projects deleted in 1977 were restored by the Senate Appropriations Committee.

Members of Congress resisted the president's proposed changes in the system of authorizing and funding projects. They consistently refused to provide full funding, as requested by the president—they wanted annual appropriations. And in 1980, the House overwhelmingly passed an authorization bill that ignored many of the criteria that Carter set forth in 1978. The president announced his intention to veto any such bill, and it was not acted on in the Senate. Congress did vote funding for a Water

TABLE 15
The Funding of Water Projects, 1977–1980

		Subsequent Action			
Year	*President's Proposal*	*House*	*Senate*	*Congress*	*President*
1977	Delete 18; modify 5	Delete 1; modify 4	Delete 9; modify 3; no starts for FY 1978	Senate bill	Signed the bill
1978	Full funding for 36 new projects	Restored 8 from 1977; approved 36 new for one year	Restored 6 from 1977; approved 36 new for one year	Restored 6 from 1977 (3 construction; 3 planning); approved 36 new for one year	Vetoed the bill (sustained in the House)
1979	Full funding for 26 new projects	Approved projects for one year; no restorations	Approved projects for one year; restoration of 2 projects (deleted on floor after veto threat)	Approved projects for one year	Signed the bill
1980	No new water projects proposed	No new construction starts; one-year funding	One new project; one-year funding.	One new project; one-year funding	Signed the bill

SOURCE: Various issues of *Congressional Quarterly Weekly Report,* 1977–1980.

Resources Council in 1980. President Carter asked that an independent body review water projects. The council had to await authorizing legislation, however, before it could act.

On one hand, many observers of congressional politics would agree with Washington *Post* reporter Haynes Johnson that "you didn't have to follow Washington politics for decades . . . to know that Carter was right in calling many of these water projects wasteful and largely unnecessary." On the other hand, this method of doing legislative business was ingrained. One could agree with Carter's goals, therefore, and still be critical of the president's tactics, as many in Washington were. Yet, according to Johnson, "the way Carter acted, and why, went to the heart of his idea of how he should function as a president." The president himself confirmed this assessment. He professed to understand the importance of such projects as "major political plums," "tangible symbols of the representative's influence in Washington." But, in his view, these advantages for the members and their districts or states did not justify continuing projects that were economically and environmentally costly. The president wrote:

> Other recent Presidents, graduates of the congressional system, had looked on the procedure as inviolate. I did not, and dove in head first to reform it.
>
> I demanded that we reassess every proposal to determine if it was still economically and environmentally justified, and insisted that the full price of the dam or canal . . . should be covered in the budget when the project was first approved. Otherwise, I threatened, I would veto the public-works appropriation bill. There was a furor on Capitol Hill, but I stood fast and began recruiting support among the more junior members of Congress who were not committed to the system (and who had not been there long enough to get a project of their own!).

The president then explained that he went along with the 1977 compromise bill that represented "a partial victory." Later he regretted doing so.

> I made some mistakes in dealing with Congress, and one that I still regret is weakening and compromising that first year on some of these worthless dam projects. The Speaker had called me during the heat of the congressional debate to say, "Mr. President, we have worked out a good compromise on the water projects. . . ." I thought for a few seconds, considered the progress we had made in changing an outdated public works system, decided to accommodate the Speaker, and then agreed to his proposal.
>
> The compromise bill should have been vetoed because, despite some attractive features, it still included wasteful items. . . . Signing this act was certainly not the worst mistake I ever made, but it was accurately interpreted as a sign of weakness on my part, and I regretted it as much as any budget decision I made as President.
>
> Later . . . I was not so timid. In October 1978, I vetoed the annual public-works bill because it included some of the same water projects. It was rewarding to prevail even though almost every Democratic leader lined up against me, but the battle left deep scars.[30]

Not unexpectedly, the congressional liaison team faced severe problems in building support for a proposal with "almost every Democratic leader lined up against [the president]." One liaison staff person spoke about the situation:

30. Haynes Johnson, *In the Absence of Power* (New York, 1980), 158; Carter, *Keeping Faith*, 78–79.

President Carter really believed in it. He thought it was a waste of public money. We predicted what the outcome would be and he said, "I'm going to do it anyway." I think we maybe underestimated it and certainly other people underestimated it. It caused a bitterness that took a long time to get over. The hit list [of projects to be deleted] was leaked. Of course what caused so much of a problem were the projects that were falsely listed. Some imaginary lists had dams on them that we had no intention of cutting. . . . I guess every dam in the United States was on some of those lists that were floating around.

Another of the liaison staff explained that the politics of water projects from the member's perspective was not quite as simple as the president had described.

From the congressional side, most of these guys had put up with some personal agony in their own congressional districts in order to start those projects. I mean it wasn't a unanimous decision in their own districts to do some of these things. They had to pay some political price to get some of these projects going. And I remember [one committee chairman] telling that it was a personal thing that [his project] was stopped. He said, "You know, they're going to drive by there and blame me for that hole in the ground forever. I mean it: forever. How could he do this to me?" I mean there was that personal kind of thing.[31]

There is perhaps no better illustration of the president's determination to do the right thing than his actions on the water projects. Nor is there a more important issue for explaining the cool and cautious attitudes of congressional Democrats toward the president. As he himself observed: "The issue of water projects was the one that caused the deepest breach between me and the Democratic leadership." Congressional liaison staff reported "the shock of it" on the Hill. The chairman of the House committee with jurisdiction for such projects called one staff member and said, according to this person, "I just got up and I've never been so upset in my whole life. I just read it in the paper."[32]

The controversy appeared to extend beyond substantive concerns. The president challenged the method by which these projects were developed and funded. He was rather explicit in condemning congressional politics on this issue. Thus, members were faced with losing both their projects and their self-esteem.

31. Transcripts, IV, 118, 119–20.
32. Carter, *Keeping Faith*, 79; Transcripts, IV, 119.

THE BERT LANCE MATTER

"We first realized the adverse consequences of still being outsiders when we had to face the allegations raised against Bert Lance."[33] Carter's assessment reveals his resentment toward the way he and the Georgians were treated in Washington. In his account of the Lance affair, Carter blames the press—in particular the Washington *Post*. Whatever the precise cause, it is unquestionably true that Lance's problems resulted in severe damage to a new administration seeking to establish its trusteeship.

There is no need to recount all the details of the various allegations regarding Lance's management of his financial responsibilities prior to coming to Washington. Suffice it to say that a sequence of revelations raised doubts about the propriety of having such a person directing the Office of Management and Budget. But the affair itself distracted congressional attention from the president's program and tarnished the image of an administration that had emphasized morality and ethics in government. The adverse effect on the Carter White House finally convinced Lance to resign.

The timing of a congressional inquiry was particularly unfortunate, coming as it did so early in the administration when the president's extensive program was still being absorbed on Capitol Hill. Ironically the inquiry began after Carter asked that Lance be released from a pledge to sell certain of his bank stocks in order to prevent significant financial losses. This request led to media and congressional attention to Lance's banking practices. Once his portfolio was opened, it proved very hard to close again. "[The president] . . . had a letter addressed to the Senate Committee [on Governmental Affairs], asking for an extension of a year for [Lance] to sell his stock. It was a perfectly fair and a just request. . . . They first approved it and then it was one thing after another."[34]

There were two major effects of the Lance matter: its immediate impact on the White House and the Carter program, and the longer-term result of Lance's resignation. Among the first order of effects was the amount of the president's time that was devoted to Lance's problem. Press conferences came to be dominated by questions about Lance. Thus the matter was distracting—in the White House and on Capitol Hill. And

33. Carter, *Keeping Faith*, 127.
34. Transcripts, XX, 22.

it diverted attention from a large policy agenda. An aide said: "It wasn't self-paralysis. It was just that every time we would try to talk about other issues, we would be asked, but what about Bert Lance? We'd try to lobby stuff on the Hill. Frank Moore's people would go to see senators and congressmen. Moore's staff would try to talk about the votes on the bill, and be asked what is the president going to do about Bert Lance? We ended up being paralyzed by it." Another of the first-order effects was associated with the high moral standards promised by Jimmy Carter. Many aides discussed this problem, all lamenting that it had arisen because, as one observed, "he [Lance] was the best liked person in the entire White House. Everybody . . . from the janitor to the president liked Bert Lance." Evaluations were offered:

I go back to the Lance issue as the single biggest turning point in Carter's presidency early on. . . . The courts have ruled Bert was not guilty, but the questions of impropriety were there certainly and it went right at the heart of Carter's strength. Carter was a man who would always tell the truth. . . . All of a sudden Bert Lance comes along and Carter did not recognize and look at the evidence more carefully, and he did not have a staff that would have presented it to him, and not want to gloss over the problem. . . . That he stuck with Lance, I suppose, is admirable, but at the point when you become president . . . if it means having to say good-bye to your friend quickly then you have to do it. I think that the fact that he hung on and went through all those hearings, the shabby bank dealings and the peanut loans and all the rest of it flew right in the face of what people's perception in the country was of Carter. . . . Even though we were not doing as well in Washington, we were still doing well in the country.

I think that the president did very well with the media. . . . He did well until the Lance situation came to a head. He got into trouble by coming strongly to Bert Lance's defense. It was clear . . . within a 48 hour period that Lance was in bigger trouble than the president thought he was. . . . It turned out that there were enough grounds . . . to indict Bert. The public perception of his defense of Lance hurt him very badly. That began to turn the press. It also began to turn the public who cynically determined that this president was just like every other president. His cronies were his cronies, and there were rules for some people and there were different rules for other people. That was unfortunate because it vastly increased the cynicism of the press about Jimmy Carter. It probably colored most everything that happened after that.[35]

The president himself is the best authority on the second type of effect, the loss of a trusted adviser. "It is difficult for me to explain how

35. Transcripts, VII, 62, XII, 89, V, 67, I, 78–79.

close Bert was to me or how much I depended on him. Even my closest friends in Georgia have never fully understood the extent of our relationship." His loss meant not just the departure of the OMB director—as important as that official was during the crucial early months of the new administration. Lance had that extraordinary ability to move easily among different types of people—politicians, business leaders, government officials. He was the type of person a Jimmy Carter needed, a translator and a communicator for the Carter program. He could make deals, he could forgive, he had a sense of humor, he appreciated politics. The president understood these strengths. "Bert was able to engender support for our programs among the political and professional leaders of the state. The business community looked on him as one of its own, but he also had good relations with labor and other special groups interested in civil rights, consumer affairs, and social progress. He took this skill in human relations to Washington. Of all the Georgians I brought to the White House, he was the best at cementing ties with key members of Congress, and with business and financial leaders." One of the president's close associates developed this same theme in responding to questions about the impact of Lance's resignation. "We didn't miss his financial skills as much as we did his management of problems like budget problems. You have all different sides and arguments about the thing and when to do it and all that. Bert could grapple with those things and work them out pretty well to the point where [the president] just had the issue to pass on. Furthermore, most any person, and particularly the business person, was comfortable with Bert. He knew how to deal with big shots and people who had money, and he served a good purpose in that."[36]

It is, of course, hard to say how the first year might have turned out had Bert Lance been able to stay. His strengths were precisely those that Washington insiders judged as necessary for effective presidential-congressional relations. Furthermore, there was no one to take his place in Washington. Charles Kirbo, the president's close friend from Atlanta, provided a great deal of counsel over the telephone and during his many visits to the White House. But his was not a continuous presence, nor did he have Lance's personal qualities.

36. Carter, *Keeping Faith* 128; Transcripts, XX, 21.

Many Democratic congressional leaders offered positive evaluations of the work done in 1977. House majority whip John Brademas (Indiana) likened it to the first-year accomplishments of Franklin D. Roosevelt. Speaker O'Neill compared it favorably with Lyndon B. Johnson's first year. Other reviews were considerably more negative. And no amount of partisan gloss could change the realities of troublesome presidential-congressional conflicts during 1977.[37] Still, the president had a sizable and politically unattractive program in 1977, and much of it passed. Some of the less positive assessments were no doubt reactions to the president's independent style of politics as well as the high promise that style projects. Whatever the precise explanation, it was a difficult first year—a view shared by the president's own staff.

THE SECOND YEAR, 1978

No modern president had experienced as difficult a first year with Congress as did Jimmy Carter (at least among those elected to office). The president's problems were not confined to Capitol Hill. His ratings in the polls had slipped badly. Editorial comments at the start of his second year were unflattering, to say the least. A Washington *Post* editorial began this way: "The most tiresome cliche of the political season is the hearty comment that President Carter learns quickly. It's like saying that a pitcher going into the third game of the World Series is showing a knack for picking up the rules of the game." The *Post* did, however, give President Carter credit for "good intentions and a steady spirit."[38]

There was a definite need for reflective analysis of what had gone wrong. Hamilton Jordan prepared one of his famous memorandums for the president, stressing the need to set priorities. The president had an opportunity to specify his agenda in 1978 that was not available to him in 1977—the State of the Union message. The speech acknowledged the ten-

37. For details on these reactions, see Ann Cooper, "Congress Adjourns Without an Energy Bill," *Congressional Quarterly Weekly Report*, December 17, 1977, pp. 2583–85.

38. "The Year's First Lessons," Washington *Post*, January 13, 1978, p. A12. The New York *Times* editorial following the State of the Union message set much the same tone. Carter "is a soothing flatterer and a sensible President, but not yet a leader, or teacher, even for a quiet time" ("The State of Mr. Carter's Country," New York *Times*, January 22, 1978, p. 18).

dency to inaction during noncrisis periods. "There are times of emergency, when a nation and its leaders must bring their energies to bear on a single urgent task. . . . There are other times when there is no single overwhelming crisis—yet profound national interests are at stake." He spoke of a "new spirit," as he had during his inaugural address. One of his speechwriters pointed out, however, that "this 'new spirit' business . . . went nowhere because you couldn't say a 'new spirit program.'" Responding to a question about having "21 items that you're simultaneously advocating," the speechwriter said: "You can do that [write a good speech] if you have an ideological framework for those 21 items. Roosevelt had much more of an eclectic and crazy mass of programs that he proposed but they were all part of the one idea of the New Deal. Carter had this program but there was never a unifying idea which, in my opinion, is basically, in American politics, an artificial construct. One of the struggles that we had over the four years was what was the theme of the Carter administration and he very much resisted a slogan."[39]

Then the president outlined a number of noncrisis matters, and the speech was not memorable. By this time the task force under the chairmanship of Vice-President Mondale was at work trying to produce and project more order into the Carter program. Besides a lack of crisis, several other factors militated against developing the kind of overriding theme that other presidents—Ronald Reagan, for example—were able to establish. First, the president's true policy positions tended to be more conservative or consolidative than was then acceptable to most congressional Democrats. His statements on limited government "were greeted numerous times by applause, but frequently that applause was led by the Republicans in the House chamber, who obviously found much in the speech that could be applauded."[40] Thus, for strategic reasons it did not make sense to symbolize the president's position with a conservative slogan.

Second, much of his 1978 message dealt with reform or reorganization of the tax system, welfare, and civil service. Other proposals included a plan to reduce unemployment through private business initiatives; a vol-

39. Congressional Quarterly, *Congress and the Nation, 1977–1980*, V (Washington, D.C., 1981), 1134; Transcripts, VIII, 21.

40. Barry M. Hager, "Carter's State of the Union . . . ," *Congressional Quarterly Weekly Report*, January 21, 1978, p. 100.

untary anti-inflation program; reductions in federal spending; and ratification of the Panama Canal treaties. It was not easy to find an appropriate label for these proposals. One can understand why the nondescript "new spirit" phrase was used.

Third, as noted before, the Carter agenda was lengthy, and the president was interested in seeing it all enacted into law. A fifty-page message accompanied the State of the Union address. It contained more than one hundred subtitles listing proposals to be acted on by Congress, and many were left over from the first session.

Thus the problems of the first year were not easily overcome. Much of the 1977 agenda was still lodged in the committees on Capitol Hill. The president faced the dilemma of moving to other issues while still trying to get many of his original proposals adopted. Further, 1978 was an election year. Members of Congress were anxious to adjourn early so they could campaign, and they were especially sensitive to the effects legislation would have on their constituents.

I have selected three issues to illustrate presidential-congressional interaction in 1978. The issues are suited to the trusteeship model in the sense that they were either politically risky or offered little political payoff. They were the right things to do. The first is the ratification of the Panama Canal treaties. The president had an opportunity to demonstrate the correctness of his position in the face of difficult odds. It was to be one of his most impressive victories on Capitol Hill. The second is civil service reform—one of those important building blocks for effective government. There are, however, few if any rewards back home for members of Congress. The third issue is hospital cost control, another thorny policy problem of the type that naturally attracts the trustee president. As had happened with the energy programs, powerful interests could be expected to turn out in force on Capitol Hill to lobby for or against whatever the president proposed. These three cases were frequently cited by the White House staff as important examples of their work with Congress.

Note that energy legislation is not included in this group. There is little to add to the earlier discussion. The struggle over energy continued throughout the session, and a bill was finally passed at the last minute. The principal issue was the matter of natural gas pricing. White House activity was better coordinated than it had been in 1977, primarily because of a new task force that included people from the Department of

Energy, OMB, and the White House staff. The task-force technique was important in getting the Panama Canal treaties approved and was subsequently used for several legislative issues.

APPROVING THE PANAMA CANAL TREATIES

The issues associated with the future of the Panama Canal were complex, and previous administrations had been unable to resolve them. President Carter became convinced that relations with Panama would deteriorate unless there were new arrangements. Other presidents' difficulties with Congress on this issue did not bode well for any treaty if it compromised U.S. control of the Canal. "Despite the opposition of Congress and the public, I decided to plow ahead, believing that if the facts could be presented clearly, my advisers and I could complete action while my political popularity was still high and before we had to face the additional complication of the congressional election campaigns of 1978."[41]

The treaties were signed on September 7, 1977. An initial wave of criticism and opposition was forestalled because senators were asked not to commit themselves until they had heard directly from the president. The Senate was in recess when the treaties were first initialed, so telegrams or cables had to be sent to each senator. That was the first major lobbying action. One staff person noted: "I think that probably saved us. By the time they came back from that recess, we had had a chance to regroup a little bit and make some strategic decisions."[42]

Hearings were held in the Senate Judiciary and Foreign Relations committees during the fall. The former provided a forum for opposition; the latter, with formal jurisdiction, reported favorably on the treaties in late January, 1978. Attention then shifted to the Senate floor, where a two-thirds vote was required for ratification.

The White House effort to gain ratification was impressive and multidimensional. First and foremost was the need to change public opinion. Every schoolchild had learned that American know-how triumphed over adversity in the building of the Panama Canal. "Panama was fundamentally a domestic political issue for us" was the way one member of

41. Carter, *Keeping Faith*, 156.
42. Transcripts, V, 13.

the White House staff put it. Response to the Gallup Poll on this issue showed initially that many Americans strongly opposed relinquishing control of the Canal. Among the more knowledgeable respondents polled (that is, those who could correctly answer three questions about the Canal and the treaties), only a bare majority (51 percent) approved of the treaties in late September, 1977. By January, 1978, the percentage had risen to 57. Among those less aware of the actual details, the opposition was reduced even more.[43]

Second, as a means for changing public opinion it was necessary to obtain bipartisan support from respected officials. If the people learned that former presidents and secretaries of state, for example, were in favor of the treaties, then their mood would be more positive. The White House mobilized to legitimize the treaties in this way.

Third, it was necessary, indeed essential, that there be favorable Republican votes in the Senate. The key to getting this support was the leadership of Howard Baker of Tennessee, the Senate minority floor leader. Members of the White House staff were uniform in their praise of his role. One observed that "I came out of all this with more respect for Baker than almost any Senator I know."[44] The president frequently negotiated directly with Baker in building the coalition needed for a two-thirds majority. Finally, the lobbying effort had to result in votes for the treaties. That meant maintaining the base of support among Senate Democrats and then working individually with each undecided senator. The president was very active in this effort—he even called and met with senators who had announced their opposition.

An ad hoc task force was organized to coordinate the lobbying effort for ratification. The technique would be used frequently thereafter on other issues. One such group, established in the State Department during the early stages of treaty development, provided speakers as well as literature to promote the treaties. The idea carried over to the White House, where a great deal of coordination of effort was required. Robert Beckel, the new congressional liaison staff member for foreign and defense policy, chaired the interagency task force.

43. Transcripts, VII, 53; *Gallup Opinion Index*, CXLIX (December, 1977), 14, CLIII (April, 1978), 24.

44. Transcripts, V, 28.

The story of the lobbying for the treaties is told in many places, including the president's book. Suffice it here simply to identify the range of techniques, since they illustrate that the White House was quite willing to pull out the stops for a policy the president judged to be "right." These techniques included:

1. An extensive public liaison effort by knowledgeable officials in the State Department and the White House (participation in hundreds of meetings, television and radio shows, speaking engagements)
2. Organization of the Committee of Americans for the Canal Treaties to publicize the support of major political figures (among the members were former president Ford, Lady Bird Johnson, and AFL-CIO President George Meany)
3. White House briefings by the president and others for local officials, editorial writers, educators, labor leaders, heads of civic organizations
4. A fireside chat by the president to emphasize the importance of the treaties to future American foreign and defense policy
5. Trips to Panama for senators, including meetings with General Omar Torrijos and other Panamanian leaders
6. Continuing contact with Torrijos to explain the nature and purpose of the Senate debate and to prevent precipitate reaction by the Panamanian government
7. Direct negotiation with individual senators (providing immediate responses to their questions, doing favors for them, providing support for them at home when they were criticized).

This impressive effort surely had its effect on getting a favorable vote in the Senate. Earlier predictions of failure proved to be wrong. The Carter administration demonstrated a capacity to change public opinion and build a coalition for an unpopular issue and policy. Both treaties passed the Senate by one more than the required two-thirds vote (see Table 16).

The White House gained more than a victory on Capitol Hill, however. A lobbying technique for mobilizing public support and developing coalitions had been discovered and put into practice. The Office of Public Liaison, under the leadership of Anne Wexler, began to use the task-force mechanism to generate outside support for Carter's legislative initiatives in order to create pressure on Congress. Inevitably this effort led to contact with interest groups and opinion leaders, as one aide explained:

TABLE 16
The Panama Canal Treaties in Congress, 1977–1978

	Senate	*House*
1977		
Sept. 7	(Treaties signed)	
Sept. 8; Oct. 13, 28; Nov. 3, 15	Hearings—Committee on Judiciary (on president's authority to cede the Canal by treaty)	
Sept. 8, 14, 15, 20, 26, 28; Oct. 11, 20		Hearings—Committee on International Relations
Sept. 26, 27, 29, 30; Oct. 4, 5, 10–14, 19, 1977; Jan. 19, 20, 25–27, 30, 1978	Hearings—Committee on Foreign Relations	
Aug. 17, 1977; Jan. 17, 18, 1978		Hearings—Committee on Merchant Marine and Fisheries
1978		
Jan. 24, 31; Feb. 1	Hearings—Committee on Armed Services (on military and economic impact of Canal transfer)	
Jan. 27, 30	Mark-ups—Committee on Foreign Relations	
Feb. 3	Report—Committee on Foreign Relations	
Feb. 8–Mar. 16	Floor debate on first treaty	
Mar. 16	Vote on first treaty (68–32)	
Mar. 16–Apr. 18	Floor debate on second treaty	
Apr. 18	Vote on second treaty (68–32)	

SOURCE: Various issues of *Congressional Quarterly Weekly Report,* 1977–1978.

We also added extensive consultations and participation by interest groups on the policy development side. This was done on all the major priority issues of the president and before we ever got to legislate language. We tried, in very general terms, to be sure that people who were going to be helping us sell the president's program to the country and to the Congress were in on the take-off as well as the landing. It was pure self-interest on our part because we could not get people to work with us unless they felt they had a piece of the action.[45]

45. Transcripts, I, 4.

Of course, as with all important victories, the cost was significant. One staff member speculated that approval of the Panama Canal treaties was gained at the expense of getting a SALT II treaty approved. The electoral risks for senators were great in both cases, and it may have been impossible to run through the exercise twice. The president himself said: "If I could have foreseen early in 1977 the terrible battle we would face in Congress [on the Panama Canal treaties], it would have been a great temptation for me to avoid the issue—at least during my first term. The struggle left deep and serious political wounds that have never healed; and, I am convinced, a large number of members of Congress were later defeated for reelection because they voted for the Panama treaties." In the end, however, the president thought this political sacrifice was in the best traditions of American politics as he understood them. "Some fine members of Congress had to pay with their political careers for their votes during these long and difficult months. Their courage represents the *best of American government*; I am proud of the role they and I played in this dramatic and historic event."[46] Again, Carter's analysis is consistent with the trustee's approach to policy making. The issue transcends political careers and electoral defeat. Supporting the right cause provides its own rewards.

REFORMING THE CIVIL SERVICE SYSTEM

Civil service reform was a priority reorganizational matter for the Carter administration in 1978, as the president said in the State of the Union message. It was not an issue likely to generate much public interest. Nor could one expect that enacting the reforms would result in many bragging rights for those on the campaign trail. Here was another "right thing to do," with no perceivable electoral benefits for Congress or the president. One of the liaison staff members summarized the challenge as he saw it: "It was an unknown. No bill had been put up there like it. There wasn't an identifiable constituency. You couldn't look at previous votes and see how somebody would vote on the thing."[47]

46. Carter, *Keeping Faith*, 184, 185 (emphasis added).
47. Transcripts, IV, 66.

This is not to say that legislation was unnecessary. No reforms as extensive as Carter's proposals had been made since the Pendleton Act of 1883. Nor could it be assumed that the lack of public interest and attention meant that the bill was noncontroversial. The federal work force itself is important and well represented in Washington. Further, the questions of veterans' status and labor practices were vital to the powerful groups representing those interests.

The White House employed an interagency task force to coordinate the lobbying on civil service reform, as had been done for the Panama Canal treaties. The task force was headed by Les Francis of the congressional liaison staff. The group met two or three times a week to discuss strategy and make lobbying assignments.[48] Cabinet secretaries were asked to call individual members of Congress. The president was very much involved, calling members and directing his cabinet to support the bill. The task force therefore provided a means for mobilizing White House and departmental lobbying on Capitol Hill. But it also served another purpose, as one aide explained: "The other thing it did was to provide a place to get quick reaction, reports and be able to react quickly to problems that were occurring on the Hill." In other words, the task force offered a means for getting a response from the White House to developments within a subcommittee or at some other stage of the legislative process. Without that mechanism, one liaison staff member noted, "you're left to my judgment. That's not always the best."[49]

An effective White House task force was necessary on this bill since Congress is not normally that motivated to act forcefully on civil service reform. The subject itself is not high on the congressional agenda. Members are not exactly clamoring to resolve problems associated with personnel policy in the bureaucracy. Further, the committees with jurisdiction on civil service matters are low in prestige. The House of Representatives does retain the Post Office and Civil Service Committee. It is one of the least-sought-after assignments, and membership turnover is very high.[50]

48. Johnson, *In the Absence of Power*, 252.

49. Transcripts, IV, 65.

50. See George Goodwin, *The Little Legislatures: Committees in Congress* (Amherst, Mass., 1970), 114; and Charles S. Bullock III, "Committee Transfers in the United States House of Representatives," *Journal of Politics*, XXXV (February, 1973), 85–120.

The Senate abolished its Post Office and Civil Service Committee in 1977 and transferred the bulk of its jurisdiction to Governmental Affairs, also a minor committee in that chamber.

The civil service reform legislation was introduced as two bills, the reorganization plan to create new agencies and the proposal to alter personnel procedures. In the Senate both bills were treated in the same committee, so there was coordinated action. In the House, however, the bills went to separate committees. The Committee on Government Operations, headed by Jack Brooks (D-Texas), handled the reorganization plan, and the Committee on Post Office and Civil Service had jurisdiction on employment matters. The ranking Democrat, though not the chairman, of the latter committee was Morris Udall, who was not anxious to take on the responsibility of shepherding this bill through the committee. "But Carter appealed to him personally, as an act of patriotism, for the good of the country and the government, to take it on, and Udall, who thought of himself as a Hubert Humphrey sort of Democrat, confessed to being 'a sucker for that kind of appeal.' He agreed to lead the fight."[51]

Table 17 summarizes the legislative history of the bill. Udall was successful, with Republican support, in getting it out of committee. Senate committee action was delayed by Senator Charles Mathias (R-Maryland), who represents many government employees in the Maryland suburbs surrounding Washington. In both the House and Senate, floor action was characterized by a great deal of amending, but the bills were passed overwhelmingly.

The president tackled a thankless task in reforming civil service. For that, he received a good press in Washington. White House lobbying and liaison operations were acknowledged to have been well managed in this case. Difficult struggles over veterans' preference and labor rights were resolved, and the reform bills received nearly unanimous support in the final vote in each chamber.

HOSPITAL COST CONTAINMENT

Two congressional liaison staff members summarized the problem with getting a hospital cost containment bill passed. The first said, "It was one

51. Johnson, *In the Absence of Power*, 254.

TABLE 17
Civil Service Reform in Congress, 1978

	Senate	*House*
Mar. 2	(Presidential message)	
Mar. 3	Bill introduced	Bill introduced
Mar. 14–May 23 (intermittent)		Hearings—Committee on Post Office and Civil Service
Apr. 6–May 9 (intermittent)	Hearings—Committee on Governmental Affairs	
June 29	Committee on Governmental Affairs votes approval	
July 10	Report—Committee on Governmental Affairs	
July 19		Committee on Post Office and Civil Service votes approval
July 31		Report—Committee on Post Office and Civil Service
Aug. 11		Floor debate begins
Aug. 24	Floor debate and vote on bill (87–1)	
September 7		Floor debate continues
September 13		Vote on bill (385–10)
Oct. 3	(Conference report)	
Oct. 4	Voice vote on Conference report	
Oct. 6		Vote on conference report (365–8)
Oct. 13	(President signs into law)	

SOURCE: Various issues of *Congressional Quarterly Weekly Report,* 1978.

of those things where you just couldn't get the engine going." The second observed that "it's just one of those issues that had all of the trappings of a loss."[52]

No one disputed the facts of escalating hospital costs. The increases had been astronomical (two and one-half times the overall inflation rate) and were likely to rise just as rapidly in the future if no action was taken.

52. Transcripts, IV, 78, 79.

President Carter sent a proposal to Congress to reduce costs in April, 1977. He asked for quick action but did not receive it. Only one of the four House and Senate committees with jurisdiction had approved a bill by the end of 1977, and in that case (the Senate Committee on Human Resources) the bill was a rather substantial revision of what Carter requested.

It was the judgment of the president that some action to reduce hospital costs was a necessary preliminary step to a national health plan. Thus a proposal to reduce hospital costs was inevitably associated with that larger issue. During the 1976 presidential campaign, Carter himself had promised a comprehensive health insurance system. This goal clashed with that of reducing the budget, however, and thus his proposal was to phase in such a system over time. A comprehensive health care plan had long been supported by Senator Edward Kennedy, a ranking member of the committee with jurisdiction for health issues. Senator Kennedy did not favor the Carter plan. According to the president, he met with Kennedy to gain his support and the meeting, which was just prior to the announcement of the administration's program, went well. Kennedy asked for a delay so he could have an opportunity to study the plan, and Carter agreed. "We shook hands and parted in fairly good spirits. Within a few hours, any hope of cooperation was gone. Kennedy held a press conference at three o'clock that afternoon to condemn our plan and to announce that he and his associates would oppose it. There was no prospect of congressional support for his own program, which was announced the following year."[53]

The cost containment bill, having been introduced in 1977, lacked the coordinated support that characterized subsequent lobbying efforts. A task force was created in 1978, but by then the formidable opposition to this legislation had had ample opportunity to prepare its case and organize on the Hill. Thus the 1978 task force was in the unenviable position of having to repair the damage done the year before as well as build public support for a new program.

It was difficult to escape the inherent problems associated with this issue, however. Even if a task force had been organized from the start, and if Anne Wexler had been on the staff to conduct briefings for interest groups, it is entirely possible that the bill would not have moved any far-

53. Carter, *Keeping Faith*, 87.

ther than it did. This was another of those issues with a limited constituency and powerful lobbies in opposition. The general public is protected from the actual costs of hospitalization by a third-party payment system. And the liaison staff talked about trying to organize community support for the proposal.

> Hospital administrators were a force who were hard to deal with. If you just think about your own home towns and your hospital board, think about who's on the board. It's usually the blue ribbon committees; usually a philanthropist who they put on. . . .
>
> The hospital administrators have some damn good people in Washington who understood hospital and community politics. They mobilized the trustees and the boards of the hospital to call the congressman. You're getting ready to vote on this thing, the administration presented their views and it makes sense. Suddenly you get a call. Maybe you've got four or five towns of any size in your district, and in three days you get calls from fifteen people who are the wealthiest, most powerful people in those towns. In addition, they're people who said, "I've never called you before. You've been my congressman for six years or eight years and I'm just asking you this one thing for me. Vote against that. We can't run our hospital if we're constrained. We'll have to go to the county commissioners if it's a public hospital, raise additional money." If it's a university hospital, you know, "I'm the president of the university and a powerful, powerful force, and one that you can't combat on a one to one." We couldn't go into that town and pick somebody that's equally influential and get them to call their congressmen to say, "No, it's not true."[54]

This staff member is describing a very difficult political situation. The president may have been right about the issue, but he was opposed by highly respected people at the local level. In this case it was virtually impossible to get adequate support for alleviating what everyone acknowledged was a serious problem. Even those who were anxious to solve the problem of rising costs were not necessarily willing to do it from Washington.

Table 18 shows the lengthy and unsatisfying consideration of this issue in the two houses of Congress. It provides a very brief outline of what was basically a situation out of control. On the House side, the legislative action can only be described as chaotic. Two committees had jurisdiction, Ways and Means and Interstate and Foreign Commerce. The for-

54. Transcripts, IV, 77.

TABLE 18
Hospital Cost Containment in Congress, 1977–1978

	Senate	House
1977		
Apr. 25	(President's message)	
May 11–13		Hearings – Committee on Interstate and Foreign Commerce
June 15, 16, July 6	Hearings – Committee on Human Resources	
Aug. 2	Report – Committee on Human Resources	
Oct. 12, 13, 21	Hearings – Committee on Finance	
1978		
Feb. 1		Chairman Rostenkowski (Committee on Ways and Means) announces reprieve
June–July		Votes – Committee on Interstate and Foreign Commerce
July 18		Bill defeated in Committee on Interstate and Foreign Commerce (22–21)
Aug. 3	Committee on Finance approves counterproposal	
Oct. 12	Compromise plan passed (64–22)	
Oct. 15		Rostenkowski announces no further action by his committee

SOURCE: Various issues of *Congressional Quarterly Weekly Report,* 1977–1978.

mer was unable to complete action in 1977. Chairman Daniel Rostenkowski (D-Illinois) could not even muster a quorum to work on the bill toward the end of the session. In 1978, Rostenkowski first announced that he favored allowing hospitals a period of one year to cut costs. The administration was opposed to this approach. The Ways and Means Committee was never able to produce a bill for floor consideration. Meanwhile, the Committee on Interstate and Foreign Commerce was divided on what to do. Throughout much of June and July, 1978, the committee struggled to formulate an acceptable compromise. In addition to the problems of satisfying hospital and medical groups, the committee members had to contend with labor union opposition to proposals that might reduce wages. After six weeks of marking up the bill, the committee voted to scrap it—22 to 21—and substitute a bill that dropped mandatory controls altogether. No further action was taken in the House.

Senate action was equally protracted and full of conflict. The Finance and Human Resources committees had jurisdiction. Both held hearings during 1977, but neither was successful in reporting a bill to the floor. Senator Herman E. Talmadge (D-Georgia) prepared his own bill for consideration by the Senate Committee on Finance. His proposal was more limited than that offered by the president and concentrated primarily on Medicare and Medicaid hospital costs. Late in the 1978 session, the Talmadge bill was reported out by the committee. The White House sought to use that bill as a means for salvaging its original proposal. A compromise offered by Senator Gaylord Nelson (D-Wisconsin) was endorsed by the administration and was introduced as an amendment to the Talmadge bill. To everyone's surprise, it passed by a voice vote after a failed move by Talmadge to have it tabled. The victory was built on "hardball lobbying, compromise, parliamentary ambush and pervasive belief that a 'yea' on the controversial bill was 'safe' because the House couldn't pass it before adjournment."[55]

Indeed, the House did not pass the Nelson substitute. The Committee on Ways and Means had not yet reported out a bill, and there was some hope that it might do so. But the end-of-session overloading of the agenda prevented tackling this thorny issue again—particularly given members' anxiety to return to their districts for the fall campaign. Thus the end of the session found the administration busily searching for a bill it could support and a strategy for enacting it. Unfortunately, time ran out. It is likely, however, that the encouraging signs were there only because time was short and senators understood that the House would not act. "It's just one of those issues that had all of the trappings of a loss."[56]

55. Congressional Quarterly, *Almanac*, 95th Cong., 2nd Sess. (Washington, D.C., 1979), 624.

56. For the account of this congressional battle by Secretary of Health, Education, and Welfare Joseph A. Califano, Jr., see his book, *Governing America: An Insider's Report from the White House and the Cabinet* (New York, 1981), 142–53.

SUMMARY

By 1978, there was no lack of realism regarding the strengths and weaknesses of the Carter administration. There was also no escaping the problems of the first session, many of which carried over for lack of action in 1977. Still the legislative record showed definite victories for the president in the ratification of the Panama Canal treaties, airline deregulation, and civil service reform. A compromise natural gas pricing bill was also finally passed, and President Carter asserted himself strongly by vetoing the public works appropriations bill that contained funding for water projects he opposed.

There were also some important developments during 1978 that helped identify a method for working with Congress for this trustee president. The breakthrough was the treaties' ratification, for Hamilton Jordan managed a full-scale lobbying operation that changed probable defeat into victory. The task-force mechanism for building public support and fashioning coalitions became standard in subsequent major legislative efforts. It was an essential device for a president drawn to issues that were sure to be politically troublesome on Capitol Hill. Of course, no one procedure can guarantee success for such a president. But he is less vulnerable if supported from the outside. One can only wonder what might have happened in 1977 had the task-force mechanism been in place.

☆ 7 ☆

Jimmy Carter and the Ninety-sixth Congress

The Ninety-fifth Congress adjourned on October 15, 1978, a little more than three weeks before the election. According to form, the Democratic margin in Congress was reduced as a result of the 1978 election. The Republicans had a net gain of three Senate seats and eleven House seats. The shift in the House was less than the average loss for a presidential party at midterm and left the Democrats with commanding majorities in both chambers (59 to 41 in the Senate; 276 to 159 in the House). Yet the election results were not interpreted as favoring the president. In fact, they were hardly identified with the Carter administration at all. An ABC/Harris Poll analysis of 104 marginal congressional districts "indicated that the President had no measurable influence in the districts he visited." And the president himself was quoted as saying: "I doubt my presence had much of an impact on the outcome of those who won. I don't look on it as a referendum on whether I have done a good job or not."[1]

On the other hand, there did appear to be a policy message in the returns, one that may have presaged changes in 1980. The changes in the Senate, in particular, were interpreted as moving that chamber to the right. Several liberal Democrats were defeated by conservative Republicans. Clearly the Republicans were encouraged by the results and were in a good position to seek a greater advantage in 1980. And it is important to point out that the conclusion of a midterm election almost immediately focuses attention on the next presidential election. For the Republicans, speculation began about who would be the 1980 candidate. For congressional Democrats, concern began to be expressed that a Carter reelection bid would hurt their electoral chances. For the administration,

1. *Time*, November 20, 1978, p. 17.

attention would naturally begin to focus on reelection. The president faced very different electoral circumstances than he had in 1976. By definition, reelection poses a dilemma for the trustee president. He must give an accounting of and renew his trusteeship. Yet in agenda setting and other policy choices, he will have downplayed the electoral benefits. The election was an event to focus staff attention, and they expressed themselves favorably on that point, but reelecting any trustee president is more than likely to be arduous.

Relations with Congress were troubled during the Ninety-fifth Congress, but the president did control the legislative agenda. Members worked on the many issues that Carter identified as deserving their attention. Further, he was in a position to manage how he spent his time and resources in treating these issues. During the Ninety-sixth Congress, external events began to command the president's time. Forces outside the administration's control were setting the agenda—these developments adversely affected Carter's leadership. As Rosalynn Carter remembers it, "[The crises] never stopped coming, big ones and small ones, potential disasters and mere annoyances."[2] Ironically, the congressional liaison operation itself received less criticism, and the staff members were quite pleased with their efforts in 1979 and 1980. But this record must be placed in the context of an administration reacting to events rather than initiating them.

Meanwhile, there were further problems for the president's program on Capitol Hill. The conservative coalition of Republicans and southern Democrats found new life in 1979. Speaker O'Neill, in particular, faced difficulties in providing majorities in the House of Representatives for administration programs.

What follows is a selected treatment of the relationships between the Carter White House and the Ninety-sixth Congress. As in Chapter 6, a few outstanding pieces of legislation are chosen as illustrations. Then a brief analysis of presidential support scores is provided, primarily to show how this president fared in comparison with other recent presidents.

THE THIRD YEAR, 1979

However ambiguous the 1978 congressional election results may have been, a new Congress was in session and so the president could sound the

2. Rosalynn Carter, *First Lady From Plains* (Boston, 1984), 304.

call for "a new foundation" in his State of the Union address. "Tonight I want to examine in a broad sense the state of our American Union—how we are building *a new foundation* for a peaceful and a prosperous world. . . . The challenge to us is to build a new and firmer foundation for the future—for a sound economy, for a more effective government, for more political trust, and for a stable peace, so that the America our children inherit will be even stronger and even better than it is today." The speechwriters were pleased with the new slogan—the "new foundation" —particularly since other attempts had fallen flat. One of the writers noted: "One sign of a successful slogan is that it gets ridiculed," and that was happening in the cartoons and on the Johnny Carson show. But the president himself "shot it down."

At his first press conference after that speech, he was asked . . . about this thing you said in your state of the union address, the new foundation, is that your idea of the theme of your administration or is that just something you had in the speech? He answered, "No, I wouldn't say that was the theme of my administration. That was just something in a speech." Jerry [Rafshoon] had sent around a memo to everybody before the speech saying this is our theme, we're going to stick with this, people are going to make fun of it, that's a good sign, if it catches on we're going to stick with it. But once the president shot it down . . . [3]

In explaining why the president did not accept the "new foundation" theme, the speechwriters stressed his desire to avoid labeling himself so he could keep his options open. I quote their discussion because it offers a near-classic description of the model trustee president's behavior. Labels confine the policy options of the free agent—particularly if others interpret what options are implied by the label.

Discussant A: I think that's the case once again where he would be willing, if they had picked it up and used it, but he didn't want to have his fingerprints on it. He wouldn't want to say "here I am saying what the theme of my administration is."

Discussant B: He never wanted to draw the line in a way that would include and exclude.

Discussant C: That went on down to our arguments about his farewell address.

Question: If he didn't want to do it himself, why couldn't he have had surrogates do it, building up some sort of October surprise, so to speak?

Discussant B: If he was unprepared to accept it, it couldn't be done.

3. Congressional Quarterly, *Congress and the Nation, 1977-1980*, V (Washington, D.C., 1981), 1137 (emphasis added); Transcripts, VIII, 22. For the president's exact response, see the transcript of his news conference, reprinted in *Congressional Quarterly Weekly Report*, February 3, 1979, pp. 201-202.

Discussant A: He could have slipped that question. He didn't have to answer it so directly. He could have said "well if that's what you want, sure, it's up to you guys." He didn't have to say "that's what I'd like you to call it." He obviously was so self-conscious about it that he had to say "no, that isn't it," which really undermines the whole effort.

Discussant B: What we would have liked him to have said naturally in answer to that question was: "Well, I don't like labels. Labels are always dangerous. But I think the idea of a new foundation is a pretty good description of what I'm trying to do." Or: "We're going back to basics. We're not dealing with the new superstructure, we're going back and trying to sort out basic problems like energy and nuclear arms."[4]

It is not certain that the "new foundation" theme would have established a recognized continuity even if the president had endorsed it. Such labels as *New Deal*, *Fair Deal*, and *Great Society* convey little substance in and of themselves. One must discover meaning by examining the content of presidential messages. Furthermore, if a president is not comfortable assigning a label to the programs—as this president was not—then it will be difficult for others to do so.

In the case of the 1979 State of the Union message, the substantive continuity of the "new foundation" remained ambiguous. The principal subtopics were: the 1980 budget, regulatory reform, a stable world community, multilateral trade negotiations, and the SALT II treaty. The construction of the speech is interesting for what it tells us about the problems of the Carter administration in 1979. The space was allocated as follows: introduction and discussion of the "new foundation" (20 percent); the budget and other domestic matters (30 percent); international issues and foreign policy (36 percent); summary and closing (14 percent).

The first observation to make is that the domestic content (the budget and regulatory reorganization) again demonstrated the complications for a Democratic president in an era of consolidation. Carter wanted to cut the budget and make government work more effectively. But these were not traditional Democratic party themes. Thus he emphasized the need to stabilize the economy through budgetary actions while still paying obeisance to standard social welfare goals. Perhaps the best example of his effort to work both sides of the street is a single sentence planted in the middle of the section on the budget. "This year, we will take our first steps to develop a national health plan." No more was said. Yet here was a major initiative—one with significant budgetary implications.

4. Transcripts, VIII, 22.

Second, the increased attention to foreign policy represented a trend that concerned Hamilton Jordan in 1978 when he summarized the problems of the president's first year in office. Less than 30 percent of the 1978 State of the Union address was devoted to foreign policy issues; nearly half of that speech was on domestic matters. As we have seen, the proportions shifted more heavily toward foreign policy in 1979. One of Carter's advisers viewed this development as perfectly natural: "Every president in the end becomes much more absorbed in foreign policy and national security issues than the domestic issues. That's in part because he can deal with them. He is really able to make decisions and carry them out in the foreign field to a much greater extent than in the domestic field. . . . In the domestic field, whatever you do is controversial. You've got all those welfare mothers and budget balancers on your hands. It's much more of a mess."[5] This allocation of time results in a shift in the president's posture toward Congress. Just as the adviser suggests, the president is drawn away from the parochialism of constituency politics and toward the global issues of world peace. For Carter, in particular, working out agreements between the leaders of nations (as at Camp David) was more satisfying and rewarding than was negotiating which unwanted water projects would survive. Ironically, however, one international incident—the Iranian hostage crisis—contributed to the president's undoing.

What the 1979 State of the Union address signaled to Congress was that President Carter had few more new initiatives. His domestic program was before them in essentially the same form as it had been during the Ninety-fifth Congress. Subsequent interaction would be more a consequence of events than of presidential initiative. And members of Congress would also be active in responding to those events.

Table 19 lists events that affected the administration in 1979. As one recalls them, it was clearly a bad year for the president. Events rather than policy began to command his attention and, by July, even force him to evaluate the structure and course of his administration. I have selected three issues to illustrate the nature of the president's relationships with Congress. First is the one that would not go away—the continuing energy crisis. "I was getting most of the blame from the public for these trou-

5. Transcripts, XVIII, 6.

TABLE 19
Major Events Affecting the Carter Presidency, 1979

Date	*Event*
Jan.	Shah of Iran falls
Jan. 16	Shah leaves Iran
Feb. 1	Khomeini returns to Iran
Mar. 26	Egyptian-Israeli peace treaty signed
Mar. 28	Three Mile Island nuclear plant accident
June 18	SALT II treaty signed
July 3–12	Camp David retreat
July 15	"Crisis of confidence" speech
July 17–20	Cabinet and White House staff shakeup
Oct. 20	Decision to admit the shah into the United States
Nov. 4	U.S. embassy in Iran overrun and hostages taken
Dec. 27	Soviet Union invades Afghanistan

bles," the president recalls.[6] The issue is selected for its salience and also because it demonstrates important changes in the way the White House developed policy and lobbied Congress. This second energy program was also comprehensive in scope, but members of Congress were consulted in a process that was much more open than had been the case in 1977.

Second, at an even more comprehensive level, the budgetary process was beginning to reorient work patterns on Capitol Hill. It had been instituted as a means by which Congress might substitute its judgment for that of the White House, thereby forcing greater consultation on the budget. The complex and lengthy procedure in 1979 was not a good omen.

Third, the creation of the Department of Education represented one of Carter's reorganization goals from the 1976 presidential campaign. The president was personally involved in lobbying for the proposal, as he was in other reorganizational plans offered by his administration.

THE CONTINUING ENERGY POLICY CRISIS

The final passage of an energy program in 1978 did not, by any means, resolve the problems facing the United States. The American public experienced even greater inconveniences in 1979 than had been the case fol-

6. Jimmy Carter, *Keeping Faith: Memoirs of a President* (New York, 1982), 114.

lowing the oil embargo in 1973. One White House staff member said: "Well, I felt the impact because I couldn't get any damn gas for my car and that was a real crisis. I mean I couldn't get to work."[7]

The first two years of conflict between the president and Congress over energy issues were sufficiently debilitating that Carter was not anxious "to stir up the energy pot all over again." But a major problem loomed on the horizon, one that was of immense political difficulty for a Democratic president. Price controls on oil, as set by the 1975 Energy Policy and Conservation Act, were scheduled to end on June 1, 1979, with presidential discretion to continue, modify, or remove controls between June 1 and October 1, 1981, when authority for all controls expired. President Carter opposed decontrol during the 1976 campaign. Yet he had no choice but to act in 1979. He proposed a phased decontrol of oil, combined with a windfall profits tax to recapture for the government a sizable portion of the costs of going to the world price for domestic oil. This policy was made in a much more open manner than had characterized the formulation of the 1977 energy program: "Under the chairmanship of Stu Eizenstat, twenty representatives of the major government agencies involved met for several hours every day. We also worked with the key members of Congress. I received such varying opinions from them that, late in March, I finally brought in a fairly large group who could represent as many different viewpoints and interests as possible. I particularly wanted them to hear each other."[8]

Since the president already had the authority to modify price controls, the principal request to Congress was for the windfall profits tax. It was decontrol and a stiff tax that the president announced to the public on April 5. He proposed the creation of an Energy Security Fund to receive the tax monies. The fund would then assist low-income families with their energy costs, build mass transportation systems, and support energy research and development.

Congress was slow to act on this difficult issue, and Carter became impatient with the delay. Consultation, it seems, did not speed congressional movement in this complex area. Given his campaign promise, the president was, understandably, anxious to soften the political effect of decontrol with the passage of the oil tax. His impatience was recorded in

7. Transcripts, XIII, 85.
8. Carter, *Keeping Faith*, 109, 110.

his diary for April 30: "I had lunch with the Vice President. We discussed . . . the energy situation that's developing in the Congress, with almost everybody trying to demagogue decontrol and the windfall-profits tax, and the irresponsibility of the Congress in not giving us authority to handle gasoline rationing and impose conservation measures if necessary in an emergency. The Congress is disgusting on this particular subject."[9]

Decontrolling prices and taxing the profits were only part of a broader energy plan to be offered by the president. Eizenstat and the DPS continued to work on other aspects of the program, in conjunction with the new Department of Energy. The process of development continued to be open, with countless late-afternoon meetings among those in the executive branch who had principal responsibilities for energy. Members of Congress and their staffs were also consulted. In fact, a bill to promote synthetic fuel development was making progress on Capitol Hill, and the White House essentially joined this effort.

This work by the DPS was to culminate in yet another speech to the nation in early July. The president was in Tokyo at an economic summit at the end of June. When he returned home he found his status in the public opinion polls at a new low. Gasoline shortages had produced higher and higher prices, long lines at service stations, and early closings. While at Camp David, the president concluded that another energy speech was unlikely to produce the desired results. Thus, in an extraordinary move, he cancelled it and decided to remain at Camp David to reassess his administration, including possible changes in the cabinet.

The Camp David retreat became a thorough review of the first two and one-half years of the Carter administration. So the speech that resulted was wide-ranging and philosophical. In fact, a serious debate occurred among White House staff personnel as to whether energy issues ought to be addressed at all. Understandably, Eizenstat argued that they should, as did Vice-President Mondale, who opposed cancelling the original energy speech.[10] Others, most notably Pat Caddell, argued for the need to concentrate attention on the larger problems of the American political system. The whole exercise caused splits among the White House staff and between the Carter and Mondale staffs.

9. *Ibid.*, 111.
10. See Rosalynn Carter, *First Lady From Plains*, 302.

The remaining aspects of the energy program were included in the speech. The whole story is well told by the speechwriters. "As I remember, when we went up there, the fight was in full cry between those who felt it should be a strong energy speech and those who felt that it should be a crisis of confidence speech and there were one hundred percenters on either side. There were people who felt that this whole crisis of confidence stuff was mumbly mush and insane and would reinforce the notion of neurosis." The speechwriters had to try to join the two aspects in the same speech—the systemic issues with the practical matter of gas lines—and to ensure that people would listen to the section on energy. The problem was "inadvertently solved by Stu Eizenstat," who became very upset with the omission of energy. "He got so angry, so incensed that there would be no energy in the speech at all, because at this point his side was losing, and we just kept telling him it's boring and he finally blew up and said it's not, it can be said in an exciting and dramatic way. He thundered out his six point program and he did it very, very well." And then "the idea of the one (energy) being a solution to the other (malaise) popped up": "It's not just two things sewn together. It's that this specific program will begin to solve this bigger problem. It's like saying your whole life's a mess, but you can't fix it all at once so pick something like experience and start there."[11] In the speech itself, the transition sentence reads: "Energy will be the immediate test of our ability to unite this Nation and it can also be the standard around which we rally." Thus, the remainder of Carter's 1979 energy program was finally launched.

By mid-July the congressional energy agenda was once again overflowing. President Carter had already proposed the windfall profits tax, standby gasoline rationing authority, and support for solar energy and other conservation programs. In his mid-July speech he requested a synthetic fuels program and the establishment of an Energy Mobilization Board that would have the authority "to cut through the red tape, the delays, and the endless roadblocks to completing key energy projects."[12] The president viewed these various proposals as an integrated energy policy, particularly when combined with actions he was able to take on his own (phasing out price controls, for example, and setting import quotas). He was also anxious for Congress to act quickly. Managing con-

11. Transcripts, VIII, 63, 64, 67.

12. Congressional Quarterly, *Almanac*, 96th Cong., 1st Sess. (Washington, D.C., 1979), 47E.

TABLE 20
The Energy Proposals and Congress, Phase II

Proposal	*Committees*	*Status at End of Session*
1. Windfall Profits Tax	Ways and Means (H) Finance (S)	In conference (passed House, June 28; Senate, Dec. 17)
2. Energy Mobilization Board	Interior and Insular Affairs (H) Interstate and Foreign Commerce (H) Energy and Natural Resources (S)	In conference (passed Senate, Oct. 4; House, Nov. 1)
3. Synthetic Fuels Program	Banking, Finance, and Urban Affairs (H) Banking, Housing, and Urban Affairs (S) Energy and Natural Resources (S) Budget (S)	In conference (passed House, June 26; Senate, Nov. 8)
4. Gasoline Rationing and Conservation	Interstate and Foreign Commerce (H) Energy and Natural Resources (S)	Passed by both houses (Senate, Oct. 17; House, Oct. 23)
5. Solar Energy	Banking, Finance, and Urban Affairs (H) Banking, Housing, and Urban Affairs (S) Energy and Natural Resources (S)	In conference (passed Senate as part of synfuels bill, Nov. 8; not passed by House)

SOURCE: Compiled from material in Congressional Quarterly, *Almanac,* 96th Cong., 1st Sess. (Washington, D.C., 1980), 606–607.

NOTE: (H) = House of Representatives; (S) = Senate

gressional action was complicated by the committee structure in the two houses, however. Table 20 shows that four committees in each house acted on the package, not including the Appropriations committees. While Congress does try to coordinate committee action, the tasks of legislative management are considerable. Committees and subcommittees disassemble integrated programs, and the various parts are acted on at different times.[13]

As shown in Table 20, only one of the major pieces of legislation actually cleared Congress late in 1979—a gasoline rationing and emergency

13. See Charles O. Jones and Randall Strahan, "Energy Politics and Organizational Change," *Legislative Studies Quarterly*, X (May, 1985), 151–79.

conservation program. The others were all still in conference at the end of the session, having passed both houses but in different form. As it happened, conference agreements were reached in 1980 on all the other proposals, but the House rejected the conference report on the Energy Mobilization Board, thus killing the bill. While action was not at the pace desired by the president, the bulk of his program was enacted in modified form. This pleased the White House staff members who had worked hard on these complex issues. They were particularly satisfied that their emphasis on consultation had resulted in increased cooperation. They attributed the defeat of the Energy Mobilization Board to election-year politics, not to their revised method of policy development and majority building.

GETTING A BUDGET

In 1974, Congress fashioned a new congressional budget process that provided for greater coordination in meeting spending and taxing goals. This process was severely strained in 1979 because of inflation and the decision by the Carter administration to reduce the deficit. As one aide explained, achieving these goals placed the administration in direct conflict with the "principles and philosophies" of certain Democrats. The struggle with the budget in 1979 was to be repeated in 1980 and in the subsequent years of the Reagan administration.

> Our '79, '80 and '81 budgets concentrated on the problem of inflation. . . . The debate that took place over those three years was one of the important characterizations of the Carter presidency. That's where all of the various viewpoints, the different attitudes about what the people in the country wanted, and differing views about what was in the best interests of the president really became evident. . . . There was no consistent presidential view on the general problem of inflation, and we all tried to get our own points of view across. We did not step back and try to define a more comprehensive point of view, and serve the president's interests as a staff should.

The president made the decision to hold the deficit below $30 billion, and that figure came to be a target at both ends of the avenue. It could only be achieved if the rates of government spending were reduced. But "the Congress was not used to budgetary restraint or to having a Democratic president coming up there and restraining Democrats whose role in life had basically been to take an expanding pie and spend it."[14] Thus, economic pressures were forcing serious examination of government spending and that examination, in turn, caused budget making on Capitol Hill to become much more difficult.

In anticipation of the problems of supporting a budget in Congress, the White House in late 1978 created a task force to coordinate their efforts. The view from OMB was that it worked. "It not only worked, it worked exceedingly well. Frank [Moore] was extremely pleased with the way it worked. It got folded into the overall White House congressional relations process."[15]

Organizational success did not mean that the budget had smooth sailing in Congress, however. The issues were difficult, and as budget analyst Glenn R. Pascall observed, "the economy and the budget were in collision." He went on to state that "the impacts of inflation were so complex, so confusing, that they sapped the energy that might otherwise have formed a basis for sustained commitment to fiscal moderation and responsibility. By 1979 a turning point indeed seemed to be reached. . . . The budget was being rewritten by inflation and recession."[16] Thus, "uncontrollability" was two-dimensional—entitlement and other programs expanded on their own, and economic instability made budgetary assumptions unreliable. As a consequence, the president's FY 1980 budget fell victim to a form of self-destruction in 1979. His best-laid plans ran afoul of events again, and the budgetary crises that were to dominate presidential-congressional relations during the 1980s had begun.

Tables 21 and 22 show congressional action on the budget resolutions in 1979. Note that the House initially rejected the conference report by a sizable vote, 144 to 260 (see Table 21). Liberal Democrats were displeased by the increases in defense and the decreases in education, training, and other social programs. Thus, the Democrats split their vote 108 to 152 against the conference report (northern Democrats voted 50 to 130 against; southern Democrats, 58 to 22 in favor). It was then proposed that the Senate should amend the conference agreement by cutting defense and international relations by $250 million and increasing social programs by $300 million. The Senate refused to make the cuts but did

14. Transcripts, VI, 7, 18.

15. *Ibid.*, 71.

16. Glenn R. Pascall, "The Carter Legacy" (Typescript in Pascall's possession), 6, 11.

TABLE 21
First Budget Resolution, 1979

Date	House	Senate
Oct. 24, 1978	(President sets goal for federal deficit—below $30 billion)	
Jan. 22, 1979	(President submits FY 1980 budget)	
Jan. 25–Mar. 8 (intermittent)	Hearings—Committee on Budget	
Feb. 6–Mar. 22 (intermittent)		Hearings—Committee on Budget
Apr. 12		Committee on Budget reports resolution
Apr. 13	Committee on Budget reports resolution	
Apr. 23–25		Floor debate on resolution
Apr. 26		Resolution adopted (64–20)
Apr. 30–May 14 (intermittent)	Floor debate on resolution	
May 14	Resolution adopted (220–184)	
May 18	(Conference report)	
May 23	Floor debate; report rejected (144–260)	Floor debate; report amended (72–17)
May 24	Floor action on revised report; vote approving report (202–196)	

SOURCE: Various issues of *Congressional Quarterly Weekly Report,* 1979.

add $350 million for social programs. This revised version of the conference agreement was then passed by the House, 202 to 196.

The congressional budget process calls for a second budget resolution to be passed by September 15. The action on this second resolution was particularly contentious in 1979, due in part to differences in House and Senate procedures. The Senate Committee on the Budget, under the chairmanship of Edmund S. Muskie (D-Maine), decided to invoke the reconciliation procedure by which authorizing committees and the Appropriations Committee are instructed to make cuts. This procedure had not been successful in the past, though it represented the enforcement mechanism for the Budget committees in producing a second budget resolution. After some serious negotiations, a compromise was reached between Muskie and the other committee chairmen, and the resolution passed on September 19 (62 to 36).

TABLE 22
Second Budget Resolution, 1979

Date	*House*	*Senate*
July 10–13		Hearings—Committee on Budget
Aug. 2		Committee on Budget votes to invoke reconciliation procedure (9–4)
Aug. 24		Committee on Budget reports resolution
Sept. 13		Reconciliation resolved (through negotiations between Budget Committee and other committees)
Sept. 14	Committee on Budget reports resolution (no reconciliation procedure)	
Sept. 17–19	Floor debate on resolution	Floor debate on resolution
Sept. 19	Resolution rejected (192–213)	Resolution adopted (62–36)
Sept. 27	Revised resolution adopted (212–206)	
Oct. (intermittent)	(Conference meetings)	
Nov. 2	(Conference report—includes reconciliation)	
Nov. 7		Conference report (with reconciliation) adopted (65–27)
Nov. 8	Conference report (without reconciliation) adopted (205–190)	
Nov. 16		Revised resolution (without reconciliation) adopted (57–20)
Nov. 28	Senate revised resolution adopted (206–186)	

SOURCE: Various issues of *Congressional Quarterly Weekly Report,* 1979.

No effort was made on the House side to invoke the reconciliation procedure, evidencing a less powerful and influential Budget Committee. Without this direction, the situation deteriorated as action moved from the committee to the floor. "Compared to the orderly and thorough Senate budget debate, the House took up its version of the second budget resolution in a disarray that grew through an evening session and culminated in the surprise rejection of the resolution Sept. 19."[17] Thus, the House initially rejected both the first and second resolutions, which was unprecedented in the short history of the congressional budget process. The vote appeared to represent the frustrations of many members with the complicated budgetary situation and with their new procedures. After a week of negotiation, the House voted to approve a slightly modified budget resolution on September 27 by the slim margin of 212 to 206.

The conference deliberations were certain to be lengthy and difficult given the differences between the House and Senate resolutions. It took twenty-three days for them to reach an agreement. The matter of reconciliation was not resolved during that period. Rather, it was left for each chamber to decide. The Senate approved the conference report on November 7 with reconciliation instructions for committees to cut spending. The House of Representatives was unable to agree to reconciliation, in part because it became an intensely partisan issue. In the end, the House agreed to the conference report by the narrow margin of 205 to 190, without reconciliation instructions. The Republican vote was unanimous —145 against the resolution. As indicated in Table 22, the Senate then compromised and omitted reconciliation but included a nonbinding "sense of Congress" advisory to the committees to make cuts. After more partisan wrangling in the House, the resolution was finally passed, 206 to 186. Only three Republicans voted in favor of the resolution. Final passage came on November 28, nearly two and one-half months after the scheduled September 15 deadline for such action.

The problems associated with the Carter budget were compounded by the new congressional procedures. In prior years, the administration and individual committee leaders would have negotiated. The new budget process forced this bargaining to take place at a very high level and on public display. So House Republicans had a forum for pressuring the Democrats to make budget cuts. The combination of a more austere budget and a congressional process that revealed both partisanship and differences resulted in significant delays. These delays cannot strictly be counted as Carter's losses. Rather, they illustrate again the confrontational nature of presidential-congressional relations during the Carter years that would have existed for whoever served in the White House. It

17. *Almanac*, 96th Cong., 1st Sess., 179.

just so happened that, as a Democrat, Jimmy Carter would suffer more criticism from a Congress controlled by his own party.

Budget politics also illustrates the growing independence of Congress. The new budget process was one of the premier reforms during the 1970s. In supporting it, most members really intended to take away some of the president's authority over a function traditionally considered to belong to the executive branch. A congressional budget represented a special challenge to a trustee president, since it presumed an institutional capability that such a president doubted could exist in a legislative body. Can an assembly of delegates produce a comprehensive spending and taxing program that is responsive to the national interest? The behavior of Congress on the budget during 1979 and 1980 tended to confirm Carter's negative response to this question.

CREATING A NEW DEPARTMENT

Creating a Department of Education was very much Carter's sort of proposal. Here was a chance to integrate several different programs into one organization. The president wrote: "Education programs were scattered all over the federal bureaucracy, and there was no way for a coherent policy to be considered or implemented. For those educators who came to Washington to seek help or resolve a question or dispute, it was almost impossible to locate the federal official who was supposed to be responsible."[18] Thus the president endorsed a new department, one that would combine education programs from the Department of Health, Education, and Welfare with those administered by other departments and agencies.

Reactions to the proposal on the Hill and among lobbyists illustrated the crisscrossing of special interests in policy making. The alliance in opposition was unusual and tested the coalition-building capabilities of the Office of Public Liaison headed by Anne Wexler. The American Federation of Teachers (AFT) of the AFL-CIO joined with conservatives to fight the reorganization. The AFT position was born out of classic coalition politics—that is, a separate department would break up the coopera-

18. Carter, *Keeping Faith*, 76.

tion among education, health, and labor groups that had been so successful in the past. Conservatives simply opposed the implied bureaucratic expansion and were prepared to introduce numerous controversial amendments to kill the bill.

The National Education Association (NEA) favored a separate department, as did organizations representing education at the local level. In fact, NEA endorsed Carter for president in 1976 when he announced his support for a Department of Education. It was NEA's first endorsement in history.[19] Thus two important groups in the education community—the AFT and the NEA—were at odds, providing conservatives with an opportunity to defeat the proposal.

Increasing the difficulty surrounding this issue was the opposition of Health, Education, and Welfare Secretary Joseph Califano to the president's position.[20] In this extraordinary situation, there was confusion about who was in charge. A White House aide explained:

> Joe Califano's efforts in opposition to the Department of Education created in-house political problems for NEA among the 1.8 million members. It forced NEA to extract an answer from the president in regard to where the Department of Education issue was going. The attitude of the membership and the leaders of the locals was, "Look, we didn't elect Joe Califano, we elected Jimmy Carter." Jimmy Carter said he was interested in establishing a cabinet level department of education as part of overall government reorganization. All we were getting was media reports about how Joe Califano thought it was a bad idea. Of course we had to do something, so we met with the president and the vice-president, Stu Eizenstat and a few others and raised the question. It was a relatively comfortable meeting with the exception of a bit of tension that was created between Califano and the president. The president made it very clear that he was still president, he remained supportive of the concept and he was directing his reorganization project committee to study it.[21]

Secretary Califano was replaced during the period of congressional action on the Department of Education proposal. His failure to support the proposal was no doubt a contributing factor to his dismissal.

19. Harrison H. Donnelly, "Separate Education Department Proposed," *Congressional Quarterly Weekly Report*, April 22, 1978, p. 987.

20. Carter, *Keeping Faith*, 76. For Califano's account of this matter, see Joseph A. Califano, Jr., *Governing America: An Insider's Report from the White House and the Cabinet* (New York, 1981), 274–93.

21. Transcripts, I, 71.

TABLE 23
Creating a Department of Education, 1978–1979

1978	*House*	*Senate*
Apr. 14	(President's proposal)	
Oct. 12, 13, Mar. 20–May 17 (intermittent)		Hearings—Committee on Governmental Affairs
July 17, 20, 31, Aug. 1, 2	Hearings—Committee on Government Operations	
Aug. 9		Report—Committee on Governmental Affairs
Aug. 25	Report—Committee on Government Operations	
Sept. 19, 20, 26, 28		Floor debate
Sept. 28		Bill approved (72–11)
Oct. 4	Bill pulled from calendar	
1979		
Mar. 27		Report—Committee on Governmental Affairs
Apr. 5, 9, 10, 26, 30		Floor debate
Apr. 30		Bill approved (72–21)
May 14	Report—Committee on Government Operations	
June 7, 11–13, 19; July 11	Floor debate	
July 11	Bill approved (210–206)	
Sept. 13	(Conference report)	
Sept. 24		Conference report adopted (69–22)
Sept. 27	Conference report adopted (215–201)	
Oct. 17	(President signs into law)	

SOURCE: Various issues of *Congressional Quarterly Weekly Report,* 1978–1979.

Table 23 shows the protracted action on the bill in Congress. The Senate approved the proposal by a wide margin in 1978, though not exactly in the form requested by the president. Opponents in the House were successful in preventing a vote, however. Members were anxious to get home in order to campaign, and party leaders had a full agenda to be acted on before adjournment. The Department of Education proposal became one of the victims when opposing members threatened delays.

In 1979 the opponents relied on the tactic of amending the bill to death. In the Senate, Jesse Helms (R-North Carolina) was successful in attaching a school prayer amendment to the bill. Senator Abraham Ribicoff (D-Connecticut), the floor manager for the bill, was quoted as saying that the Helms amendment "would tend to kill the . . . bill."[22] The amendment was removed through a series of parliamentary maneuvers by the majority leader.

If anything, opposition in the House increased between 1978 and 1979. The bill itself barely got out of committee—the vote was 20 to 19. The liaison staff was pressed hard to maintain enough Democratic support to move the bill since several urban Democrats opposed it. Conservatives sought to load the bill down with objectionable amendments, hoping thereby to guarantee its defeat. The amendments touched practically all the divisive issues associated with education. They included: an anti-quota amendment, to prevent so-called reverse discrimination (passed 277 to 126); and anti-forced busing amendment (passed 227 to 135); an amendment limiting the regulatory power of the new department (passed by a voice vote); a voluntary school prayer amendment (passed 255 to 122); two anti-abortion amendments (one passed by voice vote, the other by 257 to 149); an amendment limiting the number of employees in the department (passed 263 to 143). Among the amendments rejected were two by John Erlenborn (R-Illinois)—the first one to name it the Department of Public Education and Youth (DOPEY); the second to name it the Department of Public Education (DOPE).[23]

The situation was difficult for the conferees on this bill. Leaving the House amendments would lose liberal support for the conference report; cutting them risked loss of conservative support. Since the bill passed by only four votes, strategy had to be carefully calculated. As it happened, all amendments were dropped and the conference report was adopted in the House by a vote of 215 to 201. Fourteen Democrats and two Republicans switched from opposition to support of the bill; eight Republicans and three southern Democrats switched the other way. As expected, the Senate passed the conference report overwhelmingly, and a new cabinet department was created.[24]

Thus the president had another success in government reorganization. The lobbying effort by the White House was effective in dealing with a thorny set of issues. Reorganizations tear at the tissue that connects the

22. *Almanac*, 96th Cong., 1st Sess., 469.
23. *Ibid.*, 473.
24. *Ibid.*, 465.

federal government with the private sphere and other governments. However necessary such reforms may be, they receive few plaudits. Often as many people are disappointed as are satisfied. Members of Congress back home do not take credit because the benefits are not easily demonstrated.[25]

SUMMARY

The three cases show improved White House capability in program formulation and coalition building in the context of an ever more independent Congress. The Office of Public Liaison and a more mature and experienced congressional liaison organization contributed to a good record for the administration on some difficult and divisive issues. A system for a trustee president working with Congress was emerging.

Yet, if anything, the problems faced by the Carter administration got steadily worse. Outside events affected the president's management of the policy agenda. He sought to regain the initiative with the reorganization of the White House and the cabinet in July but was only partially successful—some would argue that he was not successful at all. Furthermore, there was evidence that House Democratic leaders were losing control of their large majority. Party unity among the Republicans and a serious division among Democrats resulted in surprise defeats for the Speaker. After a particularly difficult week in mid-September, Speaker O'Neill was quoted as saying: "Everything fell apart. . . . We came back after our August vacation and it was clear Kennedy was going to run [for president]. The members were telling us Carter was weak. What were they going to do? They were thinking, 'How am I going to protect myself?' "[26] The political situation became even more complicated. On November 4, 1979, the U.S. embassy in Teheran was overrun and embassy personnel were taken hostage.

25. On the other hand, Secretary Califano believes that the department "yielded a bumper political crop" for the president, asserting that the NEA "troops" were critical in Carter's victories in Iowa and New Hampshire in 1980 (see Califano, *Governing America*, 292).

26. *Almanac*, 96th Cong., 1st Sess., 15.

THE FOURTH YEAR, 1980

President Carter began his last year on the upswing. His steady decline in popularity during 1979 was reversed dramatically after the occupation of the U.S. embassy in Iran. The Gallup Poll approval rating was at 32 percent before the hostage crisis and 61 percent the following month, "a truly vertiginous rise of twenty-nine points in just one month." International crises often increase support for the president. Austin Ranney observes, "In this instance the mood was intensified by modern communications technology." Television brought Iranian insults directly into American homes, and the audience tended to rally around the president. Ranney quotes Haynes Johnson on this point: "The networks discovered [that] their Iranian broadcasts were attracting enormous new audiences. Iranian coverage, and competition for new angles of it, intensified. The political impact was immense. Attacks on Carter personally by Iranian leaders prominently reported via TV to Americans at home, gave the President a stature he had failed to achieve in three years in office. Carter became the personification of the nation, the symbol of American resolve, the rallying point for Americans at home to respond to insults from abroad."[27]

Nineteen eighty was a year of electoral politics for the trustee president, and, as previously noted, it was a time of accounting. But Carter himself was sequestered in the White House, having determined that the image of a president on the campaign trail was not appropriate at a time of national crisis. As one aide explained, the so-called rose garden strategy emerged as a consequence of a decision to cancel a campaign swing. "It didn't start as a rose garden strategy. It started with the fact that they [the hostages] had only been held a month and we had to announce [that the president was running]. We had a big campaign swing for that week of December 4 when he announced. There were fund raisers and all, and he said 'I just can't do that. Can't run around the country raising money and making political speeches while they had just taken our embassy.' "[28]

The president then cancelled a debate with Senator Kennedy in Iowa, one scheduled before the caucus in January. Again the president was concerned about how it would look to engage in a campaign at a crucial

27. Austin Ranney, "The Carter Administration," in Ranney (ed.), *The American Elections of 1980* (Washington, D.C., 1981), 36, 34–35.

28. Transcripts, XXI, 61.

time. He believed that he would go to Iowa as president but return to Washington as a politician seeking reelection. The Soviet invasion of Afghanistan contributed further weight to his argument. According to one aide, he wanted "to stay on the high ground on these issues" so that he could make what he judged to be unpopular policy choices, such as the grain embargo, boycotting the Olympics, and draft registration.[29] Here was the trustee president torn between his conception of his role and the imperatives of the reelection campaign.

To one White House aide, the Iranian situation appeared almost to present Carter with an escape from reelection politics, so he could be president and not just a politician. "Once the Iranian hostage situation occurred, that dramatically changed the dynamics of everything that happened in the White House. Although this might be hard for people on the outside to believe, it made the political job and the job of the politicians much more difficult. This was something that he was almost exclusively involved in. Everything else got shunted aside. People in the White House, particularly as this issue grew, suffered from a myopia on the subject. Nothing else, including politics, could get through the doors." This aide has overstated the case, to be sure. The president sought to fulfill all his responsibilities in spite of his being absorbed by the crisis. Perhaps the event could be turned to the president's advantage, at least in the short run. Nelson W. Polsby observed: "The hostage crisis was the sheer gift of circumstances and could be exploited, though not anticipated."[30]

The campaign aides naturally sought to take advantage of the issue, but as the hostage crisis wore on, "it got to be a real trap." The president was "just there" in the White House while Senator Kennedy campaigned against him. Apparently the principal campaign aides did not anticipate that the crisis might last and therefore they had no contingency plans (though some aides opposed cancelling the Iowa debate as the wrong decision from a campaign standpoint). "When he made that decision [to cancel the debate], neither he nor any of us dreamed that the thing was going to go on for weeks or months, and then ultimately for over a year. . . . We put ourselves in a hell of a box." Beyond immobilizing the president in campaign politics, the prolonged rose garden strategy had an-

29. Transcripts, VII, 85.

30. Transcripts, XII, 122–23; Nelson W. Polsby, "The Democratic Nomination," in Ranney (ed.), *The American Elections of 1980*, p. 47.

other effect. "The perception set in, whether right or wrong, and I think it was mostly wrong, in the middle of the primary season that he was using Iran for political purposes. That perception, once it had taken hold, took an enormous toll on him politically. And the rest is history. I've always been convinced that he was really single minded about Iran. . . . He cared about being reelected to be sure, but he disciplined himself to put everything else out of his mind until he could solve this problem."[31]

The president's absorption with Iran resulted in less attention than might have been otherwise paid to the domestic affairs that tend to preoccupy Congress. Foreign policy matters now came to dominate his time even more. "There were in effect three different White Houses: a campaign White House, the Iranian crisis White House and the domestic policy White House." It was the last that dealt with Congress. Of course, the president was mostly involved in the second White House. And the first suffered, in part because of "Jordan's lack of time": "Ham was calling us from all the capitals of Europe to direct the campaign," since he was intimately involved in the negotiations to release the hostages.[32]

Those staff members with direct interest in the passage of a domestic program thought that the system of development continued to improve. One aide also judged that "we had a very good year on the Hill in the sense that nothing bad happened." He pointed out that White House staff members were able to go to Congress and "talk to people in their offices and say, 'The President doesn't want this' " and "kill a couple of very controversial pieces of legislation." Part of the success was due to having gotten "consensus in the White House": "We just were beginning for the first time to do the things that a White House ought to be able to do well, which is largely tactical. It ought to be a tactical place. I thought we had a very, very good year." The same was said of the departments and agencies. "Everybody had a common objective [in 1980] from the lowliest deputy secretary to the President."[33]

In analyzing the larger context for this perceived success, one finds a preoccupied president, a more limited agenda, and a reorganized administration (cabinet and White House staff). "We weren't going to the Pres-

31. Transcripts, XXI, 62, VII, 85–86, XII, 123.

32. Transcripts, VII, 87. For details, see Hamilton Jordan, *Crisis: The Last Year of the Carter Presidency* (New York, 1982).

33. Transcripts, XIV, 70, 71.

ident all that much in 1980 for major new comprehensive decisions . . . we weren't going to the President with these gigantic memos any more. Most of his time was taken up with foreign policy . . . and the campaign. We tried to interfere with him as little as possible. The memos were smaller, the time we took up with him I think was smaller. . . . We were just kept out of the picture [regarding Iran] pretty much and just had to go about doing our business."[34]

Meanwhile on Capitol Hill, upcoming congressional campaigns focused attention on personal political futures, just as Speaker O'Neill had predicted. Thus as the year progressed and the president's popularity began to decline again, congressional Democrats became concerned about political survival. Irwin B. Arieff of the *Congressional Quarterly* found Democrats separating themselves from the president's reelection effort. "Alarmed by the steady slump in Carter's popularity—and cognizant of Carter's cool attitude toward their own survival—Democratic members of Congress found it relatively painless to disassociate their 1980 campaigns from that of the White House. Aware of the hard feelings between the two branches, Carter himself on July 29, 1980, volunteered to stay away from Democrats' districts if they thought his presence would harm their chances in 1980."[35]

The president's State of the Union address reflected the foreign policy crises of the moment. He observed that "the 1980s have been born in turmoil, strife, and change." The emphasis was on Iran, the Soviet challenge, the Middle East, Pakistan, selective service, and human rights. Space was allotted in the following way: international issues and foreign policy (77 percent; 36 percent in 1979); energy and economic issues (18 percent, equally divided); summary and closing (5 percent). The economy was mentioned last, with little indication that the president foresaw the difficulties that lay ahead. No major proposals were offered. In fact, the principal stress was on continuing past policies. As before, a lengthy document listing legislative priorities was forwarded to Congress before the address.

34. *Ibid.*, 72.

35. Irwin B. Arieff, "Carter and Congress: Strangers to the End," in Congressional Quarterly, *Almanac*, 96th Cong., 2nd Sess. (Washington, D.C., 1980), 5.

TABLE 24
Major Events Affecting the Carter Presidency, 1980

Date	*Event*
Jan. 4	Announcement of grain embargo and other sanctions against the Soviet Union
Jan. 20	Letter to U.S. Olympic Committee urging withdrawal from Moscow games
Jan. 21	Iowa caucus—Carter wins
Jan. 23	State of the Union address
Jan. 28	First budget sent to Congress
Feb. 20	U.S. withdrawal from Olympics
Feb. 26	New Hampshire primary—Carter wins
Mar. 18	Illinois primary—Carter wins
Mar. 25	New York primary—Kennedy wins
Apr. 7	U.S. breaks diplomatic relations with Iran
Apr. 21	Secretary of State Cyrus Vance submits resignation
Apr. 24	Hostage rescue attempt fails
June 3	California primary—Kennedy wins
July 16	Republicans nominate Reagan
Aug. 4	News conference on Billy Carter
Aug. 13	Democrats nominate Carter
Oct. 28	Carter-Reagan debate
Nov. 4	Reagan wins a landslide victory

Table 24 lists the major events during 1980. It is an accounting of the steady deterioration of Carter's political situation after an auspicious start. The early primary victories over Kennedy were encouraging. Then in late March, Kennedy won the New York primary, and April brought discouraging news from Iran—the failure of the rescue attempt. In June, Kennedy won the California primary. The president had enough delegates to be renominated, but the Kennedy challenge, the nagging hostage crisis, and a deteriorating economic situation were crippling blows to his chances for reelection.

As has been emphasized, the president's work with Congress in 1980 was overshadowed by Iran and the election. His most important contact during the year involved the budget and a pending economic crisis. Thus the choice of a legislative topic for this last year of the Carter administration was obvious.

BUILDING A BUDGET

The budget process in 1980 challenged the decision-making capacities of both the White House and Congress. Economic conditions steadily worsened. Assumptions upon which the budget was built proved to be so far off the mark that significant adjustments had to be made along the way. Thus, for example, when the inflation rate in January soared to 18.2 percent (on an annualized basis), the administration scrapped its initial budget and went back to work. As in 1979, "the budget was being rewritten by inflation and recession."

White House aides discussed the seriousness of the economic situation following the submission of the initial budget to Congress. First, it was pointed out that the market was reacting to miscalculations from 1979 (the fiscal year 1980 budget) when it became clear in 1980 that deficits would be much higher than predicted.

> What people reacted to was the '80 budget in which we had originally put in thirty billion a year earlier [as a deficit] and was now sixty for no one single reason. I mean it wasn't so much anybody made a policy decision, it was just higher inflation, higher interest rates, except for defense [where a policy decision had been made to increase]. We clearly just missed that. Everything was happening. Inflation was heating up, the oil stuff was coming right through, I mean they were really accumulating in the price indexes.
>
> The market saw that sixty billion [deficit], and said, "What the heck, we couldn't believe you last year, why should we believe you this year?" The bond market was drying up. For a few months the rate of inflation was running . . . at 18 percent. . . . This was all combined with the fact that this was the year in which Carter . . . had announced the big defense budget increase.[36]

Given these discouraging conditions, some of Carter's economic advisers thought it important that an effort be made to balance the budget (the first Carter budget projected a $15.8 billion deficit). The president had promised to balance the budget by the end of his first term. By the first quarter of 1980, economic and market uncertainty contributed an urgency to this goal. In an extraordinary series of meetings, White House and treasury officials met with House and Senate Budget Committee

36. Transcripts, XI, 43–44.

members to hammer out an agreement on a new anti-inflationary budget, one that would be in balance. "We had [several] days of meetings with the congressional leadership, in an atmosphere of universal recognition of the need to come in with a budget that appeared to be balanced." One aide explained the process:

> We felt we had to act. Out of that came one experience that I thought was rather good. I'm not sure it could be repeated. And in the process of putting together a new budget, three months after the other one is out for the first time in my memory, we sat down in advance in detail sixteen hours a day for a week with the major Democratic congressional leaders and put together a package that they had agreed to more or less in advance, we'd all agreed to. It was the nearest thing to a parliamentary agreement I've ever seen.

The meetings were held on Capitol Hill with the "paper . . . generated mainly by Jim McIntyre's people [at OMB]. . . . The exercise consisted primarily in line by line going through the budget."[37]

The sequence of presidential-congressional budget action is outlined in Table 25. Following the meetings with Democratic leaders, the president announced the new anti-inflation program on March 14. It included spending cuts, restraints on credit, voluntary wage and price standards, a ten-cent gasoline tax, and various measures to encourage greater productivity and savings. Then a second budget was submitted on March 31. As revised, the budget projected a $16.5 billion surplus. This shift was primarily based on a combination of cuts and the gasoline tax increase.

President Carter believed that a deal had been struck with Congress. He wrote in his diary on March 13: "In the evening I met for an hour or so with the key Senate and House Democrats who had worked on the anti-inflation package. It was an inspirational meeting. The members of Congress were so proud of themselves. . . . [They have been] willing to cooperate. . . . The outcome of it, I think, will be a good anti-inflation proposal." Two months later, the president was highly critical of Congress. Delays were apparent, and it was becoming evident that Congress would not support his gasoline tax. His diary entry on May 13 showed impatience:

> I had a disappointing meeting with the Democratic congressional leadership.

37. Transcripts, IX, 94, XI, 44, IX, 98.

TABLE 25
Sequence of Budget Action, 1980

Date	*Event*
Jan. 28	FY 1981 budget sent to Congress
Late Feb.–early Mar.	White House—congressional meetings on budget
Mar. 14	Carter anti-inflation program announced
Mar. 31	Revised FY 1981 budget sent to Congress
June 12	First budget resolution passed (with reconciliation and showing balance)
Nov. 20	Second budget resolution passed (with $27.4 billion deficit)
Dec. 3	Reconciliation bill passed

SOURCE: Various issues of *Congressional Quarterly Weekly Report,* 1980.

There is no discipline, and growing fragmentation in Congress. The Senate voted yesterday, for instance, for a budget that would be balanced only if part of the oil-import fee was to be used, and at the same time voted with only 19 dissents to put a restraint on the imposition of the import fee. . . . Jim McIntyre feels that they may not even get . . . appropriations bills in final form until after the election in November. They are running out of time, and I am running out of patience. This is a new low in performance for the Congress since I've been in office.[38]

For President Carter, the gasoline tax was "a test case" of congressional support for the new budget. He was disappointed. He had the authority to impose an oil import fee, and his plan was to pass this cost on to consumers through a surcharge of ten cents per gallon of gasoline. Presumably the tax would encourage greater conservation and produce needed revenue to balance the budget. Congress, on the other hand, had the authority to disapprove any such action with a joint resolution, subject in turn to veto by the president. Both of these things happened. The House and Senate passed disapproval resolutions by wide margins (376 to 30 and 73 to 16, respectively). President Carter predictably vetoed the resolution. The two houses then overrode the veto, the first override of a Democratic president's veto since 1952. Congressional action was swift—the House vote came just two hours after the veto. "The boisterous legislators hooted and sarcastically applauded the White House messenger carrying the veto."[39]

38. Carter, *Keeping Faith*, 527, 529.
39. *Almanac*, 96th Cong., 2nd Sess., 273.

TABLE 26
First Budget Resolution, 1980

Date	*House*	*Senate*
Jan. 28	(President submits FY 1981 budget)	
Jan. 29–Mar. 6 (intermittent)	Hearings—Committee on Budget	
Jan. 30–Mar. 11 (intermittent)		Hearings—Committee on Budget
Mar. 26	Committee on Budget reports resolution	
Apr. 3		Committee on Budget reports resolution
Apr. 29–May 1, 6, 7	Floor debate on resolution	
May 7	Resolution adopted (225–193)	
May 6–9, 12		Floor debate on resolution
May 12		Resolution adopted (68–28)
May 23	(Conference report)	
May 28	(President announces opposition to conference report)	
May 29	Conference report rejected (141–242)	
June 11	(Revised conference report)	
June 12	Conference report adopted (205–195)	Conference report adopted (61–26)

SOURCE: Various issues of *Congressional Quarterly Weekly Report*, 1980.

Carter felt betrayed by the Democratic leadership in Congress. He later wrote that "the congressional leaders simply abandoned their commitment and capitulated" to the oil companies. Charles A. Vanik (D-Ohio), who chaired the House Ways and Means subcommittee that reported the disapproval resolution, identified the following arguments for abolishing the fee: "its inflationary impact; its questionable conservation effects; and its serious legal and administrative problems." He added another important political reason: "Candidates for public office do not believe they can survive the burden of a 10-cents-per-gallon gasoline tax."[40]

Unquestionably, President Carter was in a difficult political situation. His spending reductions were attractive to many Republicans on the Hill, but his proposals to increase revenue were unlikely to find much support anywhere in Congress. The Republicans would support Carter if it would help them in an election year. In fact, the first budget resolution in 1980

40. Carter, *Keeping Faith*, 529; *Almanac*, 96th Cong., 2nd Sess., 274.

TABLE 27
Second Budget Resolution, 1980

Date	*House*	*Senate*
July 22–24		Hearings—Committee on Budget
Sept. 3		Committee on Budget reports resolution
Nov. 11	Committee on Budget reports resolution	
Nov. 18	Resolution adopted (203–191)	
Nov. 19		Resolution adopted (48–46)
Nov. 19	(Conference report)	
Nov. 20	Conference report adopted (voice vote)	Conference report adopted (50–38)

SOURCE: Various issues of *Congressional Quarterly Weekly Report,* 1980.

did receive Republican support in the committee and on the House floor. But relying on Republican votes was dangerous for a Democratic president in an election year.

Tables 26 and 27 provide an overview of the lengthy legislative action on the budget resolutions in 1980. Several factors contributed to the delay and confusion but most of these were a direct consequence of the fact that 1980 was an election year. Representative Paul Simon (D-Illinois), a member of the House Committee on the Budget, discussed the problems of that year in a statement that was remarkably prophetic (the remarks were made in late February):

> One of the immediate [problems] right now—and this would be true in any election year, when a president is running for reelection—is that the budget tends to be a somewhat political document and that it probably understates . . . the deficit figures. We also have a second problem in that members of the House and Senate want to balance the budget, but as soon as you get down to statistics, they are very reluctant to modify the specifics. And we have a third problem. We do not have, on the House side, a counterpart to Senator Henry Bellmon [R-Oklahoma, who was ranking member of the Senate Committee on the Budget]. Henry Bellmon works with Ed Muskie and has produced, on the Senate side, bipartisan support of budget action. On the House side, that has not emerged. As a result, we have a real "squeaker" every time. Sometimes we get defeated the first time around. So it becomes very, very difficult to get a budget passed on the House side. Another problem we face—really two problems combined—is that there are two major areas of expenditure: defense, and then the various welfare programs. . . . These items are destined for substantial increases.

The election, partisanship, guns versus butter, balanced-budget rhetoric—these surely were part of the politics of budgeting in Congress in 1980. They are not altogether compatible forces. Former representative Robert Giaimo (D-Connecticut), chairman of the House Budget Committee in 1980, observed: "Somehow we have got to force our colleagues to stop talking thrift one day . . . but then spending the remainder of the year voting for every program that comes down the pike."[41]

In 1980 the decision was made to use the reconciliation process to enforce limits established in the first budget resolution. Using that process at the earlier stage was rejected by the House in 1979. Reconciliation was originally designed as a device to enforce the second budget resolution. It established guidelines for the authorizing and appropriations committees. But, as Allen Schick points out, trying to reconcile spending with budget targets in September is difficult. It occurs too late. "By the time reconciliation was supposed to be completed, the new fiscal year was about to start." Thus, the decision was made in 1980 to move reconciliation forward to the first budget resolution. Chairman Giaimo explained it this way:

> So what we need is additional teeth. We need to say, "This is the total amount we're going to spend this year. Here is the pie. You cut it up and eat it the way you want, but there is no *more*. The only time there will be any more is when there is such a grave emergency that you will be willing to bite hard and vote on a resolution to breach your own, self-imposed ceilings." Reconciliation? We are going to try to incorporate that. I certainly want to. . . . But I think we're going to need more help to incorporate the reconciliation process into the budget process.[42]

It is apparent from the timetable outlined in Tables 26 and 27 that the process did not work smoothly in 1980. The first budget resolution is supposed to pass by May 15, the second by September 15. In fact, the first was not passed until June 12, the second not until November 20 (fifty days into the new fiscal year).

41. Remarks made at a conference at the Center for the Study of American Business, Washington University, St. Louis. See *The Congressional Budget Process: Some Views from the Inside* (St. Louis, 1980), 51–52, 57.

42. Allen Schick, *Reconciliation and the Congressional Budget Process* (Washington, D.C., 1981), 5; *The Congressional Budget Process*, 65.

Perhaps more than any other legislation in 1980, the budget reflected the state of presidential-congressional relations. The politics of managing the economy would be divisive, particularly in an election year. Democrats in Congress were on their own, many of them fearful of electoral defeat. The House even postponed enactment of a second budget resolution until after the election because the earlier promise of a balanced budget could not be realized. The Senate Budget Committee reported a budget resolution with a $17.9 billion deficit on September 3, but that figure ignored the probability of a tax cut reducing revenues in 1981. Thus, Congress sought to finesse the electoral effects of a politically damaging budget by postponing the final decision. As it happened, many Democrats in both the House and Senate went down to defeat along with President Carter and then had to return to Washington to finish their work.

SUMMARY

Irwin Arieff had this to say about Carter and Congress at the end of 1980: "As he left office after four years in the nation's capital, Jimmy Carter remained a stranger in a strange land."[43] Carter probably would not have wished it to be otherwise. He was unwilling to become a part of the Washington establishment. Indeed, as he read his mandate, to have accepted the dominant norms would violate his trusteeship.

In 1979 and 1980, events appeared to set the pace and the White House was never able to take charge. An effort was made in 1980 to catch up with an overheated economy, but the budgetary adjustments came too late, as is acknowledged by Carter's economic advisers. Therefore, budget politics in Congress developed a life independent of the president's wishes.[44]

43. Arieff, "Carter and Congress," 3.

44. It is interesting that Carter's principal political aide Hamilton Jordan does not even have entries in his index for *budget, Congress, House of Representatives*, or *Senate*, despite the fact that his book is about "the last year of the Carter presidency."

SUPPORT IN CONGRESS: CARTER IN RETROSPECT

At the end of each session of Congress, the *Congressional Quarterly* staff calculate a presidential support score, that is, the level of support in roll call votes that members of Congress give key elements of the president's program. In his final year in office, President Carter received his lowest presidential support score, 75.1 percent. As a matter of fact, however, his scores varied little during the four years—from a low of 75.1 percent to a high of 78.3 percent and an average of 76.4 percent.[45] In his book, President Carter concludes that these scores suggest that he "did reasonably well" in his "overall relationship with Congress." He noted that Johnson, "the masterful congressional manipulator," had an average support score "that was only a little higher—82 percent."[46] One must be exceedingly cautious about relying too heavily on such scores. The roll call votes that are the basis for the scores are not weighed for their importance; changes in legislation are not recorded (a presidential proposal may be drastically altered on Capitol Hill, and yet the president may still claim it as his); some important votes are excluded simply because the president's position cannot be identified. Still, analysis of these scores can provide a profile of support, indicate its source, and suggest variations among presidents.

Figure 5 plots the support scores for seven administrations—the Eisenhower first and second, Kennedy-Johnson, Johnson, Nixon first, Nixon-Ford, and Carter. Note that the Kennedy-Johnson administration (1961–1965) showed steady improvement even from a relatively high score in the first year. Conversely, the Nixon-Ford scores are the lowest on the chart, with 61 percent the highest score received. Eisenhower's second term produced the most erratic scoring—68 to 76, then a huge drop to 52 after the 1958 election, and to 65 in the final year. The other four administrations—including Carter's—are bunched together after the first year. In fact, the average support scores for second, third, and fourth years were: Eisenhower first, 74; Johnson, 78; Nixon first, 72; and Carter, 77. In 1977, Carter's score was just slightly better than Nixon's in his first year despite the Democrats' better than two-to-one majority in the House and a twenty-

45. The scores here are taken from the *Almanac* for the appropriate years.
46. Carter, *Keeping Faith*, 88.

Figure 5

PRESIDENTIAL SUPPORT SCORES—EISENHOWER TO CARTER

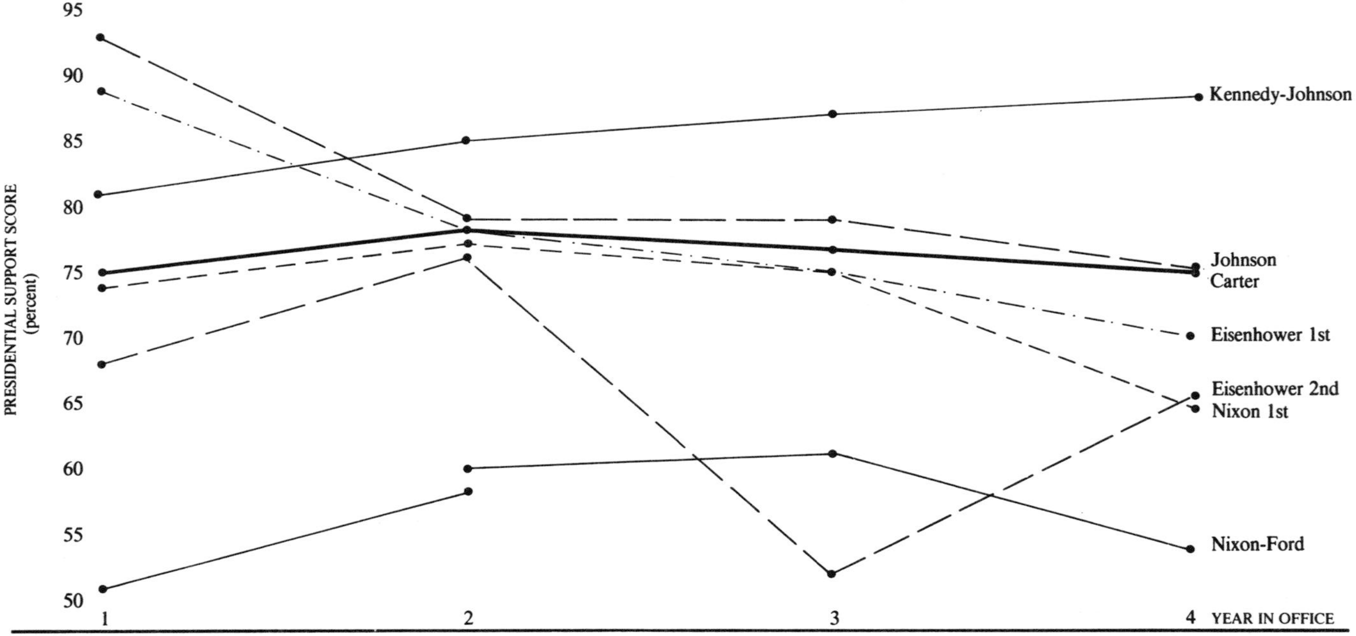

SOURCES: Congressional Quarterly, *Almanac*, various volumes for the Congresses involved.

four-seat edge in the Senate, an advantage nearly equal to Johnson's in 1965. Nixon, on the other hand, faced a Congress in which both chambers were controlled by the other party. Thus, once more we see the importance of that first year of the Carter administration.

It seemed that Carter's overall evaluation of Congress included a slightly more critical attitude toward the Senate than toward the House. Carter compared himself favorably with several senators when he was thinking about running for the presidency. His political and policy conflicts with Senator Kennedy were certain to leave negative impressions. And some of the most difficult legislative battles—the Panama Canal treaties, natural gas deregulation, the SALT II treaty—occurred in the Senate. Yet President Carter received a higher support score in the Senate than the House in three of the four years of his administration. His average Senate support score for the whole period was six points higher than that for the House. The great master of the Senate—Lyndon B. Johnson—had a lower average support score in the Senate than in the House for his five years in office. Figures 6 and 7 show that Senate Democrats supported the president with higher support scores than did House Democrats in three of four years and that Senate Republicans had higher support scores than did House Republicans all four years. Kennedy and Johnson consistently received a lower percentage of support from Senate Democrats when compared to House Democrats; they did somewhat better with Senate Republicans as compared to House Republicans.

Analysis of support scores by region shows that, as was the case for the other Democratic presidents, Carter's southern support is low. Southern Democrats in the House had the lowest presidential support scores for all four years of the administration, and southern Democrats in the Senate had the lowest scores in three of four years. On the other hand, the Senate scores show that Carter was able to attract markedly higher support among southern Democrats than was either Kennedy or Johnson. And though his average House score was below that of the other two presidents, the fall-off from the other regional scores was much less. Kennedy averaged 81 percent support in the other regions and 60 percent in the South—a 21-point difference. The comparable scores for Johnson were 76 and 55, also a 21-point difference. For Carter, the scores were 67 and 53—a 14-point difference. Since Carter's scores were uniformly lower, his southern score fell below that of the two other presidents, but the actual *proportion* of southern support to his overall support score was higher.

Figure 6
CONGRESSIONAL DEMOCRATIC SUPPORT FOR DEMOCRATIC PRESIDENTS

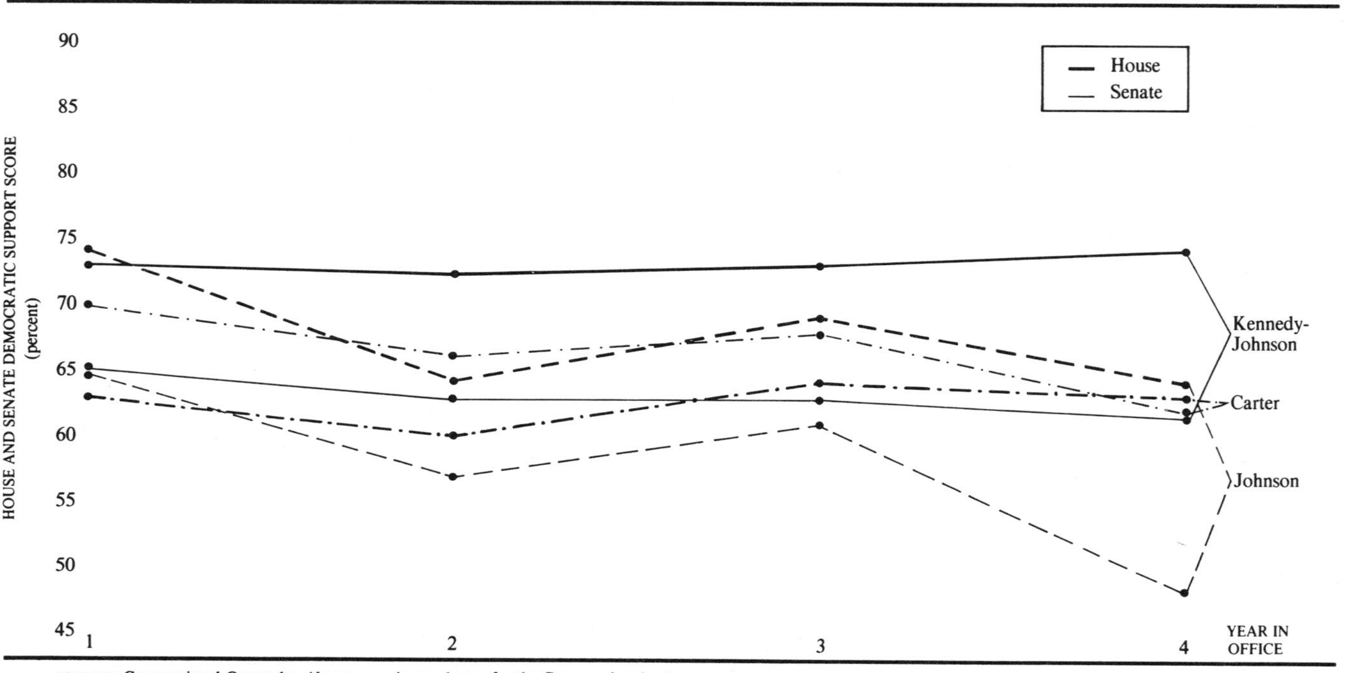

SOURCES: Congressional Quarterly, *Almanac*, various volumes for the Congress involved.

Figure 7
CONGRESSIONAL REPUBLICAN SUPPORT FOR DEMOCRATIC PRESIDENTS

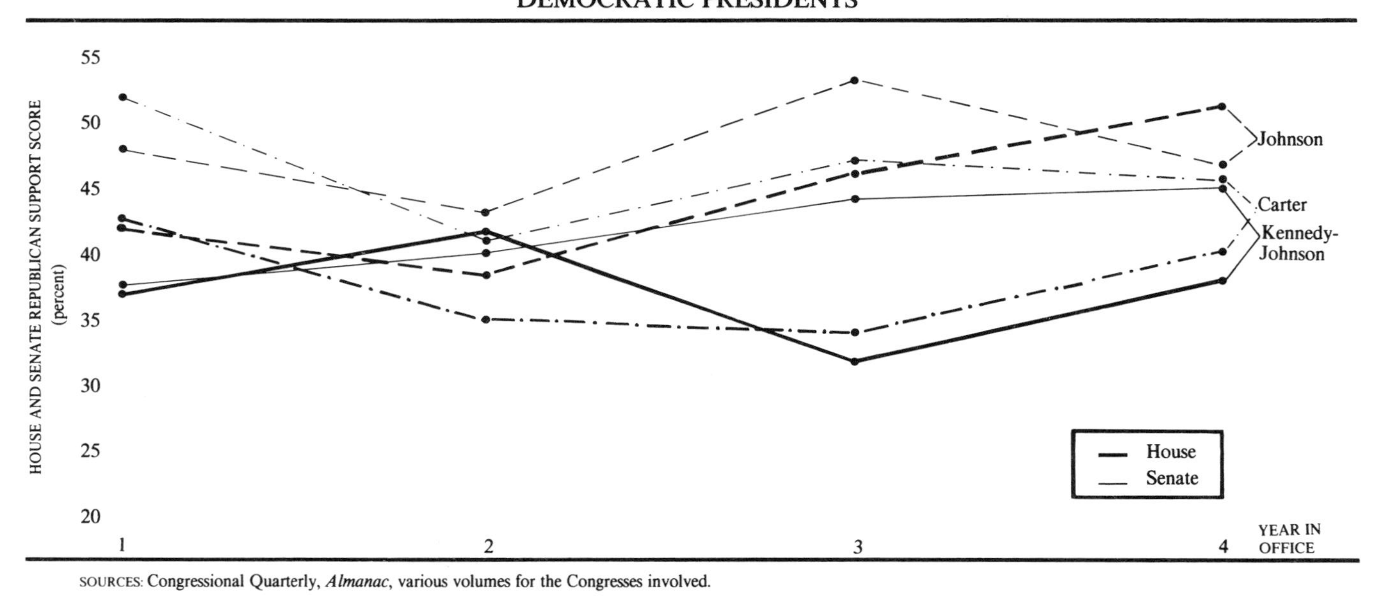

SOURCES: Congressional Quarterly, *Almanac*, various volumes for the Congresses involved.

TABLE 28
Average Presidential Support Scores by Region

	*Kennedy**	*Johnson***	*Carter*
House Democrats			
East	82	79	67
West	81	73	65
South	60	55	53
Midwest	81	75	68
Senate Democrats			
East	78	65	74
West	68	60	66
South	50	49	60
Midwest	71	63	69

SOURCE: Congressional Quarterly *Almanacs,* various volumes for the Congresses involved.
*For three years
**For five years

Still, it is interesting that this president from the Deep South did not do even better with his southern colleagues (see Table 28).

Analysis of these scores provides some surprises—the similarity of Carter's second, third, and fourth year scores to those of three other administrations; the greater support in the Senate as compared with that in the House; the limited support from southern Democrats for a Deep South president.[47] It is tempting to speculate about what might have happened had Carter been more successful in taking advantage of large congressional majorities during 1977 or in pressing his advantage with the Senate and southern Democrats. It is not inconceivable that greater harmony during that first year might have produced a curve similar to, or even more positive than, that of Kennedy-Johnson (1961–1965). However, any such speculation drives one back to who Carter is and what he was trying to accomplish. The president himself apparently believes that conflict with Congress was inevitable. Therefore, imagining conditions under which it was absent appears to be an exercise that drastically changes the man and his mission.

47. Richard Fleisher and Jon R. Bond rely on a predictive model for judging how well Carter did in the House during his first year. They conclude that he did less well than might have been expected—but that Reagan did less well too (see "Assessing Presidential Support in the House: Lessons from Reagan and Carter," *Journal of Politics*, XLV [August, 1983], 745–58).

☆8☆

"A Trust from Providence"

But [a representative's] unbiased opinion, his enlightened conscience, he ought not to sacrifice to you. . . . These he does not derive from your pleasure—no, nor from the law and the constitution. They are a trust from Providence, for the abuse of which he is deeply answerable.

—Edmund Burke,
Bristol, November 3, 1774

This study has proceeded from the fundamental propositions that a president will organize his congressional relations to suit his political experience, policy goals, and personal style, and that events will affect that organization and its performance. Accepting these propositions encourages one to understand and not merely critique the Carter experience. No president is exactly like another. Jimmy Carter was notably different, and in ways not always acceptable in Washington. In fact, his special nature appeared to prompt criticism because he did not ignore his political experience, policy goals, and personal style in organizing to deal with Congress. Seemingly it was permissible for Johnson to be as close as he was to Congress and for Nixon to be as distant as he was, but it was not permissible for Carter to remain the outsider while he resided in the White House.

Surely, there was no mistaking the president's intentions. He forcefully stated his mission and his judgment about current national policymaking before he entered the White House. And he held to his views throughout his term. *He* was not enigmatic, as is claimed in one account.[1] Rather, his being in the White House posed an enigma for others.

The president was never bashful about criticizing the dominant style of bargaining in American politics. He was distressed by policy makers' attachments to the special interests. In musing about America's success as a nation, Carter gives no credit to political leaders: "Knowing how confused and fragmented the system is, how intense the forces are that tend to induce ill-advised decisions, and how fallible the leaders who serve in public office, it is almost a miracle how well our nation survives and prospers.

1. Hedley Donovan, "The Enigmatic President," *Time*, May 6, 1985, p. 24.

The answer lies in the bountiful blessings of our natural and financial resources, the wisdom of the forefathers who shaped our government and the inherent strength of our people."[2] "Fallible" leaders are clearly a part of the problem. That the Founding Fathers shaped a government that facilitates fragmentation through diverse representation of "forces" is not acknowledged, if it is understood at all. Certainly the politicians get no credit for the miracle, for making a "confused and fragmented . . . system" work. Jimmy Carter believed in an approach that would reshape national policy-making by not succumbing to the "forces." Such an approach was strong, not weak, according to this president. Therefore accepting advice to rely on old Washington hands would result ultimately in defeat for him and the system, not victory. Indeed, it was far better to lose for the right reasons than to win for the wrong reasons.

Accompanying Carter's lofty mission is a perspective on defeat and an assurance that history will correct the record. In fact, the celebrated cellist Slava Rostropovich made this point at the last White House banquet for Carter. As recorded in the president's diary: "Slava Rostropovich gave an excellent little speech at our table, pointing out that the masses of people were often wrong. . . . He pointed out that the masses made a mistake on November the 4th, as they had when they rejected Beethoven's Ninth Symphony, rejected *La Traviata*, and in the first performance of *Tosca* the audience reacted against it so violently that they couldn't even raise the curtain for the third act. He said history was going to treat my administration the same way they did Verdi, Puccini, and Beethoven. It was beautiful."[3]

Performing as the trustee encourages one to reject a politics based on bargaining among special interests with inside access to decision makers. The trustee, in fact, has to protect his or her outsider status. In his study of the early Senate career of William Proxmire (D-Wisconsin), Ralph K. Huitt identified an "outsider role" for a senator who chose not to be in the so-called inner club of the Senate:

> The Outsider feels impelled to stand for principle absolutely, preferring defeat on those terms to half-a-loaf. He likes to tell people what they should and frequently do not want to hear. He is never so confident of the soundness of his opinions as when he holds them alone. He is as comfortable alone against the crowd as the Senate type is in the bosom of the club; indeed he is probably happiest when he stands

2. Jimmy Carter, *Keeping Faith: Memoirs of a President* (New York, 1982), 89.
3. *Ibid.*, 594.

by himself against powerful and wrong-headed foes. As a consequence few people, in the body or outside, are lukewarm toward him; they tend to like or dislike him strongly.[4]

Although Huitt is describing a different man in a different political setting, he has identified many of the characteristics that apply to President Carter and his approach to his job. The essential point is that *those in the outsider role see it as a strength, not a weakness.* As is the case with the insider or other roles, the outsider role is a consequence of meeting expectations, those of others who are important to the person in question as well as the person's own. Jimmy Carter could persuasively argue that he was *expected* to behave as an outsider in Washington—not an insider. He believed that he won by disassociating himself from Washington politics and therefore he drew his strength from outside, for example, from the town meetings and telephone chats with ordinary people and from his own personal experiences, including his religion.

Fidelity to my original proposition—that presidents organize congressional relations to suit political experience, policy goals, and personal style—requires tolerance of this independence or trusteeship model even when employed by a Democratic president encouraged to remain an outsider in dealing with a Democratic Congress. I grant that it is not easy for the Washington insider to accept this behavior. But we really limit our capacity for understanding the most interesting aspects of this presidency by refusing to concede the importance of political context and personal motivations. To wish Jimmy Carter to be Lyndon Johnson is understandable. President Johnson was judged particularly successful in his early dealings with Congress. But it is by no means clear that Senator Johnson could have won the nomination under the circumstances of the 1976 election—even in competition with Jimmy Carter. One simply cannot escape the political conditions that facilitated the nomination of Jimmy Carter. A post-Watergate mood encouraged Democrats in their new plebiscitary nomination system to look outside Washington. In fact, the record shows that Carter defeated several congressional Democrats in his quest for the nomination, including one who might be considered closest to a Johnson-type/Senate insider, *i.e.*, Henry Jackson of Wash-

4. Ralph K. Huitt, "The Outsider Role in the Senate," in Huitt and Robert L. Peabody (eds.), *Congress: Two Decades of Analysis* (New York, 1969), 107.

ington. Jackson bowed out of the race on May 1 (see Figure 2) but was eliminated before that date. It is also worth recalling in this connection that Johnson failed to win the nomination on his own in 1960 and was an incumbent president in 1964 when he was nominated.

I have sought to structure this analysis to comprehend Carter's approach and the conditions from which it developed. This quest dictated the organization of the book and has produced the following conclusions:

1. The antipolitical attitudes attributed to President Carter are, in fact, better understood as a devotion to trusteeship politics, characterized by an independent or free-agent style, a national focus, and a comprehensive or integrative method (at least where particular issues are concerned).
2. President Carter's trusteeship approach was rooted in his earlier political experiences, which were essentially negative with regard to legislators' electoral connection and the kind of bargaining this connection fostered.
3. Carter's nomination and election as president tended to reinforce his independent style. He was, in his view, a president with a mandate to change national politics and policy making.
4. Congress reacted to the events of the 1960s and 1970s with unprecedented reform, preparing itself to participate broadly in national policy making and to resist pressures to ratify policy initiatives from the president.
5. Carter selected issues and organized his congressional relations to suit the expectations of a model trustee president.
    a. Agenda setting: Politically difficult issues were identified for Congress to act on.
    b. Program development: Stress was placed on organizing an effective process with only limited participation by or consultation with members of Congress.
    c. Program support: Coalition building occurred outside Congress and typically was done on an issue-by-issue basis.
    d. Congressional liaison: Those who had direct and continuing liaison with members of Congress acted as translators and mediators between a president and a Congress committed to different forms of politics. They also had to protect the president's independence while building support for his programs.

6. The organization of this trustee president's congressional relations included important roles for the Domestic Policy Staff, the Office of Management and Budget, and the Office of Public Liaison, in addition to the Office of Congressional Liaison (and the liaison staffs of the departments and agencies).
7. Analysis of selected legislative confrontations between President Carter and Congress tends to confirm this portrait of trusteeship politics and produces the following observations:
   a. President Carter understood and represented the consolidative issues of the era, ones that were sure to cause problems for a Democratic president working with a Democratic Congress.
   b. As practiced in the first year, trusteeship politics contributed to negative impressions of the Carter White House that were impossible to dispel in subsequent years.
   c. Many efforts were made by the Carter White House after the first year to accommodate criticism and to establish a more effective decision-making process and liaison operation.
   d. During the Ninety-sixth Congress, events came to determine the president's agenda and threaten the credibility of his trusteeship.

What these conclusions suggest is that Jimmy Carter was a circumstantial president—one who benefited from the anti-Washington mood that was so prevalent during the post-Watergate era, yet one who understood and represented many of the consolidative issues of the post–Great Society period. Conditions favored a Carter-like Democratic presidency in 1976; circumstances produced a man unusually dedicated to correcting what he saw as the insufficiencies and corruptibility of American politics and policy making.

What are the tests of achievement for an outsider Democratic president relying on the independence model of congressional relations? Actually they do not differ from those for presidents acting according to other models. They include: (1) Did an organization develop that was suited to the experience, goals, and style of the president? (2) Did the organization allow the president to capitalize on his experience, realize his goals, retain his style? (3) Was there another structure or approach that would have been more suited to his experience, goals, and style?

The answer to the first question is surely positive. Again and again in the sessions with the president's staff, we became aware that what others (and we ourselves) judged to be organizational idiosyncrasies were, in fact, efforts to accommodate the man in the Oval Office. A structure was established over time that promoted issue identification, program development, and coalition building among interest groups and the public. The congressional liaison staff adjusted its role to presidential preferences. The president was available as a resource but he was unlikely very often to manage liaison activities as other presidents had. Carter selected a person to head the liaison unit more on the basis of *his needs* than on the basis of congressional needs. In so doing, he ensured access for liaison personnel to the Oval Office. A more congressionally oriented, Washington-oriented, Washington-based liaison chief was unlikely to have the confidence of Jimmy Carter. No such persons were even among his close acquaintances. The liaison unit organized itself to accommodate the manifold activities of a diverse policy-making apparatus in the White House and the departments and agencies (see Figure 4). The evaluation of Frank Moore takes on a different cast when his role in this complex policy and political environment is more fully explicated. His limited knowledge of Congress has been fully documented. His efforts to maintain access to the president for his beleaguered staff has barely received mention until now.

The central problem, of course, is that it takes time to develop an outside-in policy structure for a trustee president. As Paul C. Light, among others, has observed, time is a precious resource for a president. Light identifies the "cycle of decreasing influence" as an administration moves from its initial honeymoon period into its middle years. President Johnson pointed out that "the President and the Congress run on separate clocks. The occupant of the White House has a strict tenancy."[5] The president's clock becomes a stopwatch in the pre-inaugural period as members of Congress search for signals that a president will be sensitive to their political problems. The Carter operation suffered from two major disabilities in moving quickly to establish a confident and comprehensible organization. First, there was the inexperience of those close to the president. What was interpreted as an advantage in the campaign was a definite disadvantage in creating a government. Second was the chal-

5. See Paul C. Light, *The President's Agenda: Domestic Policy Choice from Kennedy to Carter* (Baltimore, 1982), 36–37; Lyndon B. Johnson, *The Vantage Point: Perspectives of the Presidency* (New York, 1971), 441.

lenge of establishing a different system—one unlikely to gain immediate acceptance on Capitol Hill. That it was eventually accomplished demonstrates again the extent to which the White House organization will seek to accommodate presidential interests and style. For what was finally set in place was suited to the demands of a complex model of trusteeship politics and was a result of considerable learning by the president and his staff. Unfortunately for Carter, there is a low tolerance in Washington for learning on the job, even if one is trying something new.

The second test essentially asks whether the outside-in organization facilitated the president's approach to Congress. One cannot be confident in responding positively to this question. And, in fact, if it were put to many members of Congress—including Democrats—the response would be negative. Typically, however, such analyses are based more on what members of Congress wanted the president to be rather than on what this president was. This president sought to do the right thing, which may be interpreted as a desire to focus on difficult issues regardless of perceived electoral consequences. The various White House units were obviously sensitized to that effort. The Domestic Policy Staff, in particular, was designed to assist the president in preparing policy proposals for treating major issues, with the Office of Management and Budget contributing where appropriate. The Office of Public Liaison was charged with producing supporting coalitions among interest groups for major policy proposals. Finally, in what was the riskiest (and trickiest) maneuver of all, the president's program had to be sold on Capitol Hill *with as little political bargaining by the president as possible*. It was up to the congressional liaison staff to permit the president to maintain his personal style of independence and distance, which I feel moved to reiterate, he interpreted *as a strength, not a weakness*. This unusual organization did contribute to the realization of the president's goals. It permitted him, in his words, to "keep faith" and, in Burke's words, to sustain "a trust from Providence." It also allowed him to remain quite philosophical about specific losses, though no less critical of Congress.

The third test is the most difficult to apply—it would be for any president. It asks for a judgment about whether another approach might have been more suitable. Unfortunately, we cannot back up and try the Carter administration again with different organization and tactics. As it is, the Carter record shows a number of achievements in dealing with the kind of unpopular issues the president felt bound to engage—reduction of water projects, an extensive energy program, civil service reform, and the Panama Canal treaties, to name but a few. Might other of Carter's proposals on difficult issues have been enacted with a different structure? If we do not abandon the initial proposition—that congressional relations will be organized to suit presidential experience, goals, and style—then a search for a more effective organization concentrates on perfecting a system suited to the trusteeship model that employs an outside-in strategy. It will not do to recommend methods drawn from, say, the partnership model of a Johnson or Ford, or the classic separation model of an Eisenhower or Kennedy.[6]

Any such search must begin with the consideration of what went wrong during the first year of the new administration. The record in 1977 was devastating for Carter's image as a competent manager of his own White House team. The choice, scheduling, and timing of issues; the lack of priority setting; and the seeming determination to establish the correctness and legitimacy of the White House stance on issues—these were among the sources for difficulties experienced on Capitol Hill during 1977. These problems were themselves associated with the lack of national policy experience on the part of Carter's closest aides, as well as the president's own admitted lack of knowledge about the workings of Congress. What these problems suggest, however, is that the outside-in strategy itself is not bound to fail. The differences are potentially resolvable. There may well be methods by which a trustee president can be effective without abandoning either his policy goals or personal style. Hindsight leads one to conclude that the following changes might well have contributed to a more successful first year:

1. Have more Washington-wise people on the White House staff from the start.
2. Revise the sequence of congressional agenda setting to orient Democrats to Carter's strategy and priorities.
3. Create a system for identifying and informing key members of Congress about developments in the formulation of major programs.

6. These models are developed in Charles O. Jones, "A New President, a Different Congress, a Maturing Agenda," in Lester M. Salamon and Michael S. Lund (eds.), *The Reagan Presidency and the Governing of America* (Washington, D.C., 1985), 272–73, 285.

4. Adjust the pace for sending proposals to Capitol Hill, as well as show greater sensitivity to the workload of individual committees.

5. Immediately create mechanisms to set priorities and to build outside support for major proposals.

6. Develop a less adversarial posture by the president and the White House staff as they positioned themselves in the national policy process.

It should be stressed that these are changes consistent with the goals, if not necessarily the style, of the Carter administration. In other words, I have tried to identify the means by which this independent outsider might have had a more successful first year while still being faithful to *his* purposes. In fact, most of these changes were made in later years when the White House staff members thought that they had been more effective. Thus, for example, adding more Washington-wise staff (beyond Mondale's Capitol Hill staff) is viewed as contributing a resource for accomplishing the president's purposes of dealing with unpopular issues. It is not proposed as a method for making Jimmy Carter over into someone else or for sabotaging his list of priorities. And, of course, such additions were made later, with positive effects. Likewise, the other changes are directed to establishing a working relationship with Congress that accounts for the structural and behavioral characteristics of the place and appreciates the significance of the political sacrifices being demanded of the members when they are asked to support "doing what is right." The issues that were identified by the Carter administration were, unquestionably, important and difficult. They were particularly thorny for many Democrats in Congress who were accustomed to a welfare-oriented, Great Society agenda. The harshness of the initial White House approach was counterproductive in that congressional Democrats resisted learning the important policy lessons of the 1976 election.

I earlier expressed hesitation about whether these changes in that first, crucial year were consistent with the president's independent or free-agent style. My view is that they would have facilitated the achievement of Carter's policy goals. But they may well have been impossible for this president during his first months in office. He appeared to have arrived in Washington prepared to teach that community some lessons about good government and doing the right thing. The sequence and volume of proposals were part of this instruction about who knows best. Furthermore, it is precisely those issues that pose problems back home that distinguish the trustee from the delegate. The nature of Carter's campaign and election lent legitimacy to his perceived mission of doing right. Therefore, as principal agenda-setter for Congress, he could hardly avoid the temptation of putting delegate-legislators on the spot. This does not suggest that Jimmy Carter was mean-spirited, as some have said. It simply acknowledges his view of politics—as legitimate as any other—and the conditions of his winning office.

What are we to say, then, in conclusion? Was the Carter administration bound and determined to suffer strong criticism, even ridicule, for its efforts to make Washington do the right thing? I am forced to conclude that the answer is yes. Elsewhere I observed that "President Carter was potentially a transitional president for his party. His interpretation of the issues provided Democrats with an opportunity to adjust to the realities of the agenda shifts of the 1970s. His personal style interfered with realizing any such adjustment."[7] From the first, his relationships with the press and Congress were strained, as much because of stylistic as policy or political factors. The trustee invites careful scrutiny for his announced dedication to high standards of conduct and lofty policy goals. An event such as the Bert Lance affair can be devastating to the future effectiveness of a presidency built on trust and confidence.

There is, however, the larger issue associated with this third test, whether a trustee president can be more effective than was Jimmy Carter in establishing a working relationship with Congress. In my view, the lesson of the Carter experience is that the problems associated with an independence model of presidential-congressional relations are difficult, but definitely manageable. Future trustee presidents are well advised to study the Carter years for precisely that reason.

Jimmy Carter's presence in Washington provided an unusual representation of Americans' conflicting tendencies toward idealism and realism. We want the best—just as Carter asked of us—but we are typically willing to settle for what we can get. Thus, we are prepared to listen to a politician who wants to do the right thing, but we may well abandon him

7. Charles O. Jones, "Keeping Faith and Losing Congress: The Carter Experience in Washington," *Presidential Studies Quarterly*, XIV (Summer, 1984), 444.

or her just when our support is needed most. Abraham Kaplan explains it so well:

> The American morality of power is under continuous tension between our moralization and our vulgar pragmatism. The uneasy equilibrium between what we think of as "idealism" and "realism" periodically gives way to the one tendency or the other. Like a character in Dostoevski, we hang suspended between bursts of religious ecstasy and drunken debauchery. Power is to be used by men of conscience and integrity for the common good. . . . At the same time, power is intrinsically immoral, corrupting those who have it. . . .
>
> For the moralizer, power of any sort is a trust, public office an opportunity for public service.[8]

President Carter is a moralizer—one who won office following corruption in the highest office in the land. He did not have to guess why he won his party's nomination. Democrats wanted a candidate from out of town. President Carter did not will himself into office. His views suited the mood of the times. Moods change quickly, however. The moralism of the Watergate period was directed *against a president, not necessarily toward a new politics.* Thus President Carter encountered serious opposition, criticism, even ridicule, when he sought to translate his trust into programs designed to change Washington politics and policy making. I predict that the ultimate judgment will be much less harsh, however. Jimmy Carter may never be rated a great president. Yet it will be difficult in the long run to sustain censure of a president motivated to do what is right.

8. Abraham Kaplan, *American Ethics and Public Policy* (New York, 1958), 77.

Index